A Whimsical Journey
Through India

To Vanessa & Richard
With best wishes,
Harry

A Whimsical Journey Through India

Harry Matthews

Harry Art Publishing

First published in this edition July, 2020
by Harry Art Publishing
England, U.K.
www.HarryArtPublishing.co.uk
www.HarryArt.co.uk
All rights reserved.

Typeset and designed in Venice by Harry Art Publishing.
Cover from original artwork 'Peacock Painting, Udaipur' by Harry
Matthews
© Harry Matthews 2021.
Cover design by Harry Matthews.
All illustrations from original drawings and watercolours by Harry
Matthews.
© Harry Matthews 2021.
First Printing, 2021

A CIP catalogue record for this book is available from the British Library.

ISBN 978-1-9168719-6-0

Contents

{ v }

Contents

Contents

Epitaph I

'Violent and bad, thou art Jehovah's servant still,
And e'en to thee a dream may be an angel of his will.'

-**Henry George Keene**, 'Clive's Dream before the Battle of Plassey',
Under the Rose: Poems Written Chiefly in India (1868).

Epigraph II

'And this was the reason why he (Lycurgus) forbade them to travel abroad, and go about acquainting themselves with foreign rules of morality....lest they should introduce something contrary... With strange people, strange words must be admitted...'

- **Plutarch:** *The Lives of the Noble Grecians and Romans,* trans. by John Dryden, 1683.

'Blessed the splendour of the country of Hindustan, for Heaven itself is envious of this scented garden.'

- **Isami:** *Ode to India,* 1350.

Epigraph III

'It is not mine to know Love's divine culmination.
Life is one long waiting' twixt this and annihilation.
I should of happiness have died, of joy's excess so rare.
Had I this faith Beloved, that thou didst care.

But 'twixt life and death I linger still; hoping, and in pain,
O wouldst thy mark had failed not; and I in death's lap bee lain

Tho' grief the soul destroys, but with this gift of a human heart;
Pain will not refrain: be it of love's creating, or of life's unhappy mart

Were it to die only once, I would not demur in facing. But
the pain of parted loves, is like death's finger, through life forever tracing.

Away false friends, away with your smug advice and cheap
O give me of a little love and sympathy that may perchance my grief
abate.

O give me of compassion
That might assuage my passion.'

- **Ghalib** (1797– 1869)

Epigraph IV

'And man, as he is a creature of God, capable of celestial blessedness...'

Thomas Traherne, *Centuries of Meditations*, II. 43.

Epigraph V

HE who knows himself and others

Here will also see,
That the East and West, like brothers,

Parted ne'er shall be.

1833.

Johann Wolfgang von Goethe, *On The Divan*.

Map of Journey

The Journey Begins

Monsoon[1] mists hang around the white-capped Himalayan range like a shroud that unveils from time to time a fuller glimpse of the mountain peaks. I am leaning against the railings where I once stood on a balcony at a guest house in the foothills. McLeod Ganj, the western hill station near Shimla. I am smiling, waiting for myself to catch up with the culture shock. I am smoking a cigarette from a small packet I bought at the last chai wallah stall I passed, near the bus station.

Light is defused by the vast clouds, with occasional bursts of sunshine. It is a curious solitude and I feel I am on the border of some self-discovery, some new revelation. Yet here stand the mountains, and the view towards the planes, and the monsoon swollen Ganges in the distance that flows like a giant serpent, impervious through the ages.

The Journey began a week ago, 1st July, 2001. What digressive footnotes I could add to elaborate on what may be necessary to explain? Such strange profundities strike you here when you least expect them, like the recollection of a tantalising and sensuous dream. All is rather dreamy; unreal.

Of course, I expected exciting things to happen in a place like India. Like the passage from darkness to light, I felt myself brimming with a new exuberance I had not felt before, at least not in England except when I was drunk...how much more extroverted I was...how almost everyone treated you like a long-lost friend, how people welcomed you like a god! When I said in England I would escape in haste to Eastern lands among occidental ideas, I did not expect to wade through such beauties of nature and architecture that could inspire the most reverential poetry.

Each new morning, I was excited precisely because the whole day was mine and I could go and do whatever I liked. The possibility that I might get off the plane with no fixed itinerary, and loosely improvise the general direction of travel, roughly taking in the North, South, East and West of the continent, by rail, was for me in those days the ultimate *carte blanche* of permissiveness.

I could go to the market and buy with my rupees a pair of trousers, or a dressing gown or a pair shoes or a scarf. I could go to a restaurant and have *chai* and *dahl* and rice. I could go on a camel safari when I got to the desert. Elsewhere, I could go to a decent hotel or top end one on my student credit card, for a special treat should I prefer the comparison of comfort. I could go for a hike into the mountains with a climbing fit guide whose biceps bulged from a white t-shirt, yet something held me back from fornicating in a tent on a mountain side in monsoon, with snakes and wild bears threatening, and the constant rain, even if I might not chance the indulgence in low morals for the whole of my journey.

Did I congratulate myself on my self-restraint? Did I not simply add to the pain of repressing myself. Perhaps I felt if I were less sensitive, I'd have fun easily. I think in all honesty I felt it would be a dangerous distraction from the mission to take in as much India as possible. He who travels fastest travels alone.

I always resisted being promiscuous, I could not connect with India in that way! I wondered how others could so easily do it, as a kind of sordid sex tourist? I had some ingrained subconscious belief that sex with foreigners was sinful! Besides, I was too shy and repressed, even if I wanted to indulge a passion with a particularly handsome youth, it was a mere passing schoolboy crush that never went any further than that. My heart meanwhile was too fragile. I was nursing my own soul wounds and the great pain of my childhood, and moreover the pain of disappointments back home I could not quite shake off.

There were exceptionally beautiful boys in India, who pricked the desire but as they did so my old confusion forbade it...Being a handsome twenty-one-year-old Englishman, there was some interest in me. Most felt privileged or surprised to meet me. It was like I was for them an unexpected person in their land; a charismatic enigma.

I continued to ponder my choices, pouring over that map of India. Would I go to Orissa? Or would I go into the jungle and meet the shamans of the Naga[4], or among tribes-folk in the interior of Maharashtra? The list was endless, the possibilities too vast. Ah, India! Such a rich colourful land, I would need several life times to do justice to her, yet I had only one.

And then there was the me that would project myself outward from the mountains in the coming weeks, going from state to state by bus or rail, squatting on benches at railways stations with a ruck-sack, in my chinos and pin stripe shirt with those tatty boating shoes and a battered panama hat, and walking into shops where rivers of silk would unfurl, and drinking Coca-Cola and smoking short fags, and bargaining with the latest salesman with their great deferential courtesy.

Perhaps I do not remember as well as I believed? The memories have lived as if they were in the an archive in my mind, filed away in some sealed box, separate from the one labelled 'England'. Sometimes the box opens, and a memory jumps out like a jack. Then my entire being glows with the iridescent light of the East which for a time colours my focus and gives the present field a fresh perspective on what one was culturally unprepared to see. Such a perspective does indeed make England seem quite an opposite place.

Perhaps India is like a deep root of a tree that rises upwards into the world. Its vast secret empowers and deludes by its mesmerism. It is as if India had been concealed like a school of ephemeral minnows flashing out into light of my recollection, or a darting gang of piranhas nibbling at time. At other times it is like a great ridiculous pink Irrawaddy river dolphin that suddenly breaches in the Ganga, making one wonder if Mr Blobby is suddenly floating down river after being exiled from Crinkly Bottom.

I gather them up in jars, those pesky minnows of memory, and write sentences, of impressions, extrapolations of notations scribbled in my diary on the road. And when I have turned each jar in my mind as if by hand, and held the glass up to the light, I inspect that little blighter and what he teaches, before releasing him back into the pool. Perhaps a wave will one day flush him out into the wide-open sea?

And yet to reveal my journey to others has often felt like a gross impossibility, which I could only avert by turning my gaze outwards, and trying to forget as much as possible that Self of which I could not help being conscious of. So I sought not to seek the spirit within, like an eastern adept sat on a mat, but like an Englishman, seeking the spirit outside himself, and to such an extent that while I felt it was a time when I dreamed of life in India, and life became a kind of dream, it was rather a very tangible, arduous reality, and a well co-ordinated one at that.[5]

The dream threatened at times to be so overwhelming that whilst it sat colourfully within me, it waited silently for the day to dawn, and the fragrant flower to bloom after a long black night of forgetfulness, and decadence that it nefariously wrought.

I

Himachal Pradesh

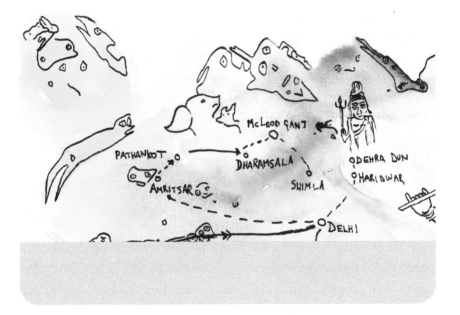

{ 2 }

A Dicey Start in Delhi

And so this radical act of courageous self-honesty begins in earnest, though I shall try not to lead you dear reader into too much appalling, humourless egoism...and with 1440 minutes in a day,[1] I hope I can make a few of them pass for you with some interest...It is a most precious gift that I should be able to give expression to that journey, that it should lead me out of myself and help me to see and love the cradle of nature to which I owe my humanity; the journey helped me to enter into my whole being the experience of a strange culture, into the essence of Indian men and women.

And there the heart is open- There one's own heart opened by spontaneous and sympathetic co-existence; to mingle with others freely. Being in India was like trying on a new personality, one both introverted and extroverted, and finding it a very congenial fit. A personality altogether poetic and philosophical, where one could buy *The Golden Bough*[2] on a street corner or some work on spirituality, and every train was on time, and flutter through the pages in the first class carriage believing oneself illuminated by an ancient wisdom as much as the conditioned air. A personality that liked to drink *chai*[3] and smoke cheap cigarettes. An Anglo-Indian personality, one that hankered after relics of the Raj[4], yet one that winced at the corruption, decay, and poverty of the Republic.

Perhaps I would discover something here, I thought, if I go and look around as though the country were a massive bazaar[5]. Of course, it is always better to go somewhere with a definite idea in one's mind where one shall begin. It might be easy to be deceived or led astray. I had a few ideas about it, but I was so overwhelmed by the possibilities open to me. I had roughly sketched out the route over the weeks before the day came to set out on the long-anticipated adventure.

I see it now upon my desk, beaten into shape, with ink-stained sketches of potential routes on the map tentatively drawn. All during the winter of 2001, when I was a student at University. It was my little secret I kept hidden in my desk draw, that I took out from time to time and made additions to or corrections to as I read more about the country I felt compelled to visit.

One evening, I even ink-drew a spontaneous map of the subcontinent with a dip pen, on a pad of blotting paper with pastel. It had begun as a hot chocolate spillage. I must have been taking some narcotic at the time because I was hallucinating, and could see these shapes in the coffee stain. It was my first most significant experience of pareidolia.[6]

So I drew them neatly in with ink. There was a sphinx where the Middle East joins Africa. There was Europe and the Cross. Africa was in the centre from which a beam of dark light emerged from the Congo and shone across towards Nigeria and Mali. Another ray of light shone in the opposite direction, South East to India- Clearly the image at the tip of the peninsula, trident or a holy grail, sparked my interested in visiting Kanyakumari... and possibly even the tear drop in the Indian ocean, Sri Lanka.

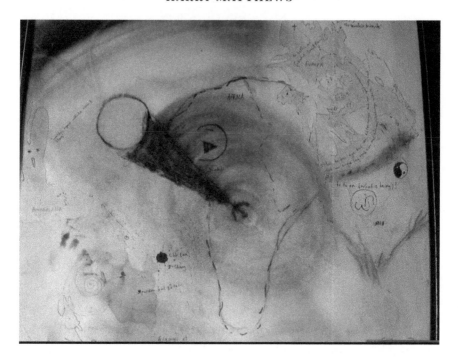

Life in England had become too stagnant for my wayfaring soul. It was a grace that inspired me to flee the drab dreary drunken days at University, to satiate the restlessness I felt. Love's disappointments were the result of the shame I carried, the self-hatred; impossible to love when one was at war with oneself. There was the fear of rejection, the rejection of self, that pushed relations away, but in lying to myself I was a fool to myself; by denying a good part of myself. It was true, not everyone could understand me. I was too complicated. To a high degree I believe my childhood had made me a complexity. I wasn't entirely sure who I was, and felt rather cursed with too much sensitivity.

Perhaps this tension would make me a poet one day? I felt a lot and drank a lot to cope. I always hoped I would survive to see the day I could be okay with myself, that I might one day be myself without any crippling shame or embarrassment. It was not something that I could be when I was twenty-one tragically. Emotional self-honesty was difficult. Feelings were tricky and easily dys-regulated. Call it a lack of confidence from being born in hostile environments; the reality was often traumatic, and inclination was always to deny and bury to survive.

Out of such grief, my journey to India was a welcome distraction. The fellow I hoped would accompany me on the journey was unable. In my boyish enthusiasm, I determined to go alone. I became fixated on India. When I look back I see it was a kind of initiation, as though I was then guided along a threshing path. Now the memories blend like sun-kissed hay in autumn mist, and sounds waver across field in light epiphanies reflected in the river's flow: purple, blue, gold and streaming clouds, and Himalayan scenery like in a Nicholas Roerich[7] painting.

Like a riven cloud in the sky that deviates from a small cloud to join a big one, then blown away by the wind. How did that journey begin? At Heathrow I suppose. And like a peaceful meditation the dream's threshold and rise, through diamond light, sparkling ahead. Above, enshrining futurist visions codified in ink on foolscap. Clear glimpses observe new worlds where bad news drips off paper like streaks of black rain. That long, eventful climb to paradise.

Ascending mountain shadows, near light-filled rock caves, charus[7] pipe smoulders pungently. Shiva carving. I Inhale it: Palatable, wonderfully smooth. Ah! Slightly nutty, flavoursome: coconut, spices, Banyan, salty breeze, Bay of Bengal, scent of wet hill mud and Himalayan Peperomia, Magnolia Tree, Jade that takes years to bloom. Parvati cream reveries: below serenity's light is clarity of mind's vision; gentle soothing deep in-breath. Dispel evil odours: passing, lingering, possessing for a time incense, bells and chanting. Then a presumption of cinnamon, *Chai* or Darjeeling? Kick of Kanyakumari air, invigorating southern flavours with coconut groves. Here is confluence at southern tip: peninsula pompom, admixture of 'ocean breeze', meeting two seas.

North India's furthest rest; snow melts, enchanted fragrance. Perfume cloud, song enriching. Iridescent purple light conjured by *rishis*. In England one often finds plants brought from here; in stately gardens...Defiant villagers gather and dance in circles, wafting strong purgative scents. Peace under a Banyan. Light: *Rishis* expunge selfishness from themselves. Perhaps it will trickle down? Strong scents: Mountain Cedar, Sandal Wood. Southern, Mango; a more cautious blend.

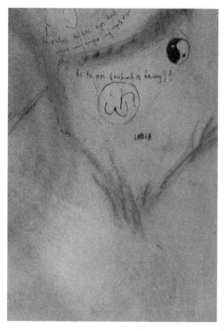

How naive of me and deluded, to appeal to Krishna, as an Englishman from the Church of Christ. He looks like a Smirth with black hair and a peacock feather. A deity I am unsure I can relate to. And yet in my superstition I am seduced by his feminine form. What can a blue skinned avatar, who looks like a children's cartoon character, have to offer me? What part of his story can I actually relate to? I can honestly say there is not a single aspect of his story I remember; that continues to have any significance to me. He is like a Greek god, a pastoral deity, with an appetite for beautiful women, who find him irresistible, innocent and playful sounding a flute. He seems to have as much holiness as the pied piper of Hamlyn. Is he a rat or child catcher?

There is nothing in his story that inspires me. It is an empty delusion. It is a denial of Christ; it is a supplanting of Christ with an antecedent who was decadent. Why are westerners more inclined to believe in Krishna than Christ? I recall with chargrin the mantra's of Hari Krishna monks. Why should I not chant Jesus Christ, Jesus Christ, Jesus, Jesus, Jesus, Jesus, Jesus? Lord make me ever mindful and observant of you: Jesus Christ, Jesus Christ, Christ, Christ, Jesus Jesus. Jesus of Nazareth,

Jesus of Nazareth, YahWeh, YahWeh, YahWeh, Jesus Jesus. (in an Indian accent).

Krishna is not Our Lord and Saviour! The entire Hindu pantheon could arguable by considered at worse satanic snake worship and at best idolatry, I could relate to it only in terms of Christ and Satan. *Every other god are the works of men, you are the most high god, there is none like you!* Is definitely my song.

How can Jesus Christ, the only God I know who took on human form and sacrificed himself for mankind's good, be considered the same as someone like Sai Baba, who as far as I know, was very holy, but not the Holy of Holy's.

I think the Indians excel in contemplative mysticism and interiority, but their spirituality seems to be altogether mental and psychological, whereas for Christ the heart is pre-eminent. I know there are Bhakti yogi's who would disagree, but Christ is the Ultimate Guru, and it was a great tragedy for India that missionaries did not proliferate as much as they did in Africa. The East India Company decided not to interfere with the traditional cultures of Indian people by supporting missionary work.

I knew in my heart it would be best to go only to Churches of the Raj, but I did go to Temples and Shrines quite strange and foreign to me. In retrospect this was a dangerous fascination. Although I went to them in a syncretic spirit, with an interest in comparative religion and Indian architecture and religious symbolism, there are a few things that are important to mention about that. As I now see it, it is a delusion to suppose there is no spiritual danger for a westerner in going within the precinct of such places...temples are places of power and ritual...who knows what has been sacrificed in these temples.....snakes? The blood of animals or even humans!?

Now I see it was all a knot of self-delusion. How could I reject my own tradition? How could it be I turned aside my faith in Christ to embrace a foreign god? A pagan deity? I conceived a mental prayer:

'In the nexus of intentions, actions, thoughts and speech release me from fetters I have formed, in knots of self-delusion. May a cosmic orgasm release the anger imprinted in my cells by misunderstanding people. Ennoble me by meditative concentration, by trust in you, on this earthly perambulation. May I come to love myself as you do. I name my afflictions so you may bless them. Heal them. May weakness turn to strength. Give me humility, the recognition of haughtiness, and when it comes may I breathe out fear that my faith may return Joyfully to You. Oh joyful, playful, musical incarnation of the Godhead! May you guide my way. Grant daily blessings, miracles, so graceful as to be unseen, that tutor me in your presence, and bring hope and mental calm in a restless world. May you draw new realisations within, integrating ever-expansive being-ness, understanding, courage and generosity in fresh, colourful, renewing landscapes of soul. May the spirit of your song glow with ever-lasting dedication, throughout the many incarnations, on the wings of prayerful praises, on my pilgrimage in this land, in honour of you Lord Jesus.'

*   *   *

I've reached here, now I appear to be lost. New Delhi is a broad horizon for my limited youth. It spreads white sails from my English shoreline, no more distant really than my skin. To this vast landscape, I am carried with a mixture of excitement and fear. I'm reading John Keay's *tour de force* of narrative history, that charts the evolution of the rich tapestry of cultures, relgions and peoples that make up India. That describes the teeming land of aboriginal Kolarians, pre- Dravidians, Indo-Chinese, pre-historic Aryans, Alexander's Macedonians, Babar's Moguls, and Anglo-Indians; a probing and provocative chronicle of five thousand years of South Asian history, from the first Harrapan settlements on the banks of the Indus River to the recent nuclear-arms race. Authoritative and eminently readable, *India: A History* is a compelling epic portrait of one of the world's oldest and most richly diverse civilizations...

My memories begin with fear and foreboding. My ink pot has spilt out onto my white linen trousers during the flight from Heathrow. The Indian man in front of me is so huge that the seat pushes backwards into my legs in economy class. There is a fumigation before we disembark the plane as we're landing at Gandhi International. Hitting the humid Delhi air and following the trail of passengers to luggage collection, it dawns on me that my intention to come here is now unfolding before my very eyes. I have miscalculated the arrival time of the flight, therefore it is 3am, and not 10pm, so I have missed the night train to Shimla. I foresaw that I would be overwhelmed by Delhi and had better flee immediately to the hills. Now this cannot be, and I am forced while tired, to find an alternative mode of entry.

This is very stressful. After passing through arrivals and the crowds of people welcoming the other passengers, I book a prepaid taxi at 4am: then out onto sooty-tar-dust road with turbaned men holding onto lorry-sides, down a slip road off the main motor course, before an unexpected man gets in at an abrupt stop.

I suddenly fear for my life and begin to panic. So I say I haven't paid for another passenger why is this man here. And he says this is my friend and he is joining us for the trip. Somehow this explanation does not allay my suspicions and fears. I ready my fruit knife in my pocket. Rough suburbs, of hotels and a terrible night's rest; past cordons manned by men in fatigues, berets, telling glances & nods down lamp-less streets with straggling matchstick-men, gaunt as dogs...

Of drivers who openly declare "Opium". Of jolting pot holes, ganja smokers, bumpy roads, rattling rigid taxi axles. Then, oasis appears, a contrived hologram covering the surrounding degradation.

Unlikely, I say to myself, in a place such as this. '24-hour tourist hotel', says the sign. A symbol of what it literally signifies? Not where I asked to go. Entering that hotel, fat man behind desk sits in stage-set office, greets theatrically like an absent friend. He seems fake. Passport thief? He jealously eyes my India Rail Pass. His money greed reflected from the wall mirror as I look aside, to see what's really going on. He's devising enlightened travel plans, presumably onward, for me?

Tempting confession makes me draw back those documents. Then clawing desk grasp seeks to revoke his extortionate plan. I see photos of less critical, pliant predecessors, each one a gullible tourist, subjected to a scam? They're sent off to Kashmir's boat people, $500 fee. Perhaps I could go trout fishing there like John Keay? Surely there is a cheaper way of getting there? What if I had gone to Kashmir? Or Assam or Maharastra Jungle or Ladak?

Tribal India is fairly unknown and requires special permits. Nagaland permits. Although free of charge, getting one can be quite a challenge, due to disturbances and political instability in the region, as Nagaland desperately strives for secession from India. A copy of a permit is supposed to be sent for review to a total number of 19 officials, and one has to stick to the approved itinerary and register at each check point, no deviation allowed, or else - a travel agency may even lose its license. In order to get a Nagaland permit, a travel agency had to produce a fake marriage certificate for my travelling companion and me. According to local rules, two opposite sex people are not allowed to enter this federal state of India otherwise than being married and we had no options how to avoid this regulation. It's much easier to get permits for a group of travelers. In that case, Indian officials perhaps perceive you as less suspicious and less politically dangerous.

People from various foreign resistance organizations render assistance to Naga struggle for independence. Therefore, tourism isn't widely promoted, and a relevant infrastructure is poorly developed. Few existing hotels and guesthouses profit from lack of competition and hugely overprice their services. It's a very costly trip. Due to complex formalities and primitive yet expensive living conditions, the region isn't much favoured by tourists. Admittedly, it helps to protect this corner of the earth.

Only the toughest and the most seasoned travellers are lavishly rewarded, gaining unique impressions and being able to enjoy friendliness and true generosity of these people. It's a truly unparalleled experience of immersing oneself into their astoundingly rich cultural heritage, with no equivalent elsewhere in the world. Nagaland was a fully closed region until 2002, and it's only recently that an extensive research work and anthropological studies have been carried out, resulting also in books written about this region and the tribes living there. The route I took seemed to just unfold by itself, le a thread in a vast teeming maze. At any point some influence could cut that thread and I would be lost? Perhaps if that happened, I would not return to England. Maybe I would drift aimlessly, and get myself into the wrong company, or walk away then from everything I had ever known. The what if's, the unknowns. Best to follow the invisible thread, and hope it would lead back out the way I came.

All up front? Is Lake Srinagar worth that? 'Do not worry my friend, we will take care of the rest!' Now their fish is off the hook. Doors guarded by stern, motionless men in military fatigues. I force my departure; pocket fruit knife waving. Despite raging, table banging (his unwelcome insults). I dart past spear-bearing security, (with cartridge belt strapped across his fatigue-shirt; no gun in view). Up the rough road I run perturbed into pace, pursued by motor rickshaw driver from hotel 24-hour; you know, the tourist sort! As he comes along side me, he grins and hopes I'll come back. Maybe my obstacle training has paid off, when finally placed in the theatre? It's the finishing line or extortion or worse.

On the main road, I realise I was the one who got away. Suddenly, a passing Sikh with sincere smile stops & extracts me from the danger zone. It would not be too far-fetched to presume I've escaped, like a special operative on a covert mission behind enemy lines, who makes it back home. 'You're in the wrong part of town, my friend', he says. The noisy motor pumps out black fumes from exhaust to hot humid Delhi air. 'Hop in! I'll take you to a nicer place. It's called Para Ganj!'

We speed off in his motor rickshaw, which feels like a safer appeal to a wiser choice. *Naïve. Aged 21. Hasn't a clue.* I am safe with a good pair of hands on a rickshaw wheel; traumatised by those rogues who use official government pre-pay taxi status from Gandhi international to enact their ploy upon innocent-looking young travellers at the early hour's morning arrivals from Heathrow.

'You are here long? Oh, three months. Well my friend, when you leave Delhi, you must go to the Golden Temple in Amritsar. Now that is worth a look. I highly recommend a charming guest house, run by my relative. I will write his details on a card, once I've taken you safely to Rajev's hotel.'

We arrive where most westerners begin: Para Ganj, the decompression district, designed for the convenience of those fresh from the long-haul. Just see how many western ruck-sacks jostle here! He leads me up a narrow alleyway, to a hotel reception and rings the bell; incense is burning beside a Ganesh. Now I meet genuine Indian courtesy and respect. It is doled out freely here. Rajev's smiling sincere welcome:

"Please relax, we have room service! ...Yes, you please enjoy your time here...There's plenty of tricksters – Beware...We look after you...New Delhi station... Is ten minutes from here...You leave by train...for Amritsar... No problem!!!!"

I enter the hotel room to rest and gather myself from shock. I order corn flakes, jam on toast, then flick the TV on, and flash through various channels with Bollywood films, or live scenes from the Indian Parliament. I settle on BBC World Service. Stock charts and updates on Dow Jones or FTSE indices. Cornflakes arrive. Are they meant to flake crumbs? A jug of hot milk and sugary chai.

The next day I walk from Rajev's hotel to New Delhi train-station. The streets of thronged with men busily going about their lives driving bumblebee motor rickshaws, past sacred cows, cycle rickshaws, westerner's with *ruc-sacs*, women in bright coloured saris, the pungent smell of filth, spices, and diesel; the heat of July. After walking down a busy road, I arrive towards the station, between Ajmeri Gate and Paharganj. It is the busiest and biggest of Indian railways. I am aiming for platform 1 on the Paharganj side. I am shocked to see the taxi rogues I encountered the day before, who took me to the 24-hour tourist hotel, operating outside New Delhi station. They are at the government prepay taxi rank and notice me, then taunt me in an obnoxious way. Those scammers I find really irritating, confusing and annoying, especially since they continue to use the government pre-pay.

Perhaps they feel clever over assumed impunity? Trusting the laws of karma will dissemble their shady racket, I race past. One seems to be very aggressive-towards me, which is disturbing. No doubt the devil's in him. Perhaps my arrival trauma, being triggered, speeds me onto the train? Where the devil pushes, I'm forced to move, hastily past all protocols.

What a crowded place to catch a train. People are sat on the floors of the railway station, and platform, occasionally there is spartan wood furniture. I am shocked by the sheer density of people rushing past. Families camped out with canteens, peddlers of pakoras, even a souvenir shop. The station has total 16 platforms. It holds the record for the largest route interlocking system in the world i.e. 48. A tout approaches me trying to convince me my train is cancelled. Another tries to take my luggage, but doesn't seem official. I realise it might have been wise to book my ticket the day before. So this is it, the station where I can reach anywhere in India. I will be coming to and from here several times over the coming weeks. It begins to feel like a second home. From the platform floor to the executive lounge, I am searching for a safe place to wait for my train, and where to book my ticket ahead of boarding the train to Amritsar.

The crowd decides where and how you're going. Perhaps this is one of the better maintained railway stations, but still dirty. Some say it is one of the dirtiest places in the Delhi, but after my experience in the suburbs I'm not so sure. Perhaps it is an eye sore by western standards, and it also smells less than the street despite the heat. Then this is Delhi where people shit on the pavements, where human excreta litters the tracks and every kind of trash imaginable. I don't see any escalators or public facilities, but hey this is the East; chaos unlimited! Organised chaos, yet every train is always on time. A Perfect flavour of India in a more sympathetic spirit. I'm told by one man that 30,000 people passed through that morning from 6 am. That's Crazy. Totally crazy.

I avoid the queues to the info kiosks, people talking through windows to officials, and check what platform my train arrive to and depart from. I'm an hour ahead of train departure as Rajev advised. This place is always crowded he told me. Do anything but look at the rail tracks, watch where you step on the platforms, steel yourself mentally. I am keen to leave Delhi before exploring it, simply as I've had enough of it already. So I turn down solicitations to go on shopping tours of Markets like Karol bagh, Connaught Place, Chandni Chowk[8], Sarojini nagar Market, Lajpat Nagar Market. I'm told here one shouldn't hesitate to negotiate.

The safest and most convenient way to book train ticket as a tourist is to go to the INTERNATIONAL TOURIST BUREAU. There is a sign saying 'Be a responsible citizen, don't create stampede', which is disconcerting. I hope it's not rush hour, but perhaps it is? Another sign says 'Help yourself & others in maintaining the queue'.

Suddenly I hear the Windows 3.1 logon chime over the loudspeakers, which sounds like an improbable announcement. Apparently, an important announcement follows this chime. I feel like I should be following it to reach there and get lost. A middle class Indian businessman joins me in the cue.

'You are in the right place. Never ever book a ticket outside. Those are bloody bastards and cheat.'

It helps to have an India rail pass to get first class reservations. So feel pretty clever I bought one through an agency when I was back in England. I feel I'd be lost without it. The trains elegant here. There might be a lot of people every-where, but mostly people are pleasant and staff polite. Deep in the throng, I feel energized by this adventure. I had been warned about the Paharganj entrance to New Delhi train station. You might end up at very different places, Rajev had forewarned. The scene at New Delhi train station is like an even greater population explosion than the traffic choked streets I'm relieved to escape. I feel the thrill of my first taste of the trains here: The Amritsar Shatabdi. I'm told it comes in on Platform 1, which is convenient as its just down the stairs from the airconditioned ticket office for foreign traveller bookings. There is a special cue upstairs, where there is an even number of tall male tourists around my age, with rucksacks speaking German.

'The 12013 and takes 6 hours 5 minutes', I'm told. It is claimed it is 'super-fast express' and will run me from New Delhi to Amritsar junction in no time, and is a daily service. This is the longest train journey I've taken. I enjoy hearing about the journey times before embarking. Time doesn't matter to me, as the experience is novel. With my India rail pass I am guaranteed a seat in an AC Chair car. It is a luxury train for the Indian middle class. It is now 4:30pm so I will arrive evening at Amritsar. There is a ballyhoo in the compartment with people setting their luggage and taking their seats. After a while I am served tea in a plastic cup. After Ambala Cant station there comes the round of soup with butter, black pepper and bread sticks. Then the dinner is served: paneer, yellow dal (Moong dal), rice, and two paranthas with curd and pickle.

The man opposite me thinks the Dal is overcooked with a very bad taste. He complains that the Paneer pieces taste stale, and the Paran-thas half cooked. He is only satisfied with the Curd and pickle as these are pre-packed so can't go wrong. There are window curtains, and light switches, and seats that move.

{ 3 }

Amritsar

I quickly enter the station flashing my India Rail Pass, bound on express train for Amritsar in a first-class carriage. Soon we're chuffing through mud-plains, swollen by monsoon rains. We arrive in misty humidity which contrasts with desert aridity. I charter a cycle rickshaw, hotel bound; leap out at a busy roundabout, question his navigational integrity, but he's fine. He finds me quite baffling.

He speaks some English. 'This hotel', I yell; conveys me on that unnamed puddled road (bewildered, he silently peddles on). I jump from the rickshaw at the cross-roads, plead panicked assurance peppered with post-traumatic stress from Delhi landing. He calmly assures me 'we go right place', where I'll see the temple, whose cupola glows with golden dawn light.

It Is a 2.5 star hotel. On the edge of the Jallianwalah Bagh off the Mahana Singh road, near the water tank of the Golden Temple. The location however is amazing. A short walk to the Golden Temple and lots of restaurants in the area. I would not stay here again and from this point on I always thoroughly inspect the bed before paying for the room.

The Sharma Guesthouse looks, politely, like it has seen better days. My room didn't look out onto the lovely garden, but onto the street with passing traffic. I stand on the balcony and look down on the traffic passing below. There is a group of people sharing a lift on the back of a truck. I shout a resounding *Hello!*

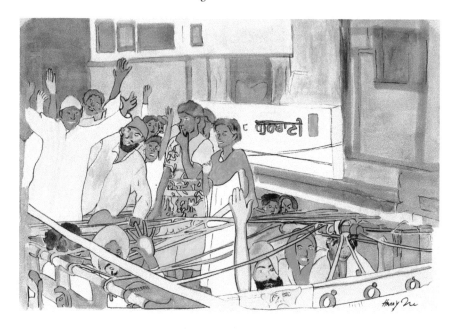

The location was good for visiting the golden temple. Unfortunately, my sleep was the sort where the bedbugs do bite. Of all the rooms I would have to stay in during my time in India, this was among the worst of the cheapest budget rooms. There were some rancid smears of brown on the white washed wall. As I entered the room, I was almost thrown back by the overwhelming wall of stench wafting from old bed sheet left to ferment, the pungent odour of rotting food. I had been wondering how I could stay the whole night here. I didn't even sleep in my insect net, perhaps a mistake, as I woke thinking I'd been bitten by mosquitoes but that was the bedbugs again. After a power cut, the lights came back on and revealed the wretched bedbugs. Those few winks of sleep, were eased with the fan 'air cooler' in the room, wafting some already warm air.

I'm not sure if it was a foraging mouse or rat that woke me early. On departure, I told the receptionist about it, and the bedbugs, but he smiled, shrugged, and didn't feel moved to apologize: "Wake up call.

Enjoy your trip!" The tap in the bathroom sink didn't work well and there were spider-webs from the ceiling. Paint peeling from the walls, filthy toilet, bed sheets stained and dead insects on it, floor and table extremely dusty and a bad smell (mould?) in the room. I know it is normal for some places to lock their doors with a padlock only, but not for a price. Perhaps a few more rupees would have bought me hot water, Air Conditioning, a clean room with clean sheets and clean bathroom. The difference between semi-deluxe and shifting to the full-deluxe room may have been worth my while. I'm still mindful of danger; cunning schemes that appear to me where they aren't. The Sahib greets me with a broad smile that beams; makes me oil-fried rice and veg on huge pan; one can see outside the monsoon drizzle. Perhaps the dimming light of a calmer night's rest?

In the old city's narrow alleys, dazed, I meander to the Temple precinct. The Sikh's hospitality has me amazed, and that ancient dome whose form is succinct, makes me think I am here as a pilgrim with the chords of an accordion poem accompanying me, as I tour this sacred place, the only compensation in this forbearance of a stay in Amritsar.[1] The Golden Temple is the centre of the Sikh faith.

Land of Akbar. Amritsar means literally, the tank of nectar of immortality. The enlightened spirit of Guru Nanak rests in Harmandir Sahib[2], the holiest shrine in Sikhism. It is located within the introverted plan of Amritsar, the central walled city, with katras[3] and narrow streets developed in the 17th and 18th centuries. Umbrellas, once held to the sun, now deflect the downpour. I escape the crowded city and enter the Sikh *temenos*. Sunset is approaching, and the dimming light enlivens the copper-gilded temple, Ram Das built, to golden glory. My bare feet greet the hot marble floor. I walk around the pool, feeling calm and placid. The spirit of the place is soothing; enfolds me tenderly in peace.

I walk through the door and view this Temple, full forty feet high, as gazing into water, penetrate an inner sky. Amrit savovar, an augury of heaven? I walk around here at halfpast seven.

Let me turn homeward, why linger in this land? Will my soul sustain itself, rising higher? As I set out across the sand, not knowing what leads me where and why; save some restless spirit's part of it.

Sikhs embrace the gods, build without idol, to the Godhead: Water of love, fire of longing. Golden temple's exemplifiable truth, where one may be washed clean by belonging: where one may have a foretaste of the nectar of God? A *sanctum* that embraces the soul, to be transported to the Eternal? It is a monumental gilding, reveals a sacred place away from the wearying world.

I see processions of people in religious robes partaking in ritual pilgrimage; long hair bound in turbans above the ear. To the shrine they go with adoration: there is but one God, without an image.

Merging with secrets unfathomable. The setting sunlight gives the formidable elixir of the nectar of Light. Perhaps there is deliverance in their worship, like my own? Prayers and songs from the heart ascend through and beyond the ritual. I see the youth present to his truth. And his religious truth precedes it? He is around 19 with white shirt and black trousers; bare feet. (In his religious faith, he is well versed). The four entrances (representing the four directions) to get into the Harmandir Sahib also symbolise the openness of the Sikhs towards all people and religions.

The present-day *gurdwara* was renovated in 1764 by Jassa Singh Ahluwalia with the help of other Sikh Misls (states of the Sikh Confederacy). In the early nineteenth century, Maharaja Ranjit Singh secured the Punjab region from outside attack and covered the upper floors of the gurdwara with 750kg of gold, which gives it its distinctive appearance and its English name.

Four months after the operation, on 31 October 1984, Indira Gandhi was assassinated by Satwant Singh and Beant Singh, who were her two Sikh bodyguards, in what is viewed as an act of vengeance. Subsequently, more than 3,000 Sikhs were killed in the ensuing anti-Sikh riots in 1984.

Within the Sikh community itself, Operation Blue Star has taken on considerable historical significance and is often compared to what Sikhs call "the great massacre", following the invasion by the Emir of Afghanistan, Ahmad Shah Durrani, the Sikh holocaust of 1762. Time magazine described Amritsar in November 1983:

"These days it more closely resembles a city of death. Inside the temple compound, violent Sikh fanatics wield sub-machine guns, resisting arrest by government security forces. Outside, the security men keep a nervous vigil, all too aware that the bodies of murdered comrades often turn up in the warren of tiny streets around the shrine. Dewan once again failed to move towards the parikarma (the pavement around the pool). Sikh Militants: 500 dead Military: 830 killed and 2360 wounded."

She [Indira Gandhi] was assassinated by Sikh nationalists in 1984. In her case, her elimination by her bodyguards was claimed to be a retaliation for the storming of the Harmandir Sahib (Golden Temple) in Amritsar that she ordered to counter the Punjab insurgency.

At the North door, illumined by the East, we share wisdom. I hear varied languages, stolen scraps; from southern door of flights, I walk inside their hidden world; for me an unparalleled sight. A melody with vague ethereal lights. I'm suffused with it.

Towards the mountain's heavenly delight, you will ascend with all your strength, whatever direction you chose to enter. Enclosed silent circle, wise voice imparts the salve to heal your heart.

Moon rises. I ask myself a question, sat by the waters of Amrit Sarowara. Gazing up at the clear night's starry rotation, while moon beams glisten on the *Gurudwara*. Holding onto inner sanctum's wealth, seeing how it represents wholeness & health. Your hidden power and inner light spark within, despite accretions of night.

Beyond the shoreless ocean there is a crossing, such as the prophets were given in vision; silent dictations, prayers always rising, from the temple within holy body's prism. 'When your soul can find its home in mirth, this they call the second birth.'

The light expands your soul's glow, ever-increasing circles; know your God. You're caught in snare, soul defiled, blood on sand, trapped in worldly, sensual enticements. You grasp heart/mind's secret, unbound, following pursuits while yet on earth. You will surely break the chain, then be found. Do not be beguiled by a well-wishing friend, or be threatened by a jealous foe: infliction of suffering, mental bends, trap you in world-mesh that slows to pain; possibly deadly ends.

Question their felt suggestions for your path, they could be distractions with ill intent. Use your discernment, whoever persuades. Remember this: reply upon your own thought. You are sovereign; you live the consequences. Would you allow another's advice? Cause you unknowing suffering? Beware. Such sufferance is an insidious sin, preventing you from enjoying the nectar of your inner sky. With the Master's advice, you hear the melody, but can't escape those intrusions: The taste of the wine is dangerously sweet. Passion fire wanes as the rod cools, should the moment pass.

Deserving soul finds sure life foundation, refuge in True Guru, peace mantra after years of strife, consuming you completely?

Shabd[4] is always, everywhere present. Feel it as you set about your way; fare-well, distant glow ignites your inner bliss; wait for fireworks.

Spineless? Finding peace, care of soul astray, forgetting your goal. Foolish pursuits, soul finding home, in God on earth: To those who are lost a mantra is always giv'n. Beware of those who live in their egos, you are not strong enough to take them on. They will overwhelm you; acting alone. I wish my ego didn't make me feel separate and obscure my equality still further with my brother or sister, in that game of projection or attack. If I infer something bad from what someone, I am always hurt by it. Then you allow it to rob you of your peace? Why? Silent reflection. The key unlocks many suns. The seeker finishes: You are that which you seek.

Head cowled in a panama hat, in lieu of tea towel or turban, to the sound of organ, wailing adoration, a question rises, conversion of view, a quest/ion mark, set to where you will go. A question of expansion, outwardly growing to glory. Do not wait for someone to knock on your box, expecting theirs to open. To create the experience, you desire, focus on your middle-mind at will.

Accessing those bars in the brain, rewrite your scripts, self-absorbed. Hold only loving thoughts. Angels act as gatekeepers, establishing love's steady stream of good thoughts to live by, through the heart.

Collecting shoes, moon perfectly aligned, from the entrance between two minarets confined. There are peculiar marble cracks. Your shoes are pigeonholed at the entrance gate. Crawling ants (giants) could carry them off? I get bitten a few times. Perhaps they are angry I got in their way?

I branch along the causeway leading to Western light, beyond the awesome gateway. Bare feet kiss eastern, fading light. 10-foot-tall ivory art panels speak of faith reformed. 'God in waiting, deeper layers foretold'.

Slabs, in laid Arabesques, flower sprays, upper cornices cascade in roof columns. Cupolas, every inch glittering mass; more gilded copper glowing in sunset. Happy blend of local faith, speaks from soul expressed; perfection of architecture, through which God in man is blessed.

A mouse must have got into my room. I retire to bed. At 4am it wakes me. Certainly, helps me catch the train as I shout to the Sahib to fetch me a broom. Sky is black, gloom lit with thunder and lightning. Banish doubt, mantra humming, excited that you're off to Himachal Pradesh.

The Golden Temple

{ 4 }

McLeod Ganj

I hear the mouse at 4am scampering along the floor. I bolt from bed, then leave by pre-arranged cycle rickshaw; the cyclist of which collects me for the train to Pathankot. Dark clouds, thunder, then lightning flashes. Gone is sunshine, broad smiles. See English frowns, or, say, Dutch water angst: Storm ravages battling them like conflicting armies in the Mahabharata.[1]

From third-floor balcony, road watching, I shout to catch the eye of a turbaned Sikh, among others, who become enlivened when they see me waving at them. Now, so many friendly faces turn up towards me as they pass by. They are shouting, smiling, dancing, eagerly waving rapture!

Like the joyous return of your long-lost friend after a prolonged absence. They are in an open trailer pulled by tractor. This moment is complete, but reminds me how responsive adults are; unlike home. This only ever tends to happen at home during the village fete, when tractors pull decorative floats in summer along the main road. Many miles away now. I reflect on the pensive, if humbling, visit to the Bagh.[2]

Sounding the depths from strong solitude, the train pulls in, far North: Punjab. From railhead, I find bus wheels stewed in hot mud; spraying everywhere. Buses clawing and reeling their way to sure air in chaos and blindness of interchange, unable to forward-fare; stationary rotation. *Who freely roams the Duhla Dhar?*[3]

Mud-stained, I eventually join a motley band and we're ushered into the bus from the stand. A man oils himself with coconut in the seat in front, combing it through his glossy black mane. I can't complain, this isn't an English bus, but you see there's no shame in it here. Men proudly assert their public right to grooming and self-care. Hindi music is played by the driver on speakers; in England this would cause a riot of titters. Here everyone loves a public singalong in transit, as though on pilgrimage.

Various folk speak in turn of the free Indian Soul. It is an extraordinarily friendly place. I smoke with impunity almost anywhere, at a fraction of the cost. There's a relaxed air on buses in India, aided by warm climate and open windows with bars across, fresh air rushes freely in, giving one an exhilarating blow-dry. People busily living and jostling on board in colourful dress. I feel at home here. No complaining. Plenty of sun.

If I went bare foot on a bus in Shropshire, I'm not sure how the locals would react. Perhaps a Salopian yokel would shout and make a fuss, lambast me for my shoeless lack of 'tact'? Still less, cool eccentricity, what is more, crass stupidity? To be judged is to receive a curious point of view; blinkers of habitual conditioning in mere custom. Generally, I feel under-travelled, though by native standards, horizons expand; it's amusing to see prejudice unravelled, perspective enlightened. Is this not what one travels for?

I read that the Kali Yuga ended in 1899, leaving a discord, profoundly bad, but then the yogi says the light shines with the strength of a thousand suns. In dark, inseparable nature, what it seems, on twists and turns in the serpentine road, this plausible world is a passing dream. Something is pressing hard on my shoulder like a load. Weariness and darkness. I am crying inside, disbelieving, unspeakably sad, as Gaddis' wander upon the wall afar. Shepherdesses, maiden nomads, under that great rock's shadow: Dhula Dhar.

The scenery of Dharmsala is peculiarly grand. I sense I am onto something special as we approach by bus as the foothills of the Himalayas come into closer view. The station occupies a spur of the Dhaola Dhar itself, and is well wooded with oak and other forest trees. Above it the pine-clad mountain-side towers towards the loftier peaks, which, covered with snow, stand out jagged and scarred against the sky.

Below, in perfect contrast, lies the luxuriant Kangra valley, green with rice-fields and a picture of rural quiet. Dharmsala is accessible. Roads connect it with the plains, via Hoshiarpur on the south and via Pathankot on the west (which serves me on the bus service).

The rainfall is very heavy, and the atmosphere is peculiarly damp during the three months of the rainy season. The annual fall averages 126 inches, by far the highest figure reached at any point of observation in the State. Trade is confined to the supply of necessaries for locals, and handicrafts for the European and Indian tourists. I read there is The Dal fair, held at the Dal Lake, close to the cantonment, in September, is largely attended by the Gaddis and other Hindus. The famous temple of Bhagsu Nath is two miles to the east of the station.

McCleod Ganj rises on the dark pine mountain-side. A holy place & quiet climb. It's on the main spur of the Himalayas, rising to the upper peaks. I put on extra layers, bearing an umbrella that doesn't yet leak. Here soar the regions of eagle, eternal snow. I am filled with calmness and serenity. A cool rain shower, near St John's in the wilderness, the sound of waterfalls and gentle breeze. Light glows through tree shadows. Monkeys appear to my delight and distress.

Immediately above the station rises a hill known as Dharmkot, the summit of which is a favourite resort. There are also some picturesque waterfalls, within a walk, at Bhagsu Nath.

Seclusion of mountain forest is preferred, McLeod Ganj is about higher altitude. River, Earth, the 'All is Oneself', as written in that Vedic text's beatitude. Alone, at One with All, I listen to the mountain's call.

Tea helps the way; uphill struggle rewarded, pleasing comfort to feel so at home. Fires of experience steadily soften to sleep. Tutored patience lives here, with kindness, and sincere compassion, as though the hills activate an evolved part of the brain?

It is essential too that all is well no matter how bad it seems; though to become listless without a caress, feels like one is gradually descending.

The great sun scripture says, 'What is enlightenment?' It is to know your own mind as it really is (end sentence with question mark; avoid answers, chant mantras). Road snakes, bus bumps from pot-holes. Neem trees rise on the vast sweep of lower Himalaya.

Crumbling road; an ox cart tries to barter shrinking road width, the driver cries. Horns honk, then wheel, mud, stationary, slips until stones forced under the wheel give it grip. Our bus punctures, past rusty pylons as we shrink to ox cart width again, and then, ascending the hill, the hinterland opens. Heavy grass banks flank the road, flatness of plain relieves the hill ascent to new altitude; teeming, lush, verdant plateau; arduous journey.

Hill-top monastery, cluster of pale houses, cubic, multi-pecked on valley hillock. Courtyard entrance, after trekking up mud paths. Prayer wheels roll in sequence, by gentle hands from crimson yellow robes, wood beads, sandalwood's sweet scents, then vegetable stew, creamy yak-curd. Pale houses rise in tiers above green fields. Crashing cymbals break the silence. Groaning horns bellow. Valley borne, deep, sonorous, vibrant echoes. Moon full, silver illumination's tinge on hill terrace, valley panorama. Dalai Lama birthday celebration.

Mountain-locked Tibet, always overrun when China was strong, by its invading army, with occupation garrison in Lhasa...Whenever China was weak, Tibet would drive the garrison out. Tibet is now an autonomous region belonging to the People's Republic. Its territory China has forcibly absorbed: 1950s invasion, they claim, was to 'liberate and modernise' Tibet; to do those Tibetan's a great 'favour'. To escape this Chinese 'favour', hardly well received, they risked sniper fire, starvation, frostbite, high altitude passes. Imperial modernisation has decimated their homeland; no favour after all.

McLeod Ganj is home to exiled Tibet, where India offers 'Tibet' asylum. The Dalai Lama's oracle told His Holiness that he must flee to India before 17/03/1959, Tibet's spiritual/ political chief decided, age 23, to slip away, disguised, through crowds, from the palace; never seen again in his homeland. Dangerous journey to asylum; Himalaya crossing on foot with a retinue of guards, ministers; night travel to avoid the Red sentries.

The prayers of Buddhist monks conjured up clouds, mist, to screen him from the Chinese search planes. Now they've brought 7.5 million Chinese to live in Tibet. (6.3 million before China invaded in 1959; today, there are 5.4 million Tibetans). The Chinese stifled Tibet's population. Remaining Tibetans dwindle annually yet risk the month-long journey through harsh conditions to reach Indian asylum. Most make their way to Dharamsala. Some are turned away, others shot by Chinese sniper teams in mountain passes. Tibet is a Chinese tax payer's gain? Infrastructure: new roads into Tibet enable natural resource extraction.

Rich with iron, copper, gold, uranium. Endless convoys on the highway carry out timber. Now they are building a 1,215-mile Qinghai-Tibet Railway, to be opened in 2006, from Beijing to Lhasa; to plunder resources as trains carry millions of Han Chinese into Tibet; now Mandarin is more often spoken; such cultural genocide. Tibetans knocked off their economic social perch, and in their own capital!

'59, that fateful, forced retreat across white peaks to India, in flight from China's shameful crime. I rise to McLeod Ganj from Dharamsala, 3 miles to government HQ, Ganchen Kyishong, Tsunglagkhong Temple's chanting throng of monks, Dhomey dancers, Stri Ngasol nomad costume, 7th-century hats, 1700m high, summoning bell toll, veneration, meditation on mats. Tsang family guest-house, wheels to pray, white in silvery moon that is full, sanctifies the Dalai Lama's birthday. Change begins in the heart.

Gliding high up in the clouds, consorting with Chandra's lights, which fill the deep, I am in a hammock, hanging, swaying cradle in crescent moon, lulled by Buddha horns, echoes through valley sleep. Deep bellows of haunting purity. Wisdom vibrates, like heart and soul-light. Happiness kept locked up tight in the breast above the tear dam, manic jests and flood-banks of compassion lodged above it. Maybe one day I'll sweep the plain, nestled on a mountain perch, beside a hill station named after Sir Donald McLeod.[3]

Inhaling sweet charus and wrapped within a silver-lined mosquito net, David is veiled like a seer inside a stilted wood hut, as I peer through the balcony door, on the mountain side. 'There is so much hidden wisdom from the past staring straight back at us', he says smoking a joint.

Certainties seem faint here. There is light, peace, contentment: what greater thing than this protects and guides me on?

A cool wind parts the mosquito net veil, as paths cross at countless chai stalls in McLeod Ganj. Handsome and muscular Westerner, my age, passes me in a white vest and red bandanna. I don't befriend him, though I want to. Elsewhere on the muddied street, I meet a Brazilian widow. She claims she is searching for inspiration. She is a painter.

As dark falls, Israelis dance to 90s rave in an unlikely building that's a discotheque. 4am: Western devotees spring from yoga mats. Crimson-robed monks pass palms in procession, along prayer wheels; flags flutter in the wind.

Morning curd consumption lines the stomach; (guards against bugs that may upset it). My shirts are meticulously washed and pressed for me; a matter of 11 rupees, folded on the guest house bed by the kind Tibetan family. Monsoon rains, roof dancing; subsiding now. Memory of nocturnal door-scratching; I confronted the door in the early hours and found a friendly hound sleeps under my bed, like some protective demi-god. The dog was probably just as lonely as me. Dogs, held in high esteem among mountain Buddhist believers, are considered Deities in disguise.

I feel heart-connected to McLeod Ganj, like Kalachakra initiation.[5] From the Tsong Tibetan Guest House, muddy tracks meander through town past Tibetan medicine outlets, with cancer cures. Temple dancers in caps, wearing peacock feathers, celebrate the birthday of HH the Dalai Lama. Paying respect to the Holy Gompas, intrigued by the mandala tantaras, high up above the cloud mist, time passes quickly; *wabi-sabi*.

'You're brave to travel alone at 21', says Shrada, the Brazilian painter. She's at the canteen, and tells me she is into Tibetan esotericism and yoga. Later, at the Nechung Gompa (where the Tibetan Parliament resides), a senior Buddhist monk is too busy to explain the mysteries, quaternity of the circle, life's essence.[6]

I trek the Bhagsu road in search of Zilnan Kagyeling Nyingma Monastery. A monk is a pedestal uttering Tibetan incantations. I eat porridge at the Mount Everest restaurant, on the open balcony, part consumed in silver-white cloud. Three English girls arrive and speak of a traumatic time in India, shaken not stirred, strong-willed as only English girls can be. Indian interest in young women traveling alone seems excessive. Who would guess English female rarity, combined with Indian male repression, and disrespect, provokes such violence?

Hundreds of monks tread up and down muddy streets. Smell of pine, incense unique to McLeod Ganj. Prayers rise. Sacred standards. Chanting mantras. Mists blacken on this Holy Day. On a bamboo balcony, a faint line of mountain strikes outward then vanishes; lightning flash. Silence follows the brief exposure; dogs howling. Mischievous monkeys skip on corrugated roofs.

I am cloud consumed, unknowingly confused. Clouds drag their silvery carpets over pine trees. A Frenchman with hashish tells me he drove overland from Paris, many years ago, and his brother is still languishing here in prison. Afterwards, I meet an 'Aussie Bum' who has been on the road since '69, leaving Southampton, he says, with a loaf of bread, and a head full of acid. I ask for advice. Curtly, he says: 'the streets are filled with filth, littered with foul-smelling piles of rubbish and crowded with beggars. You'd hardly believe there are millionaires here. Don't give them anything!

'They've enough money in the country to feed all their people. Basic hygiene goes a long way. Always wash your hands after you take a leak. Elementary, really. And if you get on a train and it's going 70 miles per hour, on the rackety rail tracks, and there are monsoon rains, you must take your chances, pray to God, hope you arrive at your destination, mate!'

David has disappeared, off in the exhaust cloud from his Harley, heading to Leh, Ladakh, made accessible by snow paths melting.Canadian, wearing Indian dress, his complexion is dark brown from much sun. He's proud to embrace the East, more than is often tolerated. (He tells me he carries a gold medal in the 'pill Olympics' and he feels 'like a Western account number'. He also warns me 'to go to the South this time of year is madness!' He is hopeful I will go north with him on motorcycle).

While in India, he feel's more human, but still needs a bank number to draw on here. I concur. However, for wearing native costume, he says he was threatened with a knife on a train by a group of Indian men. For looking different? (I like wearing English dress in the East), 'Well, you do look very English!' he replies. He'll climb higher, beyond all that fruitless hippy ganja cloud. 'Maybe I'll try the Yeti trekking North of McLeod Ganj, on the Dharamkot Road? I say I'll take another kora[7] of the Tsunglagkhang complex. There is always St John in the Wilderness, a short distance north of the Dharamsala road; I will say a prayer, I could easily do so right here.'

I trek the mountain trail towards Triund, but word of snakes and bears, lively in monsoon rains, draws me back despite the keenness of the muscular guide. I decide to leave for Shimla.

I pore over the map of India, eager for future direction. Smoke billows rise intermittently in wreath-loops, before ceiling fan dispersion. Lamp-light flickers yellow, orange with dark shadows. I see life's well-spring, picturing a cup rising from ocean teardrop isle, from roots of the Tree. Outstretched branches, Shaivite trimurti.[8] Light radiates from East to West, at the portal. Imagine a threshold to the realm of the New Earth. This is what I see. I drink from the cup, diving in secret. Fresh depths reveal good road's renewed viewpoint. On my map, branch-ends grow out to upper most reaches of West Bengal. What is Tantra? A profound reflection on the principles of reality, that grants liberation from worldly madness? Or those revealed teachings assisting God's praise within you, to cleanse the Self of filthy accretions that dim the Light. Sacred dictums glow red on the forehead of the ascetic who resonates Tat Va Hum's. The Jungle of Maharastra looks wild, with ancient caves that call me to explore. Is there not a painful mystery left here? In the loom-wheel of time, there unfolds being.

In wilderness peace, be still, and rest in majestic view of the Dhaula Dhar range. Rising higher to altitudes, gazing at misty valley, with scattered houses. There are questions which concern me greatly. Memories concealed in a store house, like an invisible library hovering a mile behind me. I feel blank, not knowing how my brain works. I feel that I AM: soul light of cosmic swirl; unfolding, expanding constantly, recreating. I know firm awareness of this is our Truth.

St. John in the Wilderness, an apt name for that beautiful parish church with stained glass window. The church is beautifully situated in a recess of the mountain. The churchyard contains a monument erected to the memory of Lord Elgin, who died here in 1863.

Though the church structure survived the earthquake of April 4, 1905, the station was destroyed, in which 1,625 persons perished at Dharmsala alone, including 25 Europeans and 112 of the Gurkha garrison, and destroyed most buildings in Kangra, Mcleod Ganj and Dharamshala; its spire, Bell tower, was destroyed. Later, a new bell, cast in 1915 by Mears and Stainbank, was brought from England and installed outside in the compound of the church. The Belgian stained-glass windows were donated by Lady Elgin (Mary Louisa Lambton), wife of Lord Elgin at St. John in the Wilderness, near McLeod Ganj.

I look at it in amazement at the church glass. Of all the religious art I saw in India, this I could personally relate to and draw strength from. The window depicting St John baptising Our Lord and Saviour in the River Jordan, and the paralell glass showing our Lord embarking upon his ministry with his Shepherd's crook with cross and raising his left hand in the teaching mudra.

*   *   *

There's no fixed recipe, preparation. Wallah makes favoured Masala chai. Each family, many variations. Some gently-picked, others organic growth. Some forced with toxic chemicals, others with preservatives for tidier profit. These latter give hurried flavours, difficult to savour. Savouring base tea-strong, black, they add spice, sweetener, here and there, with care, but not to overpower it.

Sugar is sufficient. You may prefer unprocessed? Molasses? Honey? Milk is de rigeur. Cardamom, cinnamon, clove and ginger are that with which chai is most often brewed.

You add nutmeg, peppercorn, chocolate, liquorice. Then you'll attain that special chai indeed. Bring it all to boil, allow the mixture to sleep.

{ 5 }

The Parvati Valley: The Hot Springs of Manikaran

In the bus I read an interesting tract about universal and indivisible substance of the absolute ALL. It's the greatest concept to which my mind can turn itself. It is so much larger than my brain but maybe the brain is a microcosm of the Cosmos, if Cosmos is equated as the Absolute All, or God. Maybe my brain is a map of the cosmos, and all I should do is recite a Vedic mantra to activate a sense of timelessness or time-travel?

Back in England, at university, I have read Leibnitz for seminars. His political philosophy has contributed greatly to the assumptions on which British democracy is based. He has a tremendous influence today. With regard to the Transcendent, Leibnitz says there are infinite beings both from and within the ONE; whereas Spinoza says there is only the ONE. I am inclined to agree with Spinoza, however, I am impressed by both, great philosophers in their intuitive perceptions, just as Einstein was a great scientist, because he valued the place of faith and intuition as much as reason. I suppose Leibnitz is some-what Hindu because he divides his personal Deity into several divine and semi-divine beings, and is pantheist. God or the gods are revealed in Nature, too. I am quite in sympathy with his pantheism, yet behind it all there is only ONE Eternal, Timeless Spirit. I am constantly returning to Spinoza, the absolute idealist, the Netherlandish Jew philosopher. He speaks of God, as the one underlying being; though I would eschew the term 'God' for Source or Prime Creator. Leibnitz calls God a collective unity of an infinitude of emanated monads or 'entelechies', to use Aristotle's term.

I chance upon a curious Sanskrit Word– 'Swabhava' – in the philosophy book I'm reading while travelling in India. The book tells me it is a noun derived from the root *bhu*, meaning 'to become', and hence 'to be'. I have this thought that simply to be in India, is 'to be India', as though India activates that part of me that is most truly and deeply me, and other people respond here to that. Whereas in England this does not happen. And I feel the answer to that conundrum is unanswerable; except I feel something in my East blocks me in the West. Perhaps it is the denial of one's feminine side, or true heart, one's link to the Divine Mystery, sacrificed at the altar of the Western masculine? *Swabhava* is the characteristic nature, the type-essence, the individuality, of *swabhavat*— of any *swabhavat*, each such *swabhavat* having its own *swabhava*.

I'm interested in how it changed my ability to perceive reality. For instance, when I read in Vedic literature about invisibility and dematerialisation, I would sit at the mirror and will myself to invisibility. Perhaps I had primed myself to see through myself, in a kind of pseudo-hallucination induced by mirror gazing? Sun gazing is an old yogic technique for boosting one's energy levels, and I rather liked staring into the morning or evening sun (always carefully so as not to blind myself!). When I was in Delhi, at Rajev's hotel, I would look at myself in the mirror in the bathroom, so intensely, that I disappeared. There was nothing looking back at me, there was no one there. I had disappeared. I felt like a magician or a ghost. Perhaps I had a vision of myself as pure spirit? Perhaps I was seeing the thing-in-itself, having become myself one with the mirror, the object of my perception, as pure being, reflected yet observing anything and everything in the outer world?

The book goes on with a word in old Anglo-Saxon, with the future sense completely retained and distinctly felt, to wit: ic beo, thu bist or byst, he bith or biath, etc., meaning "I, thou, he will be," in the future sense of "become." So, I began to feel the force of this meaning that being is essentially a becoming— a growth or evolution or unfolding of inner faculty. English has only two natural grammatical tenses— the imperfect tense, or the tense of imperfect or incomplete action, commonly called the present; and the perfect tense of perfected or completed action, or the past.

Now what constitutes one as different in essence— or *swabhava*— from another? It is its *swabhava*, or the seed of individuality which is it and is in it. It is that seed which, developing, makes it, and that seed, in developing, follows the laws (or rather nature) of its own essential being, and this is its *swabhava*. In *The Secret Doctrine*, H. P. Blavatsky (the Ukrainian esotericist who co-founded the Theosophical Society) speaks of one particular quality or plane of universal being, which she calls *swabhavat*, the neuter present participle of the same root bhu, and used as a noun. Like *swabhava*, it is derived from the same root, with the same prefix, and means that particular thing which exists and becomes of and in its own essential essence; call it the 'Self-Existent', if you like. It is, though, a Sanskrit word, a Buddhistic term, and its Brahmanical equivalent in the Vedanta would probably be the cosmic side of Paramatman, supreme self, the individualised aspect of Parabrahman-Mulaprakriti: Super-spiritroot-matter.

Swabhavat is the spiritual essence, the fundamental root or spirit-substance, the Father-Mother of the beginning of manifestation, and from it grow or become all things. With such lofty thoughts, I gaze at the passing scene of mountain greens, and soon fall asleep at the back of the bus. The road to Shimla has many digressions which add to the momentum of the journey. I take the road to Parvati Valley, arriving in a place called Bhuntar. It is the intersection for Parvati. At a *chai* canteen, I await my bus departure, and there are flies everywhere.

A man on my table says, 'you are very young to travel! You look like you're 16!'

I tell him I'm 21; seems you can look younger if you haven't aged fast from hard physical child labour (some auspicious genes permitting the formation of a youthful bodily frame developing still, made more athletic through the will at the gymnasium). He decides to draw something for me, which he calls "the OM and BOM! Of creation", which he adds, is the secret of all, of everything, and is also about 'black holes'. I half-wonder if he is referring to the Cosmic Vagina, or Arse-Hole.

I wonder if he means the cosmic orgasm is attained through entry into the black hole, through swirls of anti-matter. He seems to link cosmology to his religious faith and maybe his sexuality. I reflect on Shiva's benevolent wife. The black holes, he claims, hold the secrets of life. Further up the valley I search for the hot springs in my guide book. I feel as though I've passed this way, the heavy banks that meander from snowy peaks, to experience the freshness of the river Parvati from Manikaran.

A dish of trout and rice at Padha guest house, after I have settled in on arriving in Manikaran, which seems the most ancient and spectacular place I've yet seen, accessible by a rope bridge over a river cascading from a waterfall; a long distance down. I am perched on a balcony over the river cascade. Fresh water spews from rock, as steam rises from hot springs. This is the jewel in the ear of Parvati, who spears hot springs to produce soothing steam. There is an enormous rope bridge across the river that sways in the breeze wafting from the river-mountains. It is a favourite for Sikh holiday-makers, with winding market paths. It feels still more ancient.

I meet David and Jonathan, and I notice that Jonathan seems to love David, *with a love that exceeds that of woman*, to use a phrase. He doesn't seem to like me much, but David radiates a beauty that is loving and does not concern itself with petty jealousies. He jokes about me being English, and says 'cup of tea', repeatedly, which becomes irksome. I feel he dislikes me and seems to have David under his power somehow. Since I am in judgment of him as a control freak, he suspects I like his boy-friend, or travel companion. I get put down by the older Jew only because I allow him to, only because a part of me is putting myself down? Meeting someone clearly attractive always brings this up for me.

Travelling alone, I wish I had such a nice companion as David with me (maybe I'm just an unskilled empath and must love myself?). They are travelling from Israel after compulsory military service and are smoking on the neighbouring balcony to me. We have an amazing view over the river Parbati. I climb over into their balcony to chat. And immediately launch into philosophy.

'Have you read any Spinoza?', I ask.

'Ah! You are an English philosopher!'

'Yes, he is a Jewish philosopher'.

'O, I thought he was also Dutch'.

Baruch Spinoza seems to complete the false whole for me in my naive speculations, with a segment of faith, as thoughts turn to tomorrow's walk, which will involve snaking the valley path to Pulga. Do I retreat prematurely, back across to my balcony, alone?

I am beginning to see why Himachal Pradesh is referred as *dev bhoomi* or 'Land of God'. The next morning at 5am I decide to walk along the Parvati valley alone, hemmed by pinnacle peaks, twisting West from glaciers and snowfields; past hamlets perched precariously on mountain sides, lush terraces and pink forests. Sunlight shafts alight upon a curious world. Along the valley slopes, I meander towards the hot springs at Khirganga, where Shiva sat and meditated for 2,000 years.

I stop at a chai canteen for refreshment. It is made securely of wood, yet perched precariously on the valley side, overhanging the sheer gradient below, off that rough and rubble road flanked by tremendous woods along the banks of meandering Parvarti. I feel miniscule on the mountain path compared with the vast valley sides; with its dense, forest fleece, light scattered into varying shades of green, with morning mists rising like steam from the pine tops, breathing more freshness and purity into the air; valley exemplar of Himachal Pradesh's ethereal beauty. Voluptuous breathing curves, smoothed down and gentle. The life water gushing from a secret source. I taste fresh air, invigoration, and ascend a mountain path that winds ahead like a snake. I reach a rope bridge that crosses to the other side of the river, and approach three wandering ascetics (Sadhus), who are wearing orange robes, upon an enormous rock.

'COME SHARE OUR POWER MAN!' declares the obliging Sadhu, who seems more Rastafarian than Hindu Holy man. With an invitation for a puff on the pipe (pure resin is abundantly gleaned from the Parvati valley, monsoon plants secrete the legendary substance, eagerly scraped from leaves). Many travel here and disappear. I must be careful. I continue on my way; dubious Sadhu's offer to meet them next Wednesday to acquire a large consignment of their 'power'.

My gaze is fixed solemnly on the road ahead, by means of walking I'd hoped to lift the low mood that is troubling me. I can see the path extend beyond the Parvati valley. Despite the black wolf[1], I am inspired by the temple of nature at which each step is an act of devotion. *I know I'll see you again*, I say to myself. There are mists floating through the pine trees; the *champak* with its golden flowers. I am inhaling deep breaths of Brahma here, on a higher vibe.

'Hello money', says a lady in sari holding out her hand. Fingers circle the air, like prayers to the sky. It is so hot on the steep climb with short inclines. The path narrows. The women have baskets, picks and are breaking up the earth-stone; drawing dust with bare hands. There are more trail diggers further along, labourers on the path, rubble collectors in a crude, primitive way. No machinery. Just hands. I might have given them more money than they could earn in the time it takes for me to walk to Pulga. Perhaps give them working gloves? Old rope, wooden slats, another less adventurous bridge: *Chillum, charus,* dangerous valley, walk with care. Earth fire blazes. A good Sadhu lives for his fire. *Maintains his own fire*, says Dhuni.[2]

I reach a small canteen on wooden stilts on the valley side and take a *chai*, sitting at a table. There is a vase of fresh red and yellow flowers, on a wooden bench, a higher feeling here, looking across the gorge. 10 km on, and a small boy approaches. I see him on the outer turns of the narrow twists of mountain passage. He wears an embroidered beige hat, an over-garment to the knees; beads, necklaces, and holds a basket and a wooden flute. I do not break my pace to greet him. The boy speaks with excitement, walking alongside me. I eye him curiously. He reaches out, though my gaze is fixed ahead. Speaking in his dialect, persistently trying to sell me trinkets; from his basket, perhaps?

'Did you say snake?' We stop. He opens his basket to reveal a slithering serpent that sluggishly uncoils itself. I start running, about two kilometres in total. As I run, the boy and snake pursue me. The thoughts of the belly bound creature horrify me. All my associations with serpents are bad: poison, evil, sin, death by snakes. In the panic and flight, like a roller-coaster, I dash up and down. I am fit, so I can easily outrun the boy. Fear puts a lightning pace in my step I have not learned to see the snake as he does. As something precious, as something that can be tamed with a flute. As a symbol of healing; a creature to be held and befriended. The boy does not understand I don't want to see the snake. I stop. At Pulga[3], there are two men. One in a wooden canteen, another asking me what I'm running from. He assures me he will deal with the boy.

Eventually the boy arrives. And the *chai* stall keeper pulls the snake violently out of the basket, much to the consternation of the boy in the beige hat, and holds it under the head and stretches it out like a rope by the tail. I am ashamed when he swings the snake like a rope several times in the air like a lasso, then against a rock. The boy cries with horror. I was very disappointed that the *chaiwalah*[4] had taken it upon himself to punish the snake. It only upset the boy. That was the last thing I wanted. I did not realise that them dealing with the boy would involve this. Telling him to leave me alone would be enough. Heavy-handed, ingratiating corporal punishment. It is a sad, cruel scene, disproportionate to the cause, really my own inexplicable phobia. I gave the boy some ten rupee notes by way of compensation, but he is very upset, and money can't change what has just happened.

There would have been a much gentler way had I not over-reacted with abject terror and enlisted the *chaiwalah*, who I wasn't to know would deal with it like that. The magic snake boy has such an affection for his pet; his livelihood. The snake is contorted, like a zig-zag, and looks traumatised if not dead. The boy takes the snake in his arms and runs away. I decided to walk to Manikaran before night-fall. I do not feel like going onto the hot springs[5]. There would not be much time to return to Manikaran before night fall. Neither do I fancy staying in the village after the snake episode. It is just nightfall as I arrive for a hot bath and then bed. The next morning, I take the bus to Bhuntar. At a Bhuntar interchange canteen, I eat dal[6] and rice and there is the swarm of flies. I drink with trepidation from the steel cup of tap water. I do not care for intestinal bacteria. Perhaps this is more robust? I stay in Bhuntar and board the night bus to Shimla, the summer capital of the Raj. It is a long journey, and I remember waking up during a bump in the road, at an obscure stop; at a garage alighting for a roadside canteen. I join them, but it's very surreal at 3am and I am not in the mood for talking.

{ 6 }

The Road to Mandi

The road to Mandi, above mists and time in Himachal Pradesh, I leave cloud glory, and kiss mountains and the gods with the lens of my camera. Clouds scatter. In my ruck-sack is packed a golden Buddha, and a pink elephant print. I take the bus South-East, where my temperament follows the winding mountain road, and feel happier, as I enter this Himalayan region, leaving behind the plains of Punjab. I see a roadside sign that says, 'Please help keep the Environment pollution free (Punjab National Bank)', in terrain the reminds me of Wales; the green verdure of mountain valley.

The river more violent with gushing water, streaming from the glaciers now the snows are melting at the source. I am talking to a thin man who wears a lumber jack shirt, and beige combat trousers. His face is weathered, with pointed ended ears and hawkish nose; the lines of his face tell the story of a life spent travelling, with some drinking? He tells me he is Anglo-American, since his mother is English and from London. Apparently, she once told him he must go to Enoch Powell's funeral at Westminster Abbey.[1]

'Did you go?'

'No I didn't make the time.'

I tell him Powell had ambitions to become Viceroy but independence came. That I had read Simon Heffer's biography, and that his great-grandmother was probably right. How Powell had learned Urdu at SOAS.

The A.A. wonders that I'm here alone and from England, and now we are forced next to each other, he is particularly enjoying talking to me, making me feel he has been in India a longer time than I, and perhaps feels homesick? I don't necessarily find his conversation welcome, but he is garrulous talker, about all the countries he's visited, from Nepal to the Netherlands. He suggests that I go to the Andaman Isles, seeing that I have no fixed plan. Yes, maybe I go there, I think, in a roundabout way, knowing that I probably won't, as it's a flight off shore. I am content with whatever Glories of God, world gain, the cast of Indra's net may spread. Travelling while experiencing Brahma, though perhaps with less of the transcendent Bliss contained in what the Hindu's call Sacchidananda[2].

'You might go', the Anglo-American says, 'As my grand-mother said of Enoch Powell's public funeral, 'It would be rather good to go.' He says this is an English upper middle-class register of a Lady Bracknell.

Grinding noise. Axle gives, wheels jam, hopeless against holes. Open bonnet, engine hisses then steams in early morning mist, as we drop into a village garage by a Chai stall. Twenty-something sits, repairing the bus.

I jump out and chance a chai and speak to a thin Sadhu who looks Keralan. He's sat cross-legged on a blue diesel barrel beside garage, seems to preach the virtues of modesty? Foregoing marriage?

An audience of tourists at the bus window. My silver wrist watch says it is 5 a.m. Timeless consciousness that morning, inside a dream. He has understanding eyes; passes as real, not all he seems, gazes deeply with his large, dark eye glow, white-crystalline in the centre with those dim cataracts. No joyful passing, though recognition; he has a message from true faith and renunciation, a witnessing germ from his barrel-top view.

Sudden and eager, we reach in sympathy, much more than speech could give, but smoke and chillum-Parvati cream and body language, with motions up and down in the universal play of consciousness. And insight came, at this early hour, as though I knew in that face another back home; a long face, large eyes, and a mouth drawn wide with white teeth smiling.

It was as though I knew him before, reflecting on the upside sphere of memory. Here deeper things were felt, a face older but similar, and far along the path of solitary wandering, with knowledge of God. What spun his turning wheels, subtle body, each petal a spoke, from seed syllable, mantra, for balancing of mental and physical health? And what of the subtle winds of spiritual wellness, that blow in the clear light of bliss and emptiness? When the Avadhuti[3] curves up to the crown; every thought-experience filtered. When Shakti kundalini awakens for conscious creativity, empowered by cosmic energy. If self-realisation's mystery is mystery, spiritual power resides with us all. When released, enables transformation. The Padma[4] opens to ever greater levels of manifestation? The serpent may uncoil, but the Holy Spirit descends.

'Aditya has not yet risen but will always grant you strength in the long battle as a warrior, Shri Rama![5] The fruits of this prayer invoke God to give you strength in the battle field of life.'

'Worship the One, possessed of rays when he is risen, held in reverence, by Devas and Asuras[6], Lord of the Universe, by whose effulgence all else brightens. He is the totality of all Celestial Beings, He is self-luminous and sustains all rays, He is the source of All Energy and Light. The Golden-Hued Brilliance and the Maker of Dya[7], Dispeller of misfortunes, infuser of life. Salutations to thee who is One Being manifest in twelve forms of the Sun.'

'Salutations to the Hero, the one who travels fast. Salutations to the one whose emergence makes the Lotus Blossom. Gaze at the sun with devotion.'- Ādityahṛdayam[8]

I have travelled across the land, wandering, pulling back, on left path, right path, where body and spirit meet, in different shades, and seen how the realm of consciousness extends from the Great Pure White Light of the Absolute, Atman, right down to the solid matter of the clay I have breathed in heavenly diamond lights, astral, celestial. I have seen glorifications of the mystical mountain goddess; been resurrected, stayed at many ashrams, always seeking, in spiritually enclosed retreats of this world, your Peace. I have seen the extra-temporal and extra-spatial and woken up from the dream you are now seeing. I have seen a flower bloom then wilt before my eyes, and I didn't shed a tear. With the help of the language of the Gods, I have tasted Soma, slept naked as the She of Mountain and devoted my Love to Kamakshi.[9] How without her life is dry, rigid, pure materialism. All this I have seen over countless ages; seen, heard, felt, thought, walked, eaten and exhaled before resuming another in-breath in another form. I serve my suffering with heat in the fire-womb of my heart. To please Shiva and unite with him. I am poor, wretched, miserable, *tapasuin,*[10] mortified and fasting.

'I circle my temples (like this) and touch my brow like this. See how the wheel is spinning from my head down to my feet? From Sahasrara to Ajna, there is heat; there is Light. Circulate down there to the Muladhara![11] RAAM, RAAM, RAMA, RAMA, RAAAM, RAAAM, RAMA RAMA.'

He puffed the charus pipe I offered him. I bid him farewell. As I turn around, he's vanished like a phantom. The hands and wild whites of his dark eyes are gone. Empty outline of his luminous form, remains imprinted in the ether, reminding me of a distant friend, another, similar I know, many miles distant. I am concerned but impressed: Too much tapas and charus fire, rishi smoke, darkness, Rama, Rama, Rama.[12] Then 100 rupees. What spiritual suffering?

What a practitioner of austerities. Perhaps he had given his all to God. God who gives all. Back on the bus to Shimla, the man beside me wonders what the Sadhu was saying. I do not know entirely myself.

The intervening years develop memories, meaning. Distance with clarity, too young then to know. Epiphany seed waiting to sprout. Down the up and round the down of mountain road. I grow tired of a ten-hour journey after six. Dusk approaches, so I jump off at the bridge before Mandi, feeling hungry. Pavitra, Holy Awesome Queen of Shiva. Our life is inert without your *Shakti*. Shiva, You are the Himalayas-husband to Parvati, the She of the Mountain, Who destroys all fear! Hear me. (I exhale the day strain). Please Shiva, unite me with Him. I am wretched, poor and miserable. I live with austerities, darkness and suffering. A mile along the mountain road I see the black dust cloud and noxious fumes, as the quiet night stands beside me, on the bridge path with the river flowing.

A drunk shouts: *Hey Englishman,* as I walk into the *Raj Mahal* reception bar. Stunned I stand, before he trails off in rambling Hindi. Too much whiskey unsuited to his eastern constitution. 'No shame', says another man. 'This is an Englishman. Show some respect'. I turn, portly Hindu behind me, who is seated, and invites me to his table. I order a beer and eat chutney and *poppadum.*

'I am Suresh. This is Viran. Ignore that man over there. He is drunk, every night the same. Drink, drink, drink. He is nothing. At least nothing to worry about...I see you travel, first time in India and alone. Fast travel then forms your mind. Ah! The night is full of teachings, as the French proverb says. I have composed a poem...' I can see a light that is shining up ahead. Could it be my destiny? I cannot be sure (I do not know). Could it be my destiny? Each step surer of my journey. But happy to know I am going somewhere, Even if I don't know where it is.

'Tell me what you do? Oh. A student of philosophy! Do you know Osho? (no, not Oslo, Osho!) He is the one you should read. He delves richly into the depths of the cosmic ocean. He gives some fascinating and challenging insights concerning existence and experience.'

'Is he an ancient Indian philosopher?'

'No. A contemporary voice. He resounds very strongly in India today. Many people believe what he says about religion and society. '

'Is he alive?'

'No,' says Viran, who had been silent up till now.

Suresh continues: 'We once worked in Germany, on a building site. I would like to go to England. I have studied English at College. Coleridge for me was one of the greats: *The sun came up upon the left, out of the sea came he! And he shone bright, and on the right went down into the sea.* The Ancient Mariner!' Retiring now, thanking Suresh and passing the friendly elephant God, I ascend stairs lined with stuffed heads of hunted game. Comfortable recliners, colonial Artefacts; a disconcerted Italian couple sit enjoying an evening drink. They do not like the Italian PM, elected last month.[13] I share with them my own misgivings about corruption of politicians of the decade with narcissistic psychopathy?

I have a long conversation with them. They tell me about Varanasi, where a man tried to put a snake around her husband's neck, and wouldn't take it off until they gave him lots of money. It seems like an old trick; horrifying all the same. I have an idea books will soon be portable, on hand-held computer readers.[14] They doubt this could ever be true. There is an occasional flourish of tartan outside my room, upstairs along a frontal balcony.

I have a small room. There is a pervasive, musky scent of an old-fashioned, almost Edwardian polish, reminds me of my great-grand-mother's cottage.[15] as I pull open the doors to a small room. I release the padlock, brass latch, open double doors Into room with an oak wood cot, and light blue-washed walls. I sleep well, trusting the light of another day, leading me on this whimsical Indian journey.

The morning comes, and I pull back a wooden window shutter, reveal a small *pukka* courtyard. There's that European picture above my bed: two fat men in skull caps, laughing while eating from a broth-pot with long spoons. (I congratulate myself I jumped off the bus, as this is a perfect place to stop over). I continue down a long staircase, leading down into the garden. Next to the garden is a wooden house. I turn back for breakfast in the restaurant. Service, quick, polite. What a vintage place it is. The drawing room is a like museum of taxider-mic mammals hanging on the walls, Raj regalia, pictures, tiger-hunt-ing parties, objects on tables. I sit by the steps of the lawn with a hot cup of tea. It is too wet for the garden restaurant. An old man with smiles warmly, as though from the heart; takes me by surprise. After breakfast, I walk out through the gardens of the Raj Mahal, set on a plateau near the river, flanked by higher mountains, like nowhere similar in Shropshire, not even, perhaps, the Wrekin.[16]

I find a pair of cream trousers, which fit with hem adjustment. This splendid pair I take to wearing throughout my journey, mostly made of Indian cotton. The drunk is at reception again that evening, as I spruce myself up for the restaurant and conversations at the bar. He is shouting again...

'Apologies for the behaviour of our countryman. He is a national disgrace. Too many to be counted in my own motherland!', says this Indian chap, who introduces himself as Kapoor. He has a bouffant coiffure, fairly long (70s style) side burns, a red, open-collared shirt. My initial thought is: gentle, polite, Indian Elvis.

How he makes the feelings of a traveller as important as his own. From the Raj Mahal splendour, we head out on a moped through town, then up a country hill, which is exhilarating. Kapoor's moped climbs the hill to where the temple stands. There is the monkey God, with a red bhindi.

He wants to take me to a special place. Ants crawl the stinging stone floor. Kapoor is silent. I remove my shoes and socks, as it is a Temple,Venerable Shakta[17]. He blesses, with his forefingers, corpses & garlanded heads of Kali, destroyer.

'Why do you worship Kali?'[18] Nonplussed, he leaves the question in the air. Perhaps to be answered one day? His honour to the goddess is pensive, curious: Foetus earrings, having sex with a husband likened to a corpse in a cremation ground. Quite incomprehensible to my young 21-year-old mind. Perhaps Kali is just a conscientious woman pushed too far? When gentle reason and patient persuasion over so long have no effect? Queen of Wrath, a red-covered manuscript. Dice of divination. Infinite justice. Wrath descending with exquisite precision. Here is the protector and destroyer. The god who displays intense power, saying, 'Stop your madness now or you will be destroyed!'

To break through the wall of ego-driven madness that causes pain and horror, she who must take drastic measures. Is this not an act of love? Perhaps this is why Kapoor's so reverent.

'She sits on no sun, straddled across no magical rainbow. Instead, she sits on flayed skin and rides through a lake of blood. Will your wise power keep craziness at bay when I go from here? Will you protect the crazy one on the riverside from the crazier ones? Infinitely just, her wrath descends with exquisite precision. There are erotic temple scenes, sensual *kama sutra* postures.'

Here, on the temple surface, unabashed sexuality. How can such destruction and chaos be alluded to with sex? The temple precinct lies calm, concealed. Kapoor's silent glance seems to share these deeper, contradictory facets of life within me, unforced upon my youthful comprehension. Compassionate pauses.

'You see this tree? This is the sacred tree in the garden of Tarna, and it has not changed for over two hundred years.' I gaze up at the tree. An ant stings my foot. There is no word in English for *Maya*. Should you now see through *samsara*, perhaps there are glimpses through the veil of illusion? If the world is this way enclosed, and a spiritual world is enveloped around and within it, then maybe one can laugh at history, and dance through life more creatively? When the spiritual world is revealed, eternal travelling through countless fields of existence at once, where this physical world is a material experience, all the thoughts, colours, memories we know, the handiwork of that Eternal Being, are as a loom in the wheel of time, drawn by life, as an invisible necessity.

* * *

The Raj Mahal is centrally located and the bazaars are within walking distance. When I return, I recline on the kedar; chai is served. It is a chair to be cherished. Not so Spartan.

Mandi is an eccentric town. It has a unique charm, that made the journey to Shimla, by tourist bus, more tolerable. I am glad to be on my way; going somewhere...Where will I go beyond Shimla? On the veranda, for one more night, I sketch some ideas in my notebook, and leaf through the Lonely Planet India guide-book, and pour over regional maps with feverish zeal, a recent convert to an ecstatic religion, who wishes to lose himself in the Dionysian intoxication of eastern people and places. However, all this cannot be done without sober-minded Apollonian planning.

I must be up early to catch another bus.

{ 7 }

Shimla: The Viceregal Lodge

Lights flicker through bus slits, past warp and woof of wood huts, pine forest and mud. Suddenly shadows appear, and loud banging against the bus-sides at dawn light, as obscured bright rays cast warning of ninja attack of the raiding party of demented gnomes, out of the heavy mountain forest; less stocky than gnomes but muttering their dialect; sounds Ewok.[1]

Some of them jump and clasp onto the bus side, putting their hands through the windows or holding themselves onto the roof rack, as we approach the stop, shouting. Soon, off the bus as we come to a halt, they eagerly they take a bag as we file out. I am still paranoid from my experience in Delhi, and refuse to hand over my bag. My Sherpa[2] is very insistent. He must be cursing me for lost earnings Perhaps I dishonour him. The sight of a Sherpa carrying my ruck-sack (I mean, we aren't talking about a heavy luggage case).

I press on up the road, not knowing where I am or where I am going, except up the hill to the next tier in the road. Shimla is on a ridge, dominated by Christ Church, a gothic building crowning the skyline. There is a thin spectacled man in a Toyota minivan. He looks like Peter Bronkhorst[3], the Amsterdam anarchist speed-junky I will meet three years hence. I ask him to take me to the Viceregal Lodge. My bag is heavy, with books I brought from McLeod Ganj. I regret not enlisting the service of the Sherpa.

The taxi takes me to Spars Lodge, which is five minutes away, a hotel that seems promising; mid-range budget, owned by an Anglophile Indian Lady. The taxi man charges me 1,000 rupees, which must be the most expensive taxi I take in India; instant karma for spurning the Sherpa? 5 am, amid mountain mists through pine trees, after attack of the Sherpas, there is extortion, on a lay-by near Summer Hill.

I know I am being had, but I don't seem to care, as I have had enough of rackety bus travel on meandering mountain paths. I hand over the money with alacrity, then lament money wasted this way, which could have treated the whole troupe of Sherpas. 'You are in my country now, and while you are, you will pay me what you would pay if you were in England!'

His zeal is effortlessly egalitarian, for beneath his façade is the face of extortion; his tariff, the trademark of a greedy nature, using twisted logic to extract a relatively vast sum.[4]

Once I've checked into Spars lodge, which has a certain colonial charm, and a friendly welcome from the Anglophile landlady, I walk to Lord Dufferin's old place, the Viceregal Lodge, half hoping to spot some rare birds, see some rare Himalayan plants and butterflies, maybe even have silver service tea while music is played on an antique gramophone.

The Lodge is perched high on a flat plateau. At the end of the lawn there are rhododendrons, that conceal a precipice; terraced lawns with rose pergolas. Easy to fall down a precipice here with or without a horse. I turn to admire this athletic baronial Pile, built as the Government House of the Indian Empire; steadfast debouchment of native genius in Jacobethan style, architecturally, like Victorian country house, exuding the peculiar sadness of departed greatness. Eerily enticing atmosphere; I soak it in, at this early hour of the morning.[5]

Dufferin had the place built as a great romantic house in which he played a personal part in designs. Visiting the site of construction daily with his wife, who shared his enthusiasm for building, she was amused by the appearance of native labourers, especially the women, who seemed as much at ease on the top of the roof as on the ground: 'most picturesque masons they are'.

I speak to a man from the Institute for Advanced Studies, which occupies this site of historic interest. He feels the need to tell me it wasn't easy for workers to carry all that stone up the hill. *Nanos gigantum humeris insidentes.*[6] Frederick Hamilton-Temple-Blackwood, 1st Marquis of Dufferin and Ava, 8th Viceroy of India was the author of 'Letters from High Latitudes'. His son illustrated Hilaire Belloc's Books.[7]

Lady Dufferin also wrote. She published extensive travel writings and photographs.[8] It is like a house in the Highlands, with its crenelated tower and forbidding blue and grey facings of local limestone and sandstone; spectacular views. Entrance hall, gallery, huge teak staircase to upper floors, gallery; space, grandeur. I walk the state dining room, panels ten feet high, enriched with Elizabethan strap-work, carrying armorial bearings from former Governors-General and Viceroys.[9]

What surreal sense of transposed Scottish baronial grandeur here. I walk along steep mountain paths, and catch a view of Mount Jakko.[10] I wonder into town;[11] more Indian than McLeod Ganj, more English, or-dered & restrained. Each hill station has its own character; both have an Arcadian setting, informal layout, hierarchy. Gone are the English upper classes, save those that return to cottages and houses turned into smart hotels.

The middle-class Indians on holiday here in the hills, live out the English dream, offering it an unconscious respect. Place of calm recu-peration from the heat of the plains below, with dream-like visions of the snow-capped Himalayas beyond.

Impossible that Shimla and its sublimity can ever be effaced from my mind.[12] Fashionable retreat, once primitive, now luxurious,[13] with houses like alpine cottages, fretwork eaves, exposed timber framing, carpets, chandeliers, wall-shades, cricket ground, race meetings.[14] To think the British ruled from a quiet hill station. Imagine if Whitehall moved, lock, stock and barrel to St Moritz for the summer.[15] Timber-framed Post Office, intact from Kipling's Shimla, then above scandal, looks suspiciously Swiss. Below The Mall and The Ridge there are bazaars and quarters cascading down the hill, in a warren of alleys and shacks. 'The abode of the little tin gods?[16] Or pine-misted Himalayan Mount Olympus?[17]

I am amazed; balustrade terraces, hanging high over precipitous chasms; canopied balconies, with Gothic detailing: vital charm, originality, then modest villas, where colonial officials once lived, like Swiss chalets. Honey-suckle, roses. Spire of Christ Church.[18]

This place of cups of tea on the terrace, lemonade; perhaps pink gins. Back at Spars Lodge, I sit for tea, now with a German doctor called Hans. There is also the son of a disabled man who has been imprisoned for drug possession when on a charity walk. His father, he tells me, is deaf and would not carry drugs.[19] 10 years is a long sentence; he has served 2 years and 2 months of a ten-year jail term for possession of 20 kilos of cannabis.

He is a diabetic, with an artificial leg. His son is very upset, by an apparent travesty of justice; sufficiently cautionary to ward me off ever carrying Parvati cream or ganja when in transit. What if too much generosity was bad? If you bought some from a Sadhu only to forget about it being stashed in your bag, and later encounter a police search, would I remember in time? One cannot take chances, but if police are corrupt like those Delhi taxi drivers, maybe they would frame you, whether you had it or not and demand an exorbitant fee to release you? Hans tells me he was once a stoker on an Italian ship and sailed to Cape Town, Buenos Ares and the Caribbean. 'If you like to go from Bombay to Mombasa, it will take about a week. I have a friend on a cargo vessel, he could get you there very cheaply.'

I am tempted but must return to England to finish my Philosophy degree. There is a culture in the West of the pill panacea, he tells me. He is fascinated by Vedic medicine. However, he says, there are, in places, deplorable medical conditions. He says he once paid for an operation to save the life of a girl with septicaemia.

'If I always interfered, I'd have no money!'[20]

I enjoy Shimla. For me it has personal associations in that my first encounter with Indian cuisine was at the Shimla restaurant in Newport, Shropshire. Shimla is like a pleasant ski resort, set in a veritable harit aranya[21] Shimla has an astonishing mountain railway. It is one of the outstanding feats of British Imperial Engineering.[22]

A 60-mile series of tight reverse curves, gradients of over three feet in every hundred. Five miles entirely underground; 107 tunnels, two miles across precipitous viaducts balanced over yawning chasms: but not built without mishap. In 1903 all work stopped amid the excitement of the native workforce. The bones of a great snake had been discovered embedded in one of the tunnels, but on careful investigation the wonderful serpent was revealed to be an iron pipe, carrying fresh air to the workings.[23]

I leave the world of caparisoned jam pans and palanquins, the jumble of colonial dwellings and mischievous monkeys in pine trees. At the station, I meet a North African traveller, who says:

"The people of the plains, they are dirty...Dirty people!"

We descend through pines and mountains to the 'dirty' plains. I am reading Zola and speaking to an Indian youth who happens to be from Reading, Berks., and who is visiting family in India for the summer.

It seems his parents had been encouraging him to speak to me. He is living in Reading, went to school there too, now working for a company. I casually reply that I too live in Reading, at the University, and

I often pass his office when on that morning run along the Thames to Sonning. After Kalka, we reach Almora. I almost change to Saharaupar, but leave the private office of the railway station master who offers a chai and biscuit; since I'm alone, I get the twitches and decide to leave. In Delhi, I retire to the Namascar Hotel, which is hot and dirty. Four pints of lager cost 60p here, although I do not drink. Out of the smoke cloud I see the spectacle of memories unfold.

I feel quite indifferent; the hotel boy is attractive; brings a piece of *charus*. He seems quite eager, but I do not take advantage of it. In all my time in India, I do not allow myself to get that close to people. I gaze with yearning, eyes glazed, *charus* embrace, night reverie of rainbow flight. I wonder. I'm not someone other than myself? These brief joys pass as soon as they arise. It is I, myself that feels these things, but I do not yet know who my true self is. Perhaps it's an early introduction to cruelty that undermines strong self-identity? I'm running a script in a box that surrounds me, from that early life; self-hate on default. I acknowledge it as that invisible curse that takes years to throw off; from family ancestral? From weight of karmic returns?

At best, all I do is manage my limited life as it unfolds. I am used to how it has played so far; miserably. When I go on an exotic escapade, I question what it expands, reveals in me. What skins must I shed; fuller life. My mind broadens in new vistas, through this culture, new perspectives on my own. This can only aid liberation, form character.

God seems to provide the record needle and vinyl. As composer, conceives Gesamtkunstwerk, but from the moment of creation, music starts playing in the groove scratched out in one's childhood; that record player. If only you could see it!

You would certainly want an upgrade! There are certain motifs that keep reoccurring, though in different settings. You can't have a *Vivace, Scherzo, Capriccio Adagio, a Sotto, Misterioso, Pesante, Lacrimoso,* Elegy– [24] In the future, we may conquer the stars, and move through the outer stellar reaches of the unknown, just by sitting still in our hearts. In matters of the heart, still less to sit on one's hands while chugging along in an antique train. This seems to be the genius of India. Yet I am not at peace in my heart.

'Ticketless travel is a social evil', says a sign on the passing platform. I feel grateful for the three-month India Rail Pass. It means one can jump on any train. We approach the lower altitudes and stop. A girl is at a bright station decked with flowers, in a sari, puts her hand on my arm resting out the window, and hopes I will marry her, which I will not. 'Take me with you.' All I can do is press on and keep myself distracted in this place. With Wagner playing on my Walkman's cassette, I have a stirring soundtrack to accompany my voyage. Smoke and charus, I ascend to space, there are three of us, like shooting stars bursting upwards in rainbow light. Christ and Krishna.[25]

The next morning I take a train. Soon I am in Dehra Dun, Uttar Pradesh, climbing 2000m above sea level, to Mussorie, a quaint guest house with Victorian tiled floors and platitudes:

'If you cut down one tree, plant two', says a sign. My spirit is enlarged by lonely and severe wandering; discounting the angst that lends to collapse. I am never as despondent or bored here as I am in Reading. The streets are alive, engaging. People care about you to talk to you. I willed a certain fearlessness, the song of the noontide, where the sun in me shines, so my shadow is exposed, what more can I say? The greatest shadow is within, said Nietzsche, the light shines strongest in the heart.[26]

In Mussorie, I buy a book on Jung and Eastern Thought, and chance upon a page about *Tapas*. This seems to suit my temperament at this time. I am staying at the English Cottage. The warm-hearted manager is the nicest man in India. He welcomes me like his long absent friend. He takes me for a walk. We survey the Dhuladhar[27] range. We sit talking of deities and those who don't believe much at all, and what a tragedy it is if ever there was a twilight of the gods in India.

An American arrives, who has a jaded demeanour, twisted, facial skin disease which seems to reflect something dark in his soul's aspect. Foolishly I allow him to divert me from the pleasant manager, for no other reason than an American has arrived. The kind Indian sleeps in a box room beside the terrace, before the guest rooms. I go to bed early, not wishing to speak any longer to this 'guy' who wonders if I have facial herpes; clearly his game is psychological projection.

Perhaps if he got any closer to me I'd be infected? This only serves to harden my 'tapas'. Before he leaves he hands me a Vipassana[28] meditation retreat hand book, and says it is like crumbs leading back to the ginger-bread house. It confirms my prejudice that I get on better with natives here in India. I am angry I have unintentionally offended my host.

I get a taxi to Rishikesh with an excitable driver who steers the wheel with his right hand, while emptying a cigarette of its tobacco in his left. With his fingers he blends it with charus. Then deftly returns the tobacco with the charus blend into the cigarette, and packs it all back in; camouflage. He says lots of people smoke here; but if it looks like a cigarette, no one will know.

His name is Raja[29], and he is now smoking pure hash as though it were a fag, and we pull over and he offers a brief inhalation. I arrive at the Bhandar Swiss Cottage in Rishikesh, glowing. You need the digestion of an ostrich, the patience of Job, the nerve of a war veteran, and a sailor's capacity for sleep to get around India at this pace. There is the discomfort of travel, being paralysed by heat, perhaps the head marauding and occasional hallucinogenic contemplations that ganja may induce.

Having travelled at such a lightening pace, I become torpid. A man called Sandeep in Mussorie tells me: 'Mujah akele rehne do' is Hindi for 'Go away'. 'Mujah Bhandar Swiss Cottage mein chod Dijye', means, 'take me to the BhandarSwiss Cottage, please rickshaw driver wallah . I am in the Doon Valley, the camel's road, Mussorie. I feel like the poet who in the highest calenture of the brain, says, a steed that knows his rider on the crested billow of the ocean has his flowing mane. In India, everyone addresses a river (and tree) as a living being, a sovereign princess who hears and understands all they say. And it exercises a superior intelligence over all their affairs. I hear in the mountains an encouraging voice whispering.

The Master's voice will guide you like a ship's captain on a stormy sea. One must be on one's guard against self-pity. One must place one's gifts in the service of others; that we will celebrate what he has given us; in an image of his likeness. Be strong and be happy.

{ 8 }

Rishikesh

Had I become animated with perpetual vitality? Intense pleasures and trials? The bracing sweep of life? What ceaseless energy, exhilaration, pure concentration, on that higher vibration, propels further into sight-sound of the mountain? Discomfort, you can always purchase at a price you can't afford. A single ounce of drowsiness, sharpening senses; Parvati *chillum*.

You apprehend crystal clear holy Ganges, gushing down from mountains at Rishikesh, surrounded by vast green hills on three sides. Here the Beatles met Maharishi Mahesh Yogi[1] in the sixties. So, it was here that a generation was inspired to meditate and practice mental quiet; while others developed psychoses.

As I approach the huge Lakshman Jhula suspension bridge, where Rama's brother Lakshmana crossed the river on a rope I see a curious Sadhu who is smiling. He stands on the river bank awhile as I try to capture his likeness. I notice he has huge, well-worn feet from long barefoot peregrinations and has a traditional nap-sack, giving him the look of an ancient wayfarer from, say, mediaeval times. He has long matted hair, a straggly beard. Rishikesh, *faute de mieux*, means 'place of the seers'. Sadhus, yogis gather here in abundance, dressed in robes with wild, matted hair. I meet one who is bleary-eyed, smoking ganja from a pipe; scraggly beard, feet that are hobbit like; hardened by barefoot itinerancy. He is pointing discreetly at the overflowing

Ganges, from the left elbow, resting on his nap sac, camouflaged among his flowing saffron robe, giving him a proportion larger than his carriage. Imagine ending up like him, I wonder...The Sadhu turns towards the river bridge, invites me to his ashram for further talks, if not a smoke of something wild & ecstatic. I decline, afraid of false prophets in orange robes: Better be on fate's safer bank, proudly autonomous to make avoidable mistakes. What could one learn by being too obliging?

I stay at Bhandari Swiss Cottage on the hill-side, where I briefly take my longest rest, three days; in a hammock by day, a harsh bed by night. The heat is oppressive, and at night frequent power cuts. It feels like the fan on room ceiling is about to land on me like a helicopter, because suddenly the propellers have stalled, and these four blades are black shadows taunting me; forcing me to leave the protective insect shield; mosquito net.

Unable to comfortably sleep I smoke Parvati *charus* copiously in the hammock outside; ostensibly to numb myself. I'm unused to insects the size of the Koh-I-Noor Diamond.[2] And never as dazzling or appealing. Less sparkling for me, the prehistoric creature that flies at me is like a miniature Messerschmitt or drone.[3] I flash my torch and behold a locust. Perhaps it heralds from the unconscious? No mere dragon fly, being around 30cm long. Only morning light can banish these night horrors.

{ 9 }

Haridwar: The Source of the Ganges

I arrive in time for Hardiwar[1] hosting the Ganga Aarti[2] at the main Kar Ki Pauri ghat.[3] Here the Hindu worships the mythical source of the Ganga, where 13,000 feet above the sea, there is a glacier seen lying in the hollow of the valley, covered with earth, stones, (and bones?).[4] Ice melts, precipitating the titan course, in great masses of water, voyaging south in a constant artery to the very heart of India.

Haridwar leaves the mountains and enters the powerful privilege of the plains, refreshing all as it goes, packed full of miraculous minerals. Ablutions, chants and *pujas*[5] join its course in silence and ritual, where prayers and blessings are sent flowing with its course. Along the Holy River, hundreds of devout Hindus line the banks as candles are set alight on the boats, with lotus flowers. They stream down the current in passing boat lights, each on its own path to the sea, each passing boat in the night vessel joining with the Eternal ∞

I have joined a throng of pilgrims, and now find myself part of a puga ceremony. Ganga Aarti means prayer for River Ganga.[6] Prayers here are dedicated to gods and goddesses; River Ganga, Divine Mother. The same water they believe removes sins when you take a dip in its holy water; even liberation to souls.

At Ganga Aarti,[7] men on platforms, bearing caskets with huge flames rising above their outstretched arms, brighten night-fall in an ancient atmosphere surrounding this mass ritual, in which the individual dissolves into a collective adoration of God, in celebration of the departed. A priest performs an elaborate ritual upon me, and I trust it is a blessing to the Lord of Wisdom, that I may go well on my journey?

Ganga Aarti at Har Ki Pauri Ghat. 1,000 people here for Ganga Aarti; it's low season. Har Ki Pauri is the ghat to take holy dip in Ganga. Here Lord Vishnu appeared here to bless Bhratuhari.[8] Har Ki Pauri means 'footprints of god'. It's the place where nectar drops fell during the battle of Devas and Asuras for nectar. One of the holiest places to take bath in the holy river Ganga. At the point where the holy river and the holy place come together, it attracts the largest amount of people. Pundits[9] carry out the idol in a palkhi[10] to a ghat platform near Ganga, people come forward to take a blessing. Pundits start the ceremony chanting on loud speakers.

Sanskrit mantras, offering milk and honey, Ganga Lahari[11] sung; then Ganga Lahari, pundits receive promises from the crowd not to pollute river Ganga. Hands are raised in agreement. "Har Har Gange, Jai Ma Gange" the pundits light the Aartis as the Ganga Aarti song is played with bells ringing.[12] Pundits waving Aarti in front of river Ganga. Opposite is Malviya Dwip, a small island ghat. Where people line the banks on the ghat steps like a crowd at a stadium, clear view, Ganga Aarti in front. Sholkas are sung.[13] I step down to the ghat, lean forward to launch my puja with lotus, candle burning. I fall forward abruptly as I misjudge the submerged ghat step, getting soaked; fortunate I launched my boat okay, watching it flow down river with the current, and an armada of similar lights. Even here the waters are fast; high flowing, rapid in monsoon.

Under a starry night, after uttering his benediction, and marking my forehead with paste, he asks for a small fee.[14]

Har ki Pauri, Haridwar

II

Rajputana

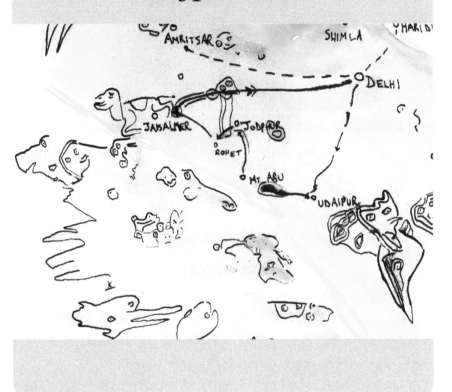

{ 10 }

Udaipur

Delhi belly. When it come is long, remorseless, during this 17-hour train journey, to Udaipur: Cramps, flatulence and a bad start to the Rajasthani leg of the journey. It must be from the jug of water from that canteen near the station before boarding the train in Delhi. Why did I drink of it?

I feel dizzy, nauseous, and visit the toilet in quick succession. Excruciating tension, belly aches. It had been a simple culinary experience: bhaaji and chickpea, I refused mango, watermelon. Always I eat curd prior to food. It encourages stomach resilience as a precaution.

I would always refuse cooked meat; drinking local water was a mistake, more so as it's vicious when traveling across vast sprawling distances in a four-berth sleeper with no incense to clear the air.

We arrive at Udaipur station. And disembark. The Indian father of the family beneath me: Is this your first time in India?

I am looking forward to Udaipur as I get to see the palace where they filmed Sir Roger Moore in James Bond's 'Octopussy'. The Lake Palace of Jagniwas Island, accessible by boat (he used a motorised crocodile from 'Q' Branch).

I walk ancient streets, perhaps used in the film's rickshaw chase. The palace stands in the distant mountain range overlooking the southern Udaipur.

I meet an Indian who has the benefit of a moped; transport to hill top for commanding panorama. We scoot along the lake with the monsoon palace, constructed by Maharana Sajjan in 19th century. It is now deserted, although a small government radio communication centre, is hidden in one room; like something out of an espionage film.

The man with the moped brings me here and I pass the caretaker some baksheesh. I take in the view of Lake Pichola, Fateh Sagar and the desert.

There has been a four-year drought, the lake is halfempty, with promise of rain. Udaipur is a tantalising sequel after my trip to Mount Abu, after a 17-hour train journey from Delhi.

'Nakki Lake' is a lake situated in the Indian hill station of Mount Abu in Aravalli range. It is a very ancient sacred Lake, according to the Hindu legend. It is called by this name because it was dug out from Nails (Nakh). One story is of dug by Gods to live in, for protection against the Bashkali rakshash (a wicked demon). The lake is in length of about a half mile and in width about of a quarter of mile and 20 to 30 ft. deep towards the dam on the west.

There is the Toad Rock on a hill near the lake. Toad rock is so called as it looks like a toad about to jump into the lake, from the side of the rock facing the lake. By the side of the lake there is a path leading to Sunset Point. It is forbidden to climb to Sunset Point due to dangerous bandits living near there. Mahatma Gandhi's ashes were immersed in this Holy Lake on 12 February 1948 and Gandhi Ghat was constructed.

I recall Mount Abu's remnant of a British Polo club, still functional, and the International headquarters of Brahma Kumaris[1], with white-robed sages who radiate insight into something unspeakably deep and peaceful.

In Mount Abu, there is a Jain Temple at Rankapur.[2] How could I forget the Jain Temple, its intricate marble carving? It contains almost 1,500 wondrous sculpted pillars. Never have I seen stone that breaths and moves in leaves over shadows. That handsome westerner, who also is a Buddhist monk, is very interested to talk to me, as I am him, if anxious. The monk is in saffron robe, with muscular biceps. I wonder how he could be a monk? 'I just felt I had to become it', he says. He seems to find me amusing and is constantly smiling. Perhaps he likes me too?

The Rang mandap or grand hall features a central dome from which hangs a big ornamental pendent featuring an elaborate carving of a lotus. Arranged in a circular band are 72 figures of Tirthankars in sitting posture and just below this band are 360 small figures of Jain monks in another circular band.

The Lake Palace was built between 1743 and 1746 under the direction of the Maharana Jagat Singh II of Udaipur, as a winter palace. The palace was constructed facing east, aligned for prayer to Surya, the Hindu sun god, at the crack of dawn; successive rulers then used this palace as their summer resort, holding their regal durbars in its courtyards lined with columns, pillared terraces, fountains and gardens. I do not try to get to it.

Perhaps I could afford a night there, but the lake is dry, half full, and algae proliferates. It is perhaps the wrong season for a stay there. My guide book tells me the walls are made of black and white marbles, adorned by semi-precious stones and ornamented niches. It has gardens, fountains, pillared terraces and columns within its courtyards.[3]

I am inclined to agree with Pierre Loti who saw it as 'slowly mouldering in the damp emanations of the lake'.[4] If I prejudice its worth, seeing only outward appearance, I would omit that Bhagwat Singh converted the Jag Niwas Palace into Udaipur's first luxury hotel. And luxurious it remains. I stand lakeside, admiring ornate white features, at the boat launch to the palace. There's a local tribal troupe, performing music; women with sword blades in their mouths, caskets upon their heads; their chief man is drumming. One of the women looks at me intently, through gritted teeth. Seems to say, you must acknowledge yourself as your own best love, own yourself, your experience, which is an expression of God's love for your Life.

There is false light drawn around a mysterious experience in sacred architecture. Where I enter temples, I choose wisely; suspicious, especially, when someone claims I must go to a specific temple, for no other reason than they think I should go! But what if I was to go, just because they suggest it? I'm not sure all temples are equally good, perhaps a mischievous spirit dwells there, or some bad presence? I wouldn't want to get mixed up in bad invocations. While I am here; the desert seems glad. One must be selective with Temples as with dentists or schools. Some dentists aren't good, and yet charge a lot of money.

There are repercussions in some temples: I seek the place where I have experience of most inner peace, and light, that encourages the growth of the sacred within, and fosters that in relations without. Bad temples make you wary; then you don't forget the good.

There is a range of Rajput[5] regalia, from saris of ancient tribes to great chapatti serving dishes, elegantly elongated sitars beside encrusted turbans, pure silver hookahs.

The Jagdish Temple is impressive. It is in Udaipur. On the temple wall there are five levels of Nature of Hindu belief: the elephant (wisdom/fortune), horse (power), mankind (engaged in Kama sutras), demi-gods. Above them are the Supreme Incarnations (Krishna, Vishnu, etc.), Jagdish Temple is a fine Indo-Aryan example built by Maharana Jagat SIng in 1651. It enshrines a black stone image of Vishnu as Jagannath (Lord of the Universe).

There are plenty of adoring women, who supplicate rain. Vishnu's incarnation, Krishna, with golden flute on his head, is next to Vishnu. Expediency. Hard currency. Usually resolves the more pressing matters. Baksheesh for photography of sacred things. This temple official is pleased to accept my contribution. The peacock's tail opens out in rapid succession, with iridescent colours. Ornamental mosaic, decorative wall feature; symbol of the astral body consciousness. Opposite Jagdish I approach a shrine, with a solitary woman, sat beside the image of Garuda. Who is Garuda, I wonder? The Indonesian airline perhaps? No, the vehicle of Vishnu, the woman tells me, that is why he has wings.

There is an elephant that you must pay 10 rupees to photograph. However, the elephant is not amused. The instant I point and click he swings his trunk and near clobbers me[6] to the ground. If the elephant represents wisdom, this is learned the hard way? Udaipur has narrow, colourful streets, an abundance of crafts, miniatures, (painted with a squirrel's hair brush). The miniaturist tells me he attended art school. The Professor of Art says, 'I studied in Amsterdam in 1997, and zis man just pulled down zhis trouzers, dipped his behind in a tin of pain, and zsmeared it over a canvas. And zhey callz zthat Art!?'

Summer scenes, distant mirage, felt from far off sands, singing, dancing, wonder of Rajasthani colour, lives on in your brightened mind. In wander folk, who do no harm; feels homelier, Aryan dark complexions, innate light beauty of soul shining through.[7]

Elephant, Udaipur

Pushkar

Pushkar's sacred Lake, one of the four most sacred dhams, a pilgrimage site for devout Hindus. The lake formed from bereft Shiva's tears for Sati: Pushkar: Most ancient of Indian cities, on the shore of Pushkar Lake.[1] Pushkar in Sanskrit means blue lotus flower. Hindus believe that the gods released a swan with a lotus in its beak and let it fall on earth where Brahma would perform a grand yagna. Everything that is offered into the fire is believed to reach God. The place where the lotus fell was called Pushkar.[2] Brahma was in search of a place for vagna.[3]

Mahayagna: A demon, Vajranash, was killing people. Brahma's mantra of the lotus flower killed the demon. The mighty yagna protected Pushkar from demons. Saraswati , god of music and arts, would have offered Ahuti for the yagna.

She was not there that time so Gayatri , a Gurjar girl, was married to brahma and performed yagna. Saraswati was angry and she cursed Brahma: 'You shall only be worshiped in Pushkar'.

All Brahma Temple priests in Pushkar to this day are from the Gurjar community. The Mahabharata says that while laying down plans for Maharaja Yudhishthara's travel, the Maharaja entered the Jungles of Sind and crossed the small rivers on the way to bathe in Pushkara.[4] Despite the abusive nature of his father, he continued his devotion towards Lord Vishnu. He is considered to be a mahājana, or great devotee, and is of special importance to devotees of the avatār Narasiṁha. Prahlāda, in his pilgrimage to holy places, visited Pushkarayana. Pushkar Lake– The prime attraction of Pushkar is the Lake, which is considered sacred, like the Mansarovar Lake in Tibet.

A knock at the door, as I lay on the single bed, travel weary. I open the door. There is a small but thin man with a pleasant, beaming smile, brandishing a bottle of massage oil. Having stiff shoulders, and feeling travel stressed, I agree to 'the procedure' which he conducts as I get on the bed, for which 'I remove my shirt and trousers and lie down on the bed?!'

His strokes vary from the deep to superficial, in flow of energy channels and nerve pathways I experience as incredibly soothing. He begins with passive delicate strokes becoming more persuasive: pinching then kneading my small muscles (with his thumb and forefinger). Soon I am completely submissive to his massage, which works on me like a hypnotic dance across my body, synchronised to his deep breathing with me as though to maintain a more profound connection.

Like a sculptor flowing with my body's mould he encourages an unprecedented, relaxing yet enlivening mood within me. My entire body is thereby summoned to an incredible sense of alignment. I had seen on a book stall a map of the human body as described by ancient Indian medicine. I was impressed by the intricacy of it, the pressure points, the chakras[5], I feel confident he has a deep awareness of subtle nerves and parts of my body to evoke these feelings of bliss. He is well versed in that chart it seems, as though he intuitively knows every millimetre of it across my body.

He knows that each chakra nourishes organs and controls various psycho-physiological aspects of our being. When they are blocked, physical disease ensues. His Ayurvedic oil massage opens and cleanses my energy channels so the current can flow freely and my latent vitality is released. He knows how to assuage these gateways to my biological and mental processes. The sense of touch, the sense of smell, sight and hearing are extraordinary. The scent of the oil coaxes my 10 million sense-detecting cells into an effortless state of harmony; aromas evoke peaceful impressions, conjure up memories of bliss; boost my immune system, triggering emotions that drive away stress; scented smells literally 'clear the air' of any negative influences and energies. He chants mantras silently in his mind; a concentrated vibration coming off his hands, cleanses subtle nerves, mind and energy channels. What mystical energy and vibrations; what unique power. I am glowing and oozing with light and peace; doshic[6] balance; transported in bliss.

I dream of an Indian lady in a palace, bathing in a pool filled with the petals of hundreds of roses, her body and hair cleansed with herbal oils of jasmine and sandalwood. What air of sensual delight intoxicates anyone entering those palace grounds. And then it is done. He gives me a bottle of rose water; says that it is for cleaning my eyes of dust and air pollution.

I am mesmerised by happy feelings; filled with the pleasing scent of summer flowers. I feel changed and renewed, as though anything I could conceive and sincerely believe in, I would achieve. Like my circumambulation of the subcontinent; and one day writing it up. His techniques are ancient and effective; for countless years, under the guide of a fierce *samkalpa*; that one-pointed resolve to do or achieve.[7]

I jump on a horse-drawn cart from the railway station, that takes me on a short journey at twilight, to the hotel near the sacred lake; to the waters where I receive a priestly blessing. Thick red paste is drawn on my brow. Then a *puja* is placed on the lake and I'm presented with a coconut, in honour of Brahma. A red band is placed on my wrist. I'm unhappy this moment as I feel coerced into giving him too many rupees.

I leave the lake *ghat* bewildered, and a kindly man at the market suggests I get a red scarf to wear with my white shirt. In all my travels, only one person took offence at this scarf, and that was in Mehrangarh Fort in Jodhpur.[8] (Luckily my panama hat survived well into my Moroccan adventure, but did not make it over the Spanish border from Morocco, as it was taken.)

The word *bazaar* naturally raises in the mind of Englishmen the idea of a place like something 'bizarre', something weird and wonderful. We merely require to take it in general sense, to understand its meaning at once. The word Bazaar is Persian, and implies market. In Pushkar, meats, alcohol and even eggs are not allowed, although I've seen Sadhus take pious pleasure in hashish pipes. In India, it is a market of provisions. Like the red scarf, a colour I am told signifies the scholarly wisdom of the Brahmin, although is that not blue? I stroll through the bazaar, suddenly stopped by a girl who could have been a vendor of earthen pots. Perhaps I wasn't being mindful?

She is standing beside an older woman who sits in the gutter, pouring forth a torrent of Shivas. She wants to see my hand, which I offer, being in a pliant, lonely moment. She begins to smear an orange paste from a tube in her hand on my palm. People stop and turn and smile. I am complicit. I walk away with a flower petal tattoo, decorated on my right palm. Despite much scrubbing, it lasts a week. I'm asked to contribute twenty rupees for this; a paltry sum for something I find embarrassing. I am scolded by an earnest Indian, further along the bazaar passage, who admonishes me.

'No, no, no, you have been made a fool. You see, you must refuse these people when they do that. You see, it is only customary for women to colour their hands. It is severely frowned upon for a male to possess such a pattern!' The November Camel Fair is five months away (by which time I'll be back in Reading),[9] but I do go on a first Camel Safari from Pushkar. I'm at a chai canteen on the literal edge of the city, which becomes pure desert. Perhaps I am imbued with a new spirit of optimism after my visit to the most sacred lake in India?

It is an ancient & important pilgrimage centre, for those individuals on spiritual perambulation. Here I am waiting for the camel to arrive, so I may undertake that desert excursion.

Chai canteen, Pushkar

{ 12 }

Deserta Rajathania

Prepare to march, prepare to march. On whose orders? On whose orders? On the order of the boss captain. The Arabic safarīyah means 'a journey', and my journey will be a matter of days in the desert. After traversing Nag Pahar[1] by means of local bus from Ajmer, I am now waiting with my ruck-sack to embark on a rural ramble from the chai canteen.

His chai canteen is encased by canvas on bamboo. The main four supports look like tree branches. There is a long wooden table, around which are rattan frette stools[2] that look like concave drums. Now all the ingredients are in the pot, he is waiting for the mixture to boil. The handsome chai wallah in black trousers, tight, white t-shirt, has his right arm resting on his hip at the wrist, fingers pointing outwards, while his other arm has its hand on a long spoon that stirs the chai concoction. His gaze is serene, out into the scene framed by the bamboo supports of his canteen. Chai is boiling in a silver pot over his wood burner.

A man in white robes passes by, pulling his four-bicyclewheel- cum-wooden-trolley, with basket, sack, stove. He looks at me, and I notice there are three boys sat above his orange turban, behind him, on the raised ledge of the concentre pavement, above the sandy road. I take a stool behind the table. The chai wallah finds my presence curious. Perhaps he's like me; shy?

He decocts the chai; a mixture of milk and water with loose leaf tea, sweeteners, and spices. He deftly shakes the pink sieve handle, drains off the solid spices from the boiled milky water. Then he pours the chai into a glass tumbler.[3] Then he returns to gazing at the street, flat roof houses, beyond them, the desert gateway; I too stare into space, occasionally look at the wallah, soon to explore rugged terrain of Thar Desert, The Great Desert of India, with a camel guide.

What an improvised journey I'm on, with some providential lines of travel; inspired satisfaction with enthusiasm. Three camels pass by the chai stall, framed by the stilts, and canopy of the chai shack, set to the flat rooftops of the sandy buildings on the dusty roadd. Tall, proud one-hump camels. Perhaps one-hump is an easier to ride?[4] We touch the Aravalli range[5]; the oldest mountain fold in India. Across the sandy fields and small dunes among beautiful hills, profound, mesmerising sun, colouring the sky.

The camel safari proceeds deeper into desert, with sparse hamlets. During the rains, enticing desert-scape, brightly subdued sky with thin orange-grey clouds, biblical thunder storms, followed by short, sharp rain. There are few comforts from the blistering heat, save bottled water and fire-cooked lunch. The third camel, part of our caravan, carries the supplies.

There are no temples here. Only the open air, aridity of desert. There's no marble work: All that breathes, moves without gold leaf, just that golden brightness of everlasting day, shimmering glint of discarded tin, refracting sun-ray, heat waves rising from scorched ground in the distance, then the apprehensions of snakes; mercifully they are just sticks basking in the distance.

No statues are found here, unlike Mount Abu, with its Jain carvings, or palm trees for that matter. Clean orange, sandy plains with frequent swathes of green scrub: This is the wild side of the land of Kings for a knight of Camel-lot.

Far from Pushkar, removed from the spiritual centre owing to its water source and religious faith, camel-journeying through barren desert which draws me deep into silence; interior peace. Lemon dawns glow through the naked trees. Sharpening faculties. Fullness of life at six am; those mesmeric silhouettes that shimmer against turquoise sky above hill crest. The desert is beautiful on monsoon mornings, few people in sight, no vehicles to impede, camel pads and footsteps silent, then clamour of rattling pans, pots fastened to the saddle of the supply camel.

We pass a small grassy swathe. I turn downward, and see crepuscular shadows form, long black lines from camel legs; silhouettes like crooked sundial readings. In the heat of midday, I feel dizzily disorientated. My throat is dry and I feel this vast space opens ever wider; with no further sign of civilisation, nor so much as a thunderous ruin.

A nomad appears, sitting obscurely, smoking on a rock, as though time is as elastic as his thin, flexible legs; he looks like he's seen it all, around the bend on repeat cycles of dusty trail. We continue our rural ramble. In time, I get used to the saddle. I have a pillow for extra cushioning; even then, *un toucher cru*. Countryside folk here, extremely friendly, a young boy decides to run alongside me with a small bowl, having appeared excitedly from the desert scrub, clad in the merest loin cloth, I half expect him to ask for money; like precocious city dwellers. Not modest. On his way to the well for water.

Fortunately, no real snakes in sight. We are amicably going our peaceful way, no one here to impose their pain pictures or with *schadenfreude* titter behind bushes, like those wildly insecure, English neighbours. Then out of nowhere, the silence is breached. In the distance, out of the fast approaching dust cloud, at break-neck speed, emerges a Mercedes 4x4; Some travel or photo-journalist on a lightning tour. French or American, the camel boy can't be sure. Surreal to see a fast and furious vehicle, during the ease of a camel trek.

Hours pass into that vast endless vanishing point, like an eternal vision, as the modern ages overtakes the slower pace of earlier times. Our consistent plod perseveres. Krishna works hard with me on top, as does his master who pulls the harness rope ahead on foot. There is no judgment here, no thoughts, just Zen-like peace, acceptance of what is. Into the sunset, continuing the desert path before setting up camp for the evening. Then off again, BJ is taking the lead with Krishna as I'm mounted. I feel it's necessary to swap places; he's tired. Krishna is content with this. If there is a camel rope in the eye of a needle it is here.

To describe my joy at taking this repast is impossible. Exposed all day to fierce rays of vertical sun, I feel insane, as though my life, which had of late become a great burden, becomes precious once again to me, if not happy. Towards the end of a very hot day, Krishna needs restful cool. He does not often feed. Krishna's legs bend, front, then back, as the camel guide encourages him to rest. Camel Krishna immediately sweeps his long neck against the sand, now he is flat on his side. soothing himself from fly irritation; lying then rolling in sand.

He lies down in shade, after day facing the sun so that only a small part of his body receives the last vestiges of the sun's rays. Then he's left us awhile, in some profound nap. 'We're near my home farm. We'll get there before nightfall.' There is an old banyan at twilight. I stand upon its huge roots. Dusk is such that the desert is distinguishable, charged with day-heat's resonance. The atmosphere cools, quietens. I'm excited as you don't see such trees back home. Our western roots are concealed beneath the earth.

All is peaceful at this serene hour in the wilderness. I look around, and derive great comfort in the desert. I like it because it's clean and enclosed by mountains. Having mounted Krishna again I am sitting securely on his hairy haunches, the camel boy proceeds ahead in sandals; patiently. For the remainder of the journey its twilight going on nightfall, towards the camel boy's family's farmstead. BJ, the camel boy, takes me to his home, where I meet his mother, brothers, little sister. It is a ramshackle old smallholding in the village of Gnigra, a sparse farming commune, whose primary produce is onions. It is not yet dark. I sit cross-legged on the single bed possessed by camel boy's family, deciding, I would prefer the starry-night in the open desert; than the comfort of a farmstead bed. It is more a wooden bed frame with tightly wrought rope cord; thread to support a body.

After dinner with his family together, his mum suggests unadventurously that I stay the night at the farm on the open bed: It is resolved that we pass the night in open desert, which seems just as arid as the land we earlier passed through.

We walk some distance into the desert: Only moonlight, constellations and torches. Under guiding glare then firelight, we make our camp. Desert night stillness possesses unrivalled peace. I climb inside a blanket bed on the dune, approaching whispers of some prophetic dream. BJ is much too tired to talk. He drinks the beer he's brought, with a younger boy, who joins him under his blanket. I am surprised by the ease in which they hold hands in that casual eastern way, and enjoy shared bodily warmth through the cold desert night.

I bid them goodnight then vanish beneath my blanket. I've quelled what passion the day heat raised. Even in the desert I cannot slake such lust. Am I secure from nocturnal intrusions!? Enfolded by a heavy top blanket, I drift in and out of deep sleep, lying entranced by exhaustion, booze.

The crystal clear starry night, fears playing games in my mind, accompanied by the disconcerting howling of a pack of dogs; distant, then suddenly all too near. I seemed to be reborn from dejection, some sulkiness persists, although I am roused from lowering my forehead, and going off into that place of dream, returning once again into focus, with the rapt fascination of the constant stream of desert unfolding. Wearing that panama hat, and buoyed up by Krishna the camel, and the guide. Feeling fatigued as the sun sinks to the west.

We wake early, and set out on a circular route returning to Pushkar. The noon heat is violent, we are determined to find some shade in the high mound of sand, by an old tree. The sands are hot. The duration of which, I wear my boating shoes and panama hat. With a thirst tormented by the heat, I drink large draughts of water.

I often call on death to relieve me of my psychological sufferings. I could fall from inanition. Always some new scene presents a sight or experience that revives my strength. I became anxious to return to England, that I might rest properly, and enjoy all those things one takes for granted back home. Pushkar is a smiling picture when I return to it, with emotions difficult to express, seeing palm trees, long yielding branches, the lake. Gone are the gazing beauties of the desert, here is verdure after the desert.

Once back at the hotel I shower, noticing how the white is such a stark contrast with my sable countenance. In the midst of misfortune, my Soul preserved all strength. Sudden changes in situations, did make me feel as though my Mind were forsaking me. Then I would recover, Tea was very important, somehow, I endured the misery and fatigue. As soon as I got to bed I fell into a profound Sleep.

There is poverty here, broken people hit by disasters, family afflictions, lack of money for adequate health care. Yet somehow they persist in living. It would be easy to sink under the complications of calamity pressing upon one here, to die destitute, of a broken heart, after that last blow, that plunged me in gloomy melancholy. It made me feel indifferent to everything. It was the special kindness of those I met, by slow degrees, helped me to recover my composure; chase thoughts of cruel recollections which afflicted me. I soon recovered my tranquillity, and dared at last, to cherish the hope of seeing more fortunate days. That hope was not delusive. Surprisingly, the camel boy is only 16. He looks older for his age; tough life leading camels. Young people in India work a lot younger and harder, than we can appreciate.

He earns something like 300 rupees a month. Given I pay his boss 1,000 rupees for the safari, I feel it is just to give him, discreetly, the same amount, not so much out of pity (in a way, I envy his life), but to treat him as an equal. The New Testament says: 'The world is a bridge, pass over it but build no house upon it.'[6]

{ 13 }

Jodhpur

Back in Jodhpur. I am fatigued here. Bazaar bustle. Bhandaars selling clothes, houseware, groceries; everything from mishtan (kitchen utensils) to bartan (sweets). Bigotry or bijouterie– gems, trinkets, etc. Virtue or *virtucurious* articles of art. The old city palatial; very hot when I arrive. Known as 'the Capital of the region of death'.[1] It was founded in 1459 by Rao Jodha, a chief of the Rajput clan known as the Rathores. The great sight here is the unmissable Majestic Fort of Mehrangarth.

Erected on protrusion from a mountain on a low range of hills, isolated, towering over all that surrounds it, table ridge, awesome feature in uninterrupted desert region. On the height of the southern extremity, the capital is thus detached. Northern height, on which is built the palace, less than three hundred feet? It is scarped. The Jayapal gates were built by Maharaj Mang Singh, following his victory over the armies of Jaipur and Bihamer. At least one hundred and twenty feet perpendicular height. Strong walls, numerous round and square towers encircle the great extent, crest of the hill, encompassing, given base-dimensions, about four miles' walk, seven barriers thrown across circuitous ascent, each with an immense portal.

Of Mehrangarh, Kipling wrote: 'The work of angels, faeries, and giants...built by Titans and coloured by the morning sun...he who walks through it, loses sense of being among buildings. It is as though he walked through mountain gorges.'[2]

Aldous Huxley wrote: 'From the bastions of Jodhpur Fort one hears as the Gods must hear from Olympus, the Gods to whom each separate word uttered in the innumerably peopled world below, comes up distinct and Individual to be recorded in the books of omniscience.' I take a final look at the white marble memorial to Maharaja Jaswant Singh II, a cenotaph to the Rathore rulers[3], containing some beautiful marble *jali* work. It commands fine views of the blue city.

After the dusty, Jodhpurean, polluted trail, to an intoxicating rampart view of sunset, from honeycombed walls on winding paths, the seven palace, cannon-pocked fort; I am transposed from such immense grandeur of royal palanquins outwards, from Jodhpur's eternal, mesmerising dream. I hail a taxi, and I leave Jodhpur, swept from Turner-like visions, luminous, of gilded magnificence across the sky, as eternal blue houses of the old city fade, from unspeakable vibrancies, leaving their mark, as orange-cum-purple-haze fades into turquoise-deep blue, azure star-night with a crescent empyrean moon; evokes for me the Lunar dynasty, Chandravansha of the Kshatriya varna.[3]

I arrive in Jodhpur after another train journey, making good use of my India rail pass. Blue city[4] skyline is dominated by Mehrangarth Fort.

*   *   *

One can hear city sounds being swept up from the noisy and stark city-scape. There is cool air on the periphery, but in central view, an austere defence fortification; humongous. A male Rajasthani sitarist sits playing a long-necked Indian lute with moveable frets. A midget (could be his daughter?) is dancing and twirling her hands in the air. I leave some baksheesh, and he offers to sell me his sitar, which I refuse because I don't want to take his means of livelihood away from him. I do not realise he wants to make a profit, and might find a replacement easily. It looks rather old and precious to me; a strange though beautiful instrument.

I walk through the gate of Mehrangarth. It might be named Fort Colossus. Kipling thought it was a palace for the Titans. There is a Rajput drummer on a rainbow-coloured mat, providing entertainment as people walk past the seven gates leading deep into the fortification. The sides of the second gate are still scarred by cannon ball hits from battles with the Mughals from Jaipur and Bikaner. Inside the Fort there is a series of courtyards and palaces. One apartment contains the flower palace of the Maharaja.

With its splendid stained glass windows reflecting the primary colours across the room: red, yellow, blue. The glass is monochrome. I feel a great sense of peace and colour healing. I then go to the Maharaja's other palace by Mercedes taxi, on the outskirts of the old city, and have cucumber sandwiches on the palatial terrace overlooking the lawn made lush by constant watering. It's called Umaid Bhawan Palace, and I won't easily forget the palm court marble, like the Taj Mahal at Agra, with an occasional tiger or leopard on the wall. I like the dainty crockery.

The Maharaja was told by a saint that a period of drought would follow the good rule of the Rathore Dynasty. Thus, after the end of the 50-year reign of Pratap Singh, Jodhpur faced a severe drought and famine conditions in the 1920s for a period of three consecutive years. The farmers of the area, faced with famine conditions, sought the help of the then King Umaid Singh, who was the 37th Rathore ruler of Marwar at Jhodpur, to provide them with some employment so that they could survive the famine conditions.

The king, to help the farmers, decided to build a lavish palace; commissioned Henry Vaughan Lanchester, who is remembered as the Edwardian architect of baroque Cardiff City Hall, to create the palace, along the lines of the Lutyens New Delhi building complex, by adopting the theme of domes and columns; an extraordinary blend of Eastern & Western architecture.

On my return, down to the city, I take in the view from Jaswant Thada, which is a white marble memorial to Maharaja Jaswant Singh II; a cenotaph to the Rathore ruler. It has beautiful jali work, and commands a specular view of the blue city. It seems they paint their houses this colour as it deters the mosquitoes.

I take a tour around antique emporiums, spy then buy two Indian ink wells, and a floral circular tray and a jewel case. There is a folding dressing screen about 40 inches tall; though I am looking for a larger item, I realise this will be portable. The antiques dealer packs it in bubble wrap, makes a string handle so I can carry it like a case. This I do, walking along the dusty humid road in the midday sun, sweating profusely, with the taste of passing motor fumes in my mouth.

{ 14 }

Jaisalmer

Jaisalmer[1] Barren, resplendent, beautiful, unique, accessible by rail from Jodhpur; took me 7 hours. Around the fort and palace areas I walk during the morning. The night revelry, *razai* held against breeze, bright star-lit sky, *chai*, rooftop view of the fort. I never hired a rickshaw here. There's a colourful Ravanahatha[2] player.

Jaisalmer is massive living fort, holding together bits of royal residences and temples made of marble, sea fossil and yellow sandstone. It is bustling with fort dwellers who sell traditional arts and crafts for a living, and antique coins, locks, block-prints, hand-made bedcovers, and souvenirs, shoes, and clothes. I feel like I haven't seen enough of it, then decide not to eat, if fluffy white rice isn't served here; cafe lantern, spicy desert beans[3], berries then panoramic view from fort rooftop, at sunset; signalling mellifluous refrain; warmest welcome.[4]

Low-walled houses and palaces, myths and realities, the archaic and the modern, all overlap; rich colour, delicate embroidery, some with shisha.[5] As with Aurora Borealis, the second sight can be so marvellous, that, as the Seer gazes into this inner world, he feels the scintillating points shoot past him, he is filled with awe at the thought of other, still greater mysteries, that lie beyond, and within, that radiant ocean of swirling energy beyond all comprehension. It is Krishna's Birthday today. He was born in 600 A.D.[6]

I take the train to Jaisalmer; there have been monsoon rains, and the train is delayed, but we eventually get there. Evidence of the flooding is found on arrival, with giant puddles surrounding the earth hardened in the blazing heat. Feeling so parched, like the cracked sandy earth here, I am constantly drinking water and drinking chai to be revived. Jaisalmer fort is spectacular, an entire fortified city, like a giant sand castle rising out of the desert.[7]

I soon encounter some helpful fellows. A man called Ganesh who runs the eponymous travel agency. He tells me Ganesh is a symbol of luck, and the swastika is a Hindu symbol for peace: 'Very holy', he says. The Nazi's reversed it, being enchanted by Eastern religion, and perverting its meaning. It is essentially a sexual creative symbol that would rotate anti-clockwise. I arrived in the extreme reaches of Rajasthan, at this 12th-century fort, with great excitement. It was a very happy place for me. I move through the sun gate, past a gaggle of men selling Rajasthani bedspreads; then through the wind-gate, round a sharp bend, the design of which I'm told keeps out the drunken elephants during a siege. I admire the outline of the fort. It is indeed an ancient place, built in 1156.[8]

The gracious havelis[9] of rich silver merchants, the kaleidoscopic

mirrors and embroideries of brilliant cloth, add sumptuous colour to the bland, sandy aridity of the landscape surrounding it. If ever there is a link between landscape and architecture it is to be seen here. It is the very colour of the desert.

Here it is perfectly blended by human hands from the earth out of which it rises, and is inseparable from the whole. Impressive mansions, mostly built by the wealthy merchants of Jaisalmer. I see the most elaborate and magnificent of all the Jaisalmer havelis. The Maharaja's seven-storey palace is next to my room. Above is the view of the outer city from the ramparts of the fort. There's a panoramic view of Jaisalmer Fort. This sandy outpost is dubbed the Golden City because of its honey colour. From above there is a closer view within the city walls of the Laxminath Temple.[10]

Being on an open roof flat, with awesome panoramic view into desert, is like being in a sauna. Cold shower needed just to come down from there into the yogi's apartment. Walking without feet, flying without wings, thinking without mind, smoking without those horrendous Chinese cigarettes, where one drag is as strong as 20 embassy number one's combined.

Between the past and the future, the past is no more and the future is not yet. Non-existential present, unable to be defined, as the cucumber sandwich filling, beyond the last slice and the slice to come, there is the present marrow between two slices of bread. It is not even part of time, it is the unmoving truth, always the same, to feel and experience that cucumber, I imagine, is to be here now! Just as in sleep or moments of love, time disappears as easily as a cucumber sandwich, stops; the mind stops. There is only ecstasy, joy and eternity.[11]

Doubt remains, perhaps I cling onto belief, the pretension of knowledge? To know, that we're part of some divine plan. The place where I'm staying. It is the former residence of the Yogi Master to the Maharaja, now a private apartment owned by his descendants. I go for a walk along those narrow market alleyways, the colour of desert sands. It is like being in Jedha, the holy city in Star Wars. I go to a fabric emporium and meet a splendid man called Pittu, who is eager to entice me with his wares!

Rajasthani fabrics are most ornate, being made from the finest materials in the whole of India. At the fabric shop I try on a Rajput dressing gown. I wish to buy it. Instead I have one made, blue with gold embroidery, though not like the one I tried on. I also purchase a bedcover, tailor-made silk pyjamas, two cushion covers, a wall-hanging, five tailor-made shirts, and a fine cut grey two-piece suit from the Pittu, who is a tailor and dress maker. Now Ganesh, the tour agent and owner of the apartment I'm staying in, transfers me to a room near the city gate, and I sleep on a camp bed beneath a mosquito net. I am roused at early morning darkness, before we traverse long stretches of dusty road in an open jeep. I am taken to the desert camp in Sam. We arrive late afternoon. Desert rises in spiralling waves to dunes; soon to meet camels; tea made by the camel man on a makeshift wood-fired stove, watching the sun sink slowly into distant, pink-tinged horizon.

This is 'the valley of death'. I am exhausted; too much under this pervasive monsoon heat. I am in the desert, with a man called Raju. There is the distant rumble of thunder around us. We are on the western reaches of the desert, from Jaisalmer. Raju cooks dinner in a desolate barn which we reach after a day's trek.

*   *   *

The first night I sleep on a wooden Indian bed, placed in the open desert, near the village of Korterie, approached like an oasis after a long trek. No mirage. Shelter for the night. A breeze soothes the air. Skin cools, then a clap of distant sky flashes, around the horizon bowl, reveals the stars. About 9km from Jaisalmer. Sleeping on a bed in the desert is surreal. Wilderness. Bright lights shine above. As I lay on my back, I see many shooting stars.

Here I have a tremendous dream; most memorable, gives me pure insight into some horrific portent: a huge tower being struck by lightning; many screaming in fire and pandemonium; awakes me in the night; gives me a feeling: something will be smashed, some great terror to be unleashed; in a destructive flash? Sunrise, stirred from your sleep: small pieces of *chapatti*[12] to eat with jam. *Chai.* A small farm in the western reaches of the Thar desert: You embark on a camel trek. After ten miles, much saddle pain; stop at a ramshackle building; gaze at the desert from this place.

This is sombre desert, desolate, beyond all expression. This isn't the place to complain about the weather, the food, and the natives. I'm sure this is just the place to make the average Western tourist feel so remote from the mechanisms of progress, that they would become peevish, if not discontented,
without Instagram.

I feel very depressed in this desert, I would almost say clinically unwell. I feel a lot of sadness is in this desert. My moods aren't entirely explicable. There is nothing too bogus about this tour, it is as close to real desert dwellers as you can get; obvious poverty but they're immured to it. Ahead, there's man & boy herders; with the coherent trail of their livestock curling like a snake mirage, from the horizon line; simple path, nomads herding goats. Sun goes down. Sand cools. Bearable heat. Monsoon lush scrub.

Ah! Snakiest fears! This season of slithering! Paranoia I can't utterly banish, haunts me, especially at night, under a canopy of starlight. Maybe the silence that follows is more promising than foreboding? Chatter-box Ragu dislikes silence in his company, rouses me from the depths, on lighter, buoyant plains of humour, keeps the conversation chugging along endlessly.

*   *   *

In Death Valley, where graves of massacred people, desert ghosts, spirits roam. Partition added to their number;[13] oppressive severance played out in raging heat. (Echoes of that quip in McLeod). Suggesting travel beyond the mountain snows is preferable! This journey through the desert border with Pakistan, now a hamlet of assorted dwellings, primitive, in balance with the surrounds; simple 'farms'. Lightning storm illumines the horizon. Rain fall breaks the heavy day-heat. Evening camp set, a hasty fire in a barn. Dripping rain waters. Gloomy, ramshackle, depressing, but seeing how chapatti is made intrigues me. Prospect of suit collection stirs me to a future from the present. Can I enjoy sitting on Rajasthani blankets laid on the floor, and feel so restless? Orange flames illuminate a smoke-filled room. Ragu boils some tea. From a roofless courtyard appears a man, who comes into fire-room. Flat ceilings, door open onto courtyard; outer door a heavy bolted gate.

I sleep in a smokeless room. Dark falls. Raju serves the tea, smoke escapes via door frames; crackling fire. Constant night rain conjures sound images, migrating snakes, shadows of flickering flame, their slithering hypnotic movement; 'perhaps less dangerous in than out; open desert?' We drink Indian whisky, enticements before sleep. To void pain, drown it, though it avenges itself. Morning frowns follow when mind-body blisters, renewed sufferings rising from a catacomb, full of obsolete rules, scripts, perceptions that have outlived their validity, that inner incarceration that comes from that delusional cloak of invisibility.

That night, after camp fire story-telling, the man from the hamlet appears, to share a drink. Portly, drunk, he seems safe enough: 'Raju is the father of my children', he says, 'I'm impotent. My family don't know this. I like to drink plenty whisky. Here, take some.' A few swigs later, he leaves. 'That was my friend', says Ragu. 'I call him 'no banana'. That is why he drink so much whisky. All the time Whisky. All the time no woman love making. You know 'no banana'? Banana look only to sand and never to sky! His parents fixed him a wife and they marry two months. But he no Banana, no sky – whisky – in the sand. Bad fruit. No fruit. He ask me to make fucking with wife. He ask me to make children. I have good banana, he bad banana...I good camel safari man. I enjoy:

No wife no life. So I sleep with friend's wife. I good Banana in sky – but no wife. He bad banana with wife. No children. So, I his wife love is making in Korterie night-time, on safari. Is good. In a hurry, chicken curry. 1, 2, 3: India Free! 4, 5, 6, nothing fixed! 7, 8, 9: India fine! Me fucking his wife. He no worry – whisky! He crazy. His family no know. Secret – no tell. You know secret?'

'What', I say.

'I Muslim. He Hindu.'

'Really?' How incredible.

Before and after partition for countless ages; human beings doing human doings. Morning hits sharply; shock of morning glory rebels against the summons; charges ahead, then with nothing to satisfy it, mere sublimation, creative heat, forward marching, dissipates into restless dissatisfaction. Masochism?

No one is in the courtyard. I leave the farmstead. There is a tall handsome lad, with sparkling silver earrings in both ears, wearing a white vest, chiselled face, doe brown eyes, muscular frame, broad shoulders. There is an awkward silence made more palpable by his lack of English and my frustration, my lack of native tongue or inner spontaneity.

His friend is much smaller; eyes me with some curiosity. Perhaps they are brothers? I don't dislike desert life. Here one's lingering self-hatred and fear gets channelled into single-minded path ahead. Pitta energy on full heat, fired by desert.

A life of desert distractions, night visions, strange dreams. That inner controller who whips me to flaming perditions of mind I banish?

O would some Power the gift give us, to see ourselves as we really are, expanding as infinite creators. I go back inside to gather my rucksack. I'm anxious of what I desire. I know what interests me when I see it. Yet it repels me. I'm diffident when faced with beauty.

I am learning to see my own self reflected at me. I feel broken inside, a part that's stuck. My burden of heart fragments. I don't know where Raju is. He returns soon enough. As we leave the farmstead, the tall lad appears out of a farmhut opposite. I'm camel mounted. He's sporting a bright new top; pastel yellow and blue. I'm led away by Raju to the camel, wanting to stay longer. I find that he wrote his name in my book: Govinda Shoken.[14]

*   *   *

I choose to open my heart to let Love in. When I delay opening my heart, thus, holding out against it, I fear I am worthless, unacceptable. May I always chose to be more open. May I attain this day Peace, Purity, Freedom: May my dark burden be Lightened. May feelings buried so long be lightened with joy. Grant health of mind, self-acceptance, love of self, respect of brother body. May my Soul seek its own expansion, free of expectation; the jostling coercion of others. Protect me from jealousy and evil eyes, misguided, negative energies blinded by love's apprehension.

Free me from unnecessary judgment, within and without; heal pain with peace, in Your full presence in the moment. May I live for each moment with equanimity, not to wait but to embrace, and may Spirit guide and clear each step I take; the Path ahead. Some more advanced souls than others; vary in intelligence; differences in language, culture, family line, childhood conditions, tradition. Can I renew every situation? I can find possibilities for fullness. I can change yourself if I face myself. I expand the light within and pray for help. It will surely come. This is all I can do, call upon the light of living light, that which is also sparkling creative light.

From the ocean of bliss there comes a ripple, to return me to the light where I'm meant to be. May I see truly, create, with clear intention. Bathe me in your radiance this day, refresh me. May I let go of what no longer serves me as I grow. May I find peace- healing within; loving myself as I walk on this earth, wherever it is I may go. And may the angels cloak me in Light, even if I go to where they dread. Protect me, showing me my higher self. May most powerful helpers be by me, as destiny leads me ineluctably on. May I transmute darkness into light, heal shame, hold space through silence, move into heart-light. Cast away all inner shadows.

Expose them in the Light so I may be free of their accustomed agenda, against my better awareness. May I serve others freely, without compunction, bringing health to this world, in speech and relationships. May I come to a truer understanding of the miracle of the soul's voice with the earth's magnetism. By this unending frequency may more Light pour forth from light-channels within, connecting me to what is above and below. Dropping what is heavy into the fire of earth. Send messengers from heaven, super-conscious mind expansion, deeper perception. Krishna, Christ, Buddha, all fields of higher consciousness, bring your Golden Light's presence into my focus. Wherever I'll be, wherever I am, here and now. If my focus be that, I am never alone. May I maintain, from my crown to my feet, this awareness. May I become more and more with you. After all, you have brought me to this point I thought I'd never see.

May this energy bring healing to my self and others. You have blessed me with a loving heart and I cannot help but attract beings of Love and Light to me. Give me grace, and dignity, when dealing with my fellow man, wisdom and clarity to become a part of the light I offer to the world. May I Trust in myself, and trust the light working through me. I would never be left adrift in this world alone. Without you; whenever I attune myself with your radiant Light of Truth divine, I know it gives me freedom to express wisdom, clarity and love.

Absolute love flows to my heart from you within me, and joy is my reward. May I release anger, up and out of me, always hold your presence close within my heart, so that the pain and confusion will drop away. May Light-giving Truth be my only reality. May I take responsibility for myself and my actions. I forgive myself for mistakes and what was beyond my control. I can't compare myself to others without doing an injustice to myself. The path I have been following, this new direction, makes my life more interesting.

Out of the blind man's cul-de-sac, in Death Valley there is rebirth. New insights. I see the grand trunk road, bumpy start, the winding path, black holes, shadow grey, sun rising on horizon; for perpetuity in Light. I know the path winds, because I am becoming it. The road that leads to Satori.[15] It is so simple, it is there shining, auspicious light, upon my blind naïveté. What sequence is my journey in. The undertaking carries me leagues deeper at varying knots. Not to death? Not to valleys of aridity, this barren infertile land? Will I reach the coconut groves, the refreshing taste, healthy for skin and enhancing vision, rejuvenation of life, potency? There is nowhere to hide. What lies beyond university? Qualification, society?Work in metropolis? Who will I serve? What freedom in conformity? In relationship? What will I serve? Will I make an income doing what I enjoy? Will I enjoy anything just to get by? Or will I just do what my parents tell me today and be unhappy, but make them happy? Will I go to the ghats and see my past lives flow by in an instant of remembrance and realisation?

Will I live in the present enough to return to my wilderness? What inescapable facts face me now? How may I turn my life around and win? I like lunching in dried-up streams, with cattle herders, and random people giggling from behind bushes in the middle of nowhere; utter barren wastes. Around a fire in the night I can forget my loneliness and disconnection. Here I can dream while wasting myself. The Indian says don't think of the morrow, just be in the moment. Spontaneous, playful, will I heal my wounded inner child? Unfurl complexes, bless neurosis as beautiful? Release it to be mentally free; return home?

Will I embrace the moment that flows in the presence of one's own self-aware, sober bloody-mindedness? If then, will they call me old or boring? With spite masquerading as listening concern, will they undermine me? I inhabit this body, I have these ancestors, this DNA, these deep memories, and all my life is constant decision making. Will I let the moment come and honour this Creation expressing itself through me, and let life happen; being available to those I love, and not listen to those who say you can't love him or her, just because they don't approve of it? Enemies of Love abound, so will I love as I can truly love myself? And then, may I stop self-sabotaging, and start selflove- aging myself. Will I bear the God-given fire in my hand?

The desert takes possession of my being, begins the process to clear away conditioned beliefs that betray the true integrity within me. I feel myself in a new light. Lying under the Rohera[16] tree without a care in the world. One hundred thousand miles from home. By midday we have stopped for tiffin in a dried-up river bed among some goat-herding nomads who have linked up with us. There is a Rajasthani boy who also joins our company.

A shepherd boy? He takes interest in my writing andsits watching me for an hour, trying to decipher my black ink pen script; mysterious scribbles to him. He has a lovely smile, and I give him my sunglasses. While preparing chai, Ragu weaves another desert story. 'I once took a New Zealand man on camel safari. Seven days by camel. He had a woman with him and many bottles of beer. Too much that we needed an extra camel; in the night, I watched them fucking. The next day at lunch, I see them behind the bush fucking. Fucking, fucking, fucking. All they did.

'I ask woman. Are you from New Zealand? She say yes. I ask woman. Are you family New Zealand?

She say Yes! She say why you keep asking this question? I say 'You Indian woman!'

'While the man is sleeping, I see her put pill in his beer. He drinks. He sleeping. Many hours. No fucking. She tell me: she Indian. I already know this. She Delhi prostitute. 140 Rupees a day. I say 'you sleep with me for free!' We fucking. Nice fruit– Indian fruit. She say white man too much fucking! She use pill in beer.

'On safari, they fucking in the dunes, in front of me, by fire. During food. I watch. I take photo. He develop and send to me. I keep safe place! He say "You good camel man. You friend. Want to fuck this woman?"

So I fuck more.'

'This went on for 1 week?'

'Eh? No! 1 month. They ask me to take on Safari: from Jaisalmer to Pushkar. Many fucking. Camel man good life! No hurry chicken curry. Lovely jubbly!

'One two three, India Free!

Four five six, nothing fixed

Seven, eight, nine, India fine!

'And whoever said three's a crowd?

And then there was the time I took two Canadian men out into the desert. And they were fucking together like this.

Two men fucking. Behind the bush and sand dune. I couldn't believe it, two men like that.'

'And what is wrong with it?' I said.

'Two men fucking. Aha! I just don't understand it.'

{ 15 }

Rohet

I leave Jodhpur's blue houses, furniture, carpets, palaces. Forty-five minutes' drive by Mercedes taxi to the south of Jodhpur; edge of the Great Thar desert. Rohet Gahr is a 17th-century converted fort with a peaceful, flower-filled garden. 'Many fragrant surprises,' says the guide book.

I arrive at the bucolic peace of a heritage hotel. If only I had someone with me. It's a sultry, hot afternoon. The receptionist tells me a room is £20 a night, an affordable treat, for a student. I am led to a room that overlooks the swimming pool; perfect setting for cooling off, reading and writing and having a rest.

I'm told the furnishings were designed and made in the surrounding villages. The walls are adorned with attractive frescoes. Dinner is usually served by the pool. Bruce Chatwin[1] resided at Rohet Garh[2] whilst writing The Songlines.[3] It belongs to the same family who, in the 1990s, transformed it into a relaxed and friendly place for tourists to stay. It is full of charm and character. There are various rooms, and suites are decorated with traditional Rajasthani printed fabrics. At tea on the veranda, later, I meet an Indian diplomat. As we look over the garden, he tells me he studied diplomacy in Leeds.

Then the owner's son joins us.[4] He enjoys chatting to me; he tells me he likes horses (there is a stud of Marwair horses nearby). The literature says Rohet Gahr has been the home of many noblemen over time; a silent witness to the progress of the Singh family for four centuries. 'It has stood steadfast through the highs and the lows of those centuries.

A kindly, if handsome, serving boy, dressed in smart maroon, gold-embraided Rajasthani long coat, serves me chai as I arrive. He senses I'm curt because I'm exhausted when he serves the long-awaited lemonade.

An Englishman must be frustrated by this heat. And travelling so far. I apologise. His eyes light up with an epiphany.

'Ah, sir! Wait!'

His second departure leaves me with thirsty longing, wondering what could possibly quench it in his eyes. When he returns he gives me a piece of brown toffee. I look at it despairingly.

'Whatever do I do with this?' I ask.

'Eat it! Eat it with water like zis!'

All the people I meet here, from all castes, are lovely towards me, and good cuisine is served. Riding is available, but after my experience with camels, I am reluctant. I feel sure it is because I am so tired. I go on a walk around the village, talking to locals, and after entering a house to see two women who are weaving a tapestry of local design,[5] I buy a pair of Rajasthani Jutti[6] from the Indian I met on my perambulation.

Village Bishnoi people have been custodians of the countryside for centuries, in their beliefs that prevent them from killing animals or felling green trees. Heritage, glimpse of life of the gentry. I feel valued as guest of honour, tea alone in courtyard garden, louche, reclining, observing the exquisite glory of the preening male peacock.[7] Perhaps it is the opium I'm taking, but I am entranced by the peacocks, and wonder off into a reverie, admiring them; marvel ling at their perennial ability to transmute snake venom into the beautiful pigmentation of their plumage. How feathers originally come from reptiles. Just when I feel they are always watching, one slow step around the garden where

I sit, with folded wings; teardrops of diamonds dangling from succulent pearls.

Glint, sparkle of the diamond-splattered breast; he parades around his palace, majestic ritual, bejewelled. Let's call it the final fling of the peacock male. Its bright blue front starts to contract and spasm, then its long feathers begin to spread out like a huge fan, its span about 6 times larger than the bird; blue, fan-like crest, spatula-tipped, wire-like feathers long train of elongated upper tail covert feathers rise bearing colourful eyespots, stiff feathers fan in quivered display of courtship. The females lack the train, and have a greenish lower neck and duller brown plumage. This Indian peacock lives on the lawn where it forages for berries, grains; but also, they prey on snakes, lizards, and small rodents. Their loud calls make them easy to detect, I wonder if they fly, their plumage some defect, if they ever wanted to roost in a tree?

From bill to tail it must be 40 inches, but with an extended train, it's more than twice that; unmistakable metallic blue on the crown, the feathers of the head being short and curled. Its fan-shaped feathered head crest is like a top knot, on bare black shafts, like an elaborate hat made with a bluish-green-tipped webbing.

A white stripe above the eye crescent, shaped white patch below; the eye are formed by bare white skin. The sides of the head have iridescent Greenish-blue feathers. The back has scaly bronze-green feathers with black and copper markings. The scapular and the wings are buff and barred in black, the primaries are chestnut and the secondaries are black. The tail is dark brown and the 'train' is made of elongated upper tail coverts (more than 200 feathers, the actual tail has only 20 feathers) and nearly all of these feathers end with an elaborate eye-spot.

A few of the outer feathers lack the spot and end in a crescent-shaped black tip. The underside is dark glossy green shading into blackish under the tail. The thighs are buff coloured, a spur on the leg above the hind toe The colours of the peacock and the contrast with the much duller peahen puzzle me. Charles Darwin wrote to Asa Gray that the 'sight of a feather in a peacock's tail, whenever I gaze at it, makes me sick!' as he failed to see an adaptive advantage for the extravagant tail which seemed only to be an encumbrance. Darwin developed a second principle of sexual selection to resolve the problem, though in the prevailing Victorian trends, the theory failed to gain widespread attention. The American artist Abbott Handerson Thayer tried to show, from his own imagination, the value of the eyespots as disruptive camouflage in a 1907 painting. How could it evolve as camouflage? From the sky? When the blue sky blends hues of peacock's neck into coherent whole? Blue sky peacock. Whose signalling is handicap, whose beautiful train is costly, causing depression from raging hormones required to enhance the feathers. Male courting female, peafowl love an ornate cock train; courtship display raises the feathers into a fan and quivers them.

Makes me wonder if the number of eyespots relates to mating success? Whether or not these displays signalled a male's genetic quality? What if one were to cut the eyespots off some of the male's ornate feathers. Would the removal of eyespots makes males less successful in mating? Male peafowls would look less interesting, and surely females would mistake these males for sub-adults, or perceive that the males are physically damaged. It is rare for adult males to lose a significant number of eyespots. Females' selection might depend on other sexual traits of males' trains. The quality of train is an honest signal of the condition of males; peahens do select males on the basis of their plumage: 'high maintenance handicap' theory.

Only the fittest males can afford the time and energy to maintain a long tail. Therefore, the long train is an indicator of good body condition; results in greater mating success. Females do not appear to use train length to choose males. Peahens do not choose peacocks based on their ornamental plumage, including train length, number of eyespots and train symmetry. Genetic variation of the trait of interest under 'the cost of trait expression may vary with environmental conditions, a trait that is indicative of a particular quality may not work in another environment. Female preference for elaborate trains; the elaborate train itself. Evolutionary adaptation. The evolved species is actually the least ornamented one. This suggests a chase-away sexual selection, 'females evolve resistance to male ploys; peacocks' train is an obsolete signal for which female preference has already been lost or weakened.'

They concluded that female choice might indeed, vary in different ecological conditions. (Shropshire vs. Amsterdam.) If you tracked the eye movements of peahens responding to male displays, they looked in the direction of the upper train of feathers only when at long distances and they looked only at the lower feathers when males displayed close to them. The rattling of the tail and the shaking of the wings helped in keeping the attention of females.

Loud pia-ows, may-awes. Then rapid series of kaaan... ka-aan kok-kok: that explosive low-pitched honk! It turns about and gives an unimpressive view, its eyes start to shimmer. I'm sure that beak could be aggressive. Peacocks strike me as the sort of bird that like to be watched, but know when you're watching. The peacock is celebrated as the national bird of India in 1963. The peacock, known as mayura8 in Sanskrit, has enjoyed a fabled place in India since and is frequently depicted in temple art, mythology, poetry, folk music and traditions. Hindu deities are associated with the bird, Krishna is often depicted with a feather in his headband, while worshippers of Shiva associate the bird as the steed of the God of war.[9] Peacock feather rituals, peacock motifs in Indian temple architecture, old coinage, textiles, kept in menageries, on this estate they are as ornaments for the large garden.

In medieval times, knights in Europe took a 'Vow of the Peacock' and decorated their helmets with its plumes. Feathers were buried with Viking warriors;[10] the flesh of the bird was said to cure snake venom and many other maladies. Numerous uses in Ayurveda have been documented. Peafowl were said to keep an area free of snakes. 1526, the legal issue as to whether peacocks were wild or domestic fowl was thought sufficiently important for Cardinal Wolsey to summon all the

English judges to give their opinion, which was that they are domestic fowl.[11]

In Anglo-Indian usage of the 1850s, to peacock meant making visits to ladies and gentlemen in the morning. In the 1890s, the term 'peacocking' in Australia referred to the practice of buying up the best pieces of land ('picking the eyes') so as to render the surrounding lands valueless.[12] The English word 'peacock' has come to be used to describe a man who is very proud or gives a lot of attention to his clothing.[13] Preening and scooting on the lawn; occasionally raising their fans, eyes watching, shimmering lights like the aura. *Pavo cristatus*. The Peacock! I wonder what the word is in Hindi? [mor] 'Our national bird is peacock; very beautiful in appearance. Each part of his body blue, the many colours are in the wings. Green blue; when the peacock opens its wings it looks even more beautiful. His eyes are long and beautiful. It is also the vehicle of the God Kartik. It is also a form of Krishna as God. When the peacock opens its wings it is a miraculous sight.

Mor in our country is found in areas of Varanasi and of course here in Rajasthan. The body is big and heavy. Because of which, it does not fly to much height. They like snakes, venom has no effect on them. It runs like a king with great pride. We like the few we have here.

'They can estimate the rains. A very important organ of her body that has feathers. In Hindu culture, it is believed that keeping its wings in the house is a benefit of happiness. People use it to mark the wings in the book.' Sidharth Singh, lovely owner of both estates.

'So what are you doing here?'

'Oh, I was in Jodhpur wondering where to go next,

And there I saw Bruce Chatwin mentioned in the guide book, so I decided to come, more on a literary pilgrimage.'

'Yes, he stayed in that room'.

There is a quiet room with shutters facing the entrance, with private balcony onto the courtyard that lends it special significance as Singh points towards it.

'He was working on one of his books when he stayed here...What was it?' he asks me breezily. (Of course, it's the Songlines, I think).

'His wife Elizabeth[14] still returns for holiday.' He recommends I view the sunset later.

'We have some French photo-journalists here who have come to view it too. There is an excellent view point up the steps onto the roof of the building there.'

I thank the Marharaja and after sitting in the garden retire to my room. Snoozing on the old Wooden-framed bed, in the room with wall paintings and the cosy swing chairs where I continue to devour The Golden Bough. which in my three days in Rohet I manage to read. The Maharaja has yoga, I walk from the courtyard garden, to view the lake. My first evening is enjoyed from the veranda overlooking the lake. My room is beside the swimming pool, which is cool and re-freshing each morning. From the courtyard, I walk onto the roof of the west facing outer wall, after some French photojournalists with tripods and telephoto lenses descend. The outer wall is lapped by a lake with an island temple on it, amid flat semidesert. I see the sil-houette of a heron. The sunset is awesome. I retire to the courtyard; as preening peacocks quietly disperse. I sit in a wicker chair and en-joy the evening's entertainment. Rajasthani musicians beating drums. Faruke Kham, Babu Kham and Pamdhi Kham (drum, harmonium and cymbals respectively). They are performing what Faruke tells says is a special benediction for me.

Music understands sound energetics, prescribes a suitable melody to reduce pain, coax one out of depression and subdue anger. I learn that utilising the Ragas (there are 72 major melodies) dispels imbal-ance; recognises cosmic vibes emitting from natural forces.

Reflecting mood and matter, listener's biorhythms resonate with the musical vibration, creating a harmony, removing obstacles to health. Ragas can be commonly used to help everything from arthritis to the hiccups.[15] Faruke tells me he will perform Hichki (Hari). It means Harry's hiccup! Although it is a slight play on the original, that is about a married man who likes to travel away from home and causes his wife the hiccups! Maybe I need to think about that?[16]

'Music gives soul to the universe, wings to the mind, flight to the imagination, charm to sadness, gaiety and life to everything' – Plato Music is a very uplifting and meditative. Transcending the intellect, music touches our deepest spiritual essence which is why the Sanskrit term for note (swara) means expression of the soul.

Transporting us to a realm of etheric vibrations, music activates the right side of the brain, which nurtures creativity, intuition, receptivity, softness, stillness, silence, dreams, relaxation, imagination and regeneration. Sound is simply a vibration eliciting change in the forms, it flows through, our atoms literally 'dancing' to the beat of the music. That night I christen Pitu's pyjamas, made in Jaisalmer, soundly sleeping in a double bed. The following day is Independence Day, 15th August, 2001. I meet His Excellency the Maharaja Singh of Rohat. It is the 52nd Anniversary of Independence. I am the only foreign guest at the village celebrations. At a sumptuous breakfast, the Singhs, along with their young son, and daughter Avijit, regaled me with accounts of life in India...and I got a cooking lesson for safed maas (white meat, in counterpoint to its more popular red version).

While Rohet Garh needed a bit of spit and polish, Mihir Garh embodied refinement, mud-plastered walls, discreet corridors, an elliptical pool overlooking the countryside, and a chef with a masterful hand (order the local beans). On my last day, as I was driving out to a Bishnoi village, I encountered black bucks. Bold young males with smart black lines slammed ringed horns into each other; behind them females, tan and white, loped nervously through shrub, briefly suspended in the air like dangling pendants. The surrounds were ascetic, dry, and level, the sky appearing to billow out from the horizon in curtains of blue. Four days, flown by, I was returning home with a design guide, a smart pair of breeches, after drinks in the shade of Mehrangarh Fort. Jodhpur, I thought, you chupa rustam of delights. In Rohet, to which I am invited. This is an honour. Seated behind the main podium where Maharaja Singh[17] stands, to give his speech to the gathered crowd. Quite a generous crowd.

At least two hundred souls. The red dusty ground reminds me of a tennis court. The stand where we are seated is fes- tooned with the national colours; Indian flags, and brightly coloured sarees dancing in the centre court. I listen to the Maharaja's[18] speech in Hindi; mostly incomprehensible to me, until he says: 'and they said the sun would never set on the British Empire.' A dance performance then Follows, given by local Indian ladies. In the morning, I swim, before departing. Mr Singh (who has now inherited the title) kindly arranges for me to be taken to Jodhpur, where he invites me to take breakfast with him, his wife and their children. We have marmalade and toast, with tea and cornflakes.

They find me most intriguing. Siddharth Singh mentions how they enjoy reading PG Wodehouse. 'Do you like him?'.

I confess I had not read much, but knew that Shifnal in Shropshire could well have been P. G. Wodehouse's fictional town Market Blandings– or rather, the town is mentioned numerous times in the Blandings Castle saga. I then gather my heavy luggage and leave. I am carrying the half-height folding Rajasthani dressing screen, which I purchased from an antiques emporium (lugging it with me on a long walk in the sweltering heat). All this was wearing white chinos, panama hat, and red scarf. Soon I arrive back at Rajev's hotel in New Delhi, where he kindly lets me squirrel away things I have collected. Hopefully I will be able to post it back by freight before I fly home. On the TV there is a character from Indian mythology in the Mahabharata; this role has been enacted by various actors over the years.

III

Uttar Pradesh

The Road to Benares: The Boat Trip and the Faqueer

Varanasi is the religious metropolis of the Hindu faith. It lies on the left of the northern bank of the river Ganges, about 120 miles below its junction with the Jumna[1], at an elevation of 264.8 feet above sea level. It is 495 miles south-east from Delhi. That is the distance I have traversed by rail. It is about the same distance again to Calcutta, in the north-west.

The Ganges forms a bay or crescent-shaped reach in front of the city, thus permitting the eye to take in at a single sweep the long line of its picturesque ghats and splendid temples. The town is built of Chanar freestone, and consists of winding labyrinths and narrow alleys, lined by temples, mosques, or palaces, and crowded with pilgrims and busy citizens, camels, asses, horses, and sacred cows.

My view is everywhere obstructed within the city itself, yet along the bank of the Ganges unrolled a magnificent panorama of palaces, capped by domes, minarets, and sacred buildings, in every variety of oriental architecture.

The people seemed to spend a large part of their time praying, bathing, or lounging by the water-side; the ghats crowded with fakirs and other ash- be-sprinkled and almost naked ascetics, practising their devotions and life-long austerities.

I read in the history books that from the earliest period of Aryan colonisation in India, a city appears to have existed there at the junction of the Varuna (Barna)[2] with the Ganges. The name of Varanasi, converted into Banaras by transposition of the liquid consonants, frequently occurs in early Sanskrit literature.

In the sixth century B.C., Gautama Buddha, on the eve of promulgating his new religion, fixed upon Varanasi as the first station for preaching the doctrine of *nirvana*, and took up his residence at Sarnath, about 6 miles away. Even before that time, Varanasi had apparently acquired a reputation as the most sacred city of the Hindu creed; it then became, for 800 years, the head-quarters of Buddhism; and about the 4th century after Christ it once more reverted to the ancient faith, whose metropolis it remains to the present day.

Hwen Thsang[3], the Chinese Buddhist pilgrim of the 7th century, found the kingdom of Benares divided between the two creeds. He mentions the existence of 30 Buddhist monasteries and 100 Hindu temples. Sankar Acharjya[4], the great opponent of Buddhism and champion of the Sivaite sect, lived in Benares in the 7th century. After the annihilation of the rival faith in Upper India, the Sivaite Hindus rebuilt a considerable portion of the city, changing its site from the northern bank of the Varuna to its present position on the angle enclosed between the southern shore and the Ganges.

Varanasi has shown a tendency to shift its position in different sections from the most ancient times. The oldest town occupied site of Sarnath, where colossal Buddhist remains still thickly scattered over the ground. At a later period, the centre of the city stood apparently north of the Varuna. Mausoleums, mosques, dargahs[5], and Hindu temples, now in ruins, stood in the vacant space to the north of the present city; thus showing that up till the Muslim period Varanasi lay close to the south bank of the Varuna; while the modern frontage faces the Ganges alone, leaving an empty suburb to the north-east.

Most of the existing buildings date no further back than the reign of Akbar. Muhammad Ghori[6] took Varanasi in 1194 and the various

Muslim dynasties continued to hold it for 600 years. Nearly all the edifices in the city which can lay claim to antiquity have been appropriated to Islamic purposes. The Muslims converted all the larger temples into mosques or tombs, destroyed or mutilated the remainder, using their walls as quarries for building material.

Ala al-Din Husayn boasted that he had razed to the ground 1000 shrines in Varanasi alone. The existing Hindu buildings are generally small, and often destitute of architectural merit or ornamental detail, owing apparently to the stringency of Muslim rule.

During the 18th century, Varanasi fell into the hands of the Oud Wazirs[7], under whom a family of local Rajas established their power in the surrounding country. The story of their rise to authority, the rebellion and deposition of Chait Singh[8], and the subsequent fortunes of their house. Varanasi was ceded to the British, with the remainder of Chait Singh's domain, in 1775, and a Resident was appointed to watch the interests of the new Government. Wazir Ali of Oudh, after his deposition, was compelled to live at Benares; and in 1799 he attacked and murdered Mr. Cherry[9], the Resident, with two other officers.

The Wazir escaped for the time, but was afterwards captured and deported to Calcutta. During the Mutiny of 1857 a serious outbreak took place at Benares. Frequent troops from Calcutta managed to put down the mob.

Benares, or Varanasi lies on the west bank of the Ganges, which flows nearly north and south as it passes before the city. The native town skirts the sacred river, with constant succession of stone steps and ornamental facades. West of this crowded labyrinth stands the suburb of Sigra[10]. Northward, towards the Varnua, the Sikraul[11] and south of the Varuna lies the church. Along the edge of the Ganges a precipitous cliff rises to a height of 100 feet, and numerous ghats or bathing stairs descend by long flights from this elevation to the level of the stream below. At intervals a handsome shrine or picturesque temple, built close to the water's edge, breaks their line.

The buildings on the edge of the cliff, being for the most part five or six storeys high, crowned with pinnacles or towers, add to the impressive effect. Within the city, the streets contain many handsome houses, substantially built and elaborately decorated ; but their narrow, dirty, and crowded state usually disappoints the visitor, after the high expectations aroused by the view from the river. The upper storeys often project beyond the lower floor, and small bridges thrown across the roadway occasionally connect the houses on opposite sides of the street. To prevent inspection from the neighbouring fronts, the windows have been made extremely small.

The facades are often tinted in fantastic patterns, to represent the mythical episodes of Hindu mythology. During the fine season most of the inhabitants sleep on the fronts of their houses. The town bristles with religious buildings, Hindu and Muslim. The temples of the ancient faith are set down at 454, most of which are diminutive shrines, while there are 272 mosques. Besides these regular places of worship, every street corner, and empty space upon the ghats and in the walls of houses occupied by some religious image, mutilated statue, *linga*[12] or square- strewn sacred stone. Raja Man Singh of Jaipur is said to have presented 100,000 temples to the city in a single day. The chief buildings are too numerous to be fully noticed, but a few among them deserve special attention.

The temple at Durga Kund, in the southern extremity of the city, is a great society of sacred monkeys attached to its precincts. It is erected by Rani Bhawani during the last century, and is remark for its simple and graceful architecture.

The Dasasamedh ghat is one of the five sacred places of pilgrimage in Benares. Raja Jai Dgh's observatory, a handsome and substantial building, erected in 693, overlooks the Man Mandil ghat. Its founder reformed the calendar for the Emperor Muhammad Shah. Close to the same spot stands the Nepalese temple, whose quaint and picturesque architecture unexpectedly betrays the influence of Chinese models.

Surrounded by pure Hindu buildings, it strikes the eye at once by its novelty and its excellent workmanship.

A little above the observatory, the burning ghat where the bodies of Hindus are reduced to ashes, leads down to the Ganges by a narrow, confined pathway, with numerous slabs of stone set up on end in honour of widows who in the past performed *sati*.[13]

The Well of Mani Karniki, filled with the sweat of Vishnu, forms one of the chief attractions for pilgrims, thousands of whom annually bathe in its fetid waters. Stone steps lead down to the edge, crowded with worshippers, whose sins are washed away by the efficacious spring. The graceful Tarakeswar shrine fronts the well.

The huge mass of Aurangzeb's mosque, built from the remains of a Hindu temple, towers conspicuously over the brink of a steep cliff, above Panchganga ghat with strong breastworks of masonry extending far down the bank. It is the most conspicuous building in the city when seen from the river ; and on a nearer view becomes remarkable for its slender minarets, 147 feet in height, and slightly inclined from the perpendicular. Bhairondth[14], the divine guardian and watchman of Benares, has a famous temple near the public gardens; while his sacred baton or stone steps, 4 feet in height, is deposited in a separate shrine near by.

Close to it is the Gopal niand'ir, containing two gold images of Krishna, is temple, though not remarkable for beauty of architecture, ranks first in wealth and in the richness of its furniture and jewels. The temple is daily attended by numbers of devotees. But the Bisheswar golden temple, dedicated to Shiva, may perhaps be selected with invidiousness as the holiest among all the holy places of the sacred city. It stands a short distance from the observatory, and contains the venerated symbol of the god, a plain *linga* of uncarved stone.

The building has a centre spire, and each corner is crowned by a dome. The temple was erected by Ahalya Bai, the Maratha Princess of Indore. The Maharaja Ran Singh of Lahore had the spire and domes covered with gold leaf, fro' which the temple derives its ordinary title.

The Buddhist remains at Sarnath, about 4 miles from the city, will be described under the proper heading.

The most remarkable relic of early antiquity in Benares itself is the Lat Bhairo, a broken pillar, supposed to be a fragment of one amon the many columns set up by the great Buddhist Emperor Ashoka in the third century B.C. Many other fragmentary or mutilate monuments strew the ground outside the city, or form portions (Muhammadan edifices, into which they have been built as ready-made masonry. Few buildings of European origin deserve special mentioi The most noteworthy is the Government college, a large structure i the perpendicular style, faced with Chanar freestone. Next to it ran the Prince of Wales Hospital, built by the gentry of Benares in commemoration of the visit of His Royal Highness to the city in 1876 ; and the Town Hall, a fine building, constructed at the expense of the lat Maharaja of Vizianagram, where the special magistrates hold court, and where public and other important meetings are held.

The wealth of Benares depends largely upon the constant influx of opulent pilgrims from every part of India whose presence lends the same impetus to the local trade as that given to European wateringplaces by the season visitors. Many of the pilgrims are Rajas or other persons of importance, who bring considerable retinues, and become large benefactors to the various shrines and temples. Hindu princes of distant States pride themselves upon keeping up a 'town residence' in holy Benares. But besides the wealth which thus flows passively into the bazars of Benares, a considerable trade is carried on by the merchants and bankers. The sugar, indigo, salt of the District find a market in the city. The trans-Gogr products of Gorakhpur and Basti, and the raw materials of Jaunpur form large items in the through traffic of Benares. Manchester good are imported in considerable quantities, and distributed to the neigh bouring local centres...

Bodies, garbage, the sick, the weak, the poor, a constant stream of people bathing and bustling past, you may think to see this kind of scene when you first reach the river side. Soon you will find out it is

quite different than one could possibly imagination. Benares is by far
the most thickly populated District in the North-Western Provinces,
having a density of 6,210 persons to the square mile. Over 100 years
ago that was only 894 persons; a seven-fold increase.

The Indian president recently announced to revive Ganga river, the
sidewalk and stairs are now more clean than when I was there. It's evident that people there want to make the city clean and welcome more
tourists.

In Varanasi it's very common to take a walk to a ghat, or to take
boat from ghat to ghat. There are ghats everywhere, and boats. Ghats
line the banks, thronged in summer by numerous bathers. Those handsome stone ghats lead down to the river beside fine Sivaite temples and
handsome masonry. Pukhra is one of the sacred ghats to which pilgrims in the neighbourhood resort to bathe in the Ganges.

Varanasi forms part of the alluvial valley deposited by the river Ganges, and occupies an irregular parallelogram on either bank of the sacred stream. The surface consists of a level plain, with a gentle upward slope on each side from the central depression; and the general monotony of its cultivated fields is only broken by the ravines of two tiny streamlets—the Varuna in the west and the Nand in the north—and by the deep gorges and precipitous cliffs of the Karamnasa on the south-eastern boundary.

The Ganges enters Varanasi as a very large river, augmented at the point of leaving Allahabad by the Jamuna, and joined 16 miles below Varanasi city by the waters of the Gumti. Before reaching the confines of Ghazipur, it presents a magnificent expanse of 4 miles in breadth during the rainy season. The Giimti also flows through the...strict for a course of some 22 miles ; while the Karamnasa skirts the south-eastern border, a heavy stream after rains, but almost dry during the hot months, though subject, like other hill rivers, to sudden flushes, which produce considerable inundations.

The city of Benares, the metropolis of Hinduism, traces its origin to the very earliest period of Aryan colonization in India, yet the District at large can scarcely be said to possess any separate history of its own until the middle of the 18th century.

—The climate of Benares is one of the hottest and dampest in the North-Western Provinces. No really cold weather diversifies the year as in the upper country beyond Allahabad; and since the hot west winds have lost their force before reaching this District, tattis or grass mats fail to perform their function of cooling the air by evaporation. The temperature more nearly resembles that of Lower Bengal than that of the North-Western plains in general.

*   *   *

There is still some trash there, and you can see bodies burning every day, but it is ok to stay there for many days. There are morning and evening ceremony everyday, no need to worry to miss any kind of ceremony. Usually people gather the place to wait for ceremony around 7 pm, you can choose to seat on the ground nearby the sacrificial altar or take seat on a boat.

Taking boat in early morning is my favorite part, because it's quiet and you can see sun rise from river. It takes 90 minutes only and you can see people swimming or showering and praying on the river side. When you look at all things happen everyday here, some moment will touch you as you were involved in their daily life or a sacrifice moment.

I was worried before I arrived Varanassi because I was afraid of seeing bodies and stinky roads. But now I'm glad that I came here, I love this place more than New Delhi. I enjoy the life of peace and calm here in a mess but beautiful city.

Indians sometimes express their surprise that I should travel so far in search of their country at the age of twenty-one, yet looking no older than sixteen. They are impressed by my adventurous spirit. I sometimes wonder why I have come here, when there's an abundance of scenery and people at home.

In a more philosophical spirit, I see there's more than mere scenery. I did not leave the River Severn or Thames unexplored, and go to India in search of the Ganges or Parvarti, or some such river with its own identical character. What I look at in this strange land is not water, and rock, and woods, but such things seen through a new medium—accompanied by the colours, contrasts, Holy men and simple folk in un-English dress, which array universal nature herself in such foreign apparel.

An un-travelled Englishman is ignorant of his own country. He must cross the seas before he can become acquainted with home. He must admire the romance of Parvarti—the sublimity of the (mountain) Kachenguna— the beauty of the Yamuna and the Vasi—before he can tell what is the rank of the Severn, in picturesque character, among the rivers of the world.

So many Sadhu's figuring in the fore-ground, resting upon staffs, holding in the left hand a gourd scooped into the form of *tota*.[1] Indian beggars who live on alms from their fellow man. What a beggar is in England, an Indian Sadhu is, with with this difference: whereas the former is considered a vagrant, and though often deserving alms which he solicits, he is held in very low esteem; the latter takes religious devotion as the apparent basis of his conduct, is not only tolerated as a privileged member of society (imposter would be a better word), but is, because his prescribed austerities, even regarded with honour and respect!)

These sadhus are, in a few instances, sad rogues, and very immoral. Religion with them is a cloak; for every species of wickedness. In most cases I like to think they are genuine. Some coat themselves with filth and are objects of disgust. The Mother Ganja is one of the seven sacred rivers, running from Haridwar, to the sacred city of Benares, more ancient than the most ancient of cities, wrote Mark Twain.

If you die at this lucky intersection of the sacred ganja and Holy City, it is believed you will be transported straight to heaven.

'If you take a dip in the holy river you will wash away one's sins, and then if you have your ashes disposed in the Ganja after death, you will achieve liberation sooner,' says the guide. 'Devout Hindus make pilgrimages to bathe in the Ganga and meditate upon its banks.'

I considered it to be the perfect place to die. And there are old people who wait to die here. If you believe in metempsychosis, as both Neo-Platonist and Hindu do, it is a curious belief that to die in Benares will free you from the cycle of reincarnation.

Perhaps this is a comforting tale, told by priests to assuage the dying? Is then Moksha that easy? There must be something greatly purifying in this water at its source in the mountains. Perhaps the sulphur in the springs, or some strange bacteria kills all the more gruesome things in the water, giving it a restorative spirit; cleansing?

The daily ablutions in the waters, elderly Hindu's waiting patiently for their days to end by the city's Ghats.

Ganga arrogantly fell on Shiva's head. But Shiva calmly trapped her in his hair and let her out in small streams. The touch of Shiva further sanctified Ganga. As Ganga travelled to the nether-worlds, she created a different stream to remain on Earth to help purify unfortunate souls there. She is the only river to follow from all the three worlds– Swarga, Prithvi[15] and, Patala[16].

Thus, is called 'Tripathagā'[17] (one who travels the three worlds) in the Sanskrit language. Because of Bhagiratha's efforts, Ganga descended to Earth and hence the river is also known as Bhagirathi, and the term 'Bhagirath prayatna' is used to describe valiant efforts or difficult achievements.

Another name that Ganga is known by is Jahnavi. The story has it that once Ganga came down to Earth, on her way to Bhagiratha, her rushing waters created turbulence and destroyed the fields and the sadhana[18] of a sage called Jahnu[19]. He was angered by this and drank up all of Ganga's waters.

Upon this, the Gods prayed to Jahnu to release Ganga so that she could proceed on her mission. Pleased with their prayers, Jahnu released Ganga (her waters) from his ears. Hence the name "Jahnavi" (daughter of Jahnu) for Ganga.

It is sometimes believed that the river will finally dry up at the end of the Kali Yuga[20] (the era of darkness, the current era) just as with the Sarasvati river[21], and this era will end. Next in (cyclic) order will be the Satya Yuga[22] or the era of Truth.

Generously strewn Ganges; pilgrim sites, temples. Holiest of cities that Shiva founded, mid-way between Delhi & Calcutta. Seventeen hours it took me to arrive here from Haridwar via Delhi. The old city is teeming with ghats, soaring temples rise from river banks, as sunshine sparkles; diamonds on water ripples, channels of torrent; lethal top surface.

Vast channel of majestic water undulates in the monsoon swell. It is truly huge; like an enormous estuary about to open out to the sea.

Holy men stride into their ablution. Descending the ghat, a tout ushers me to a long boat. I walk the plank, take my seat, no other tourists join me. All to myself. The tout unties the rope, also gets in boat with oarsman & me. Many other boats on the riverside, heavily laden with American, Chinese, Japanese tour groups; dangerously so.

There are boatman struggling with the current, using long poles and oars in their fight against the flow.

The river is too powerful. Boats get swept away from the river sides, into the stronger channel of the river current. I see panicked faces and screaming tourists pass me by, then disappear into the long distance downstream, swept at surprising speed. At Shiva Ghat we alight.

The guide reveals he gave a lift in a boat to Luc Besson[23], who directed the 5th Element. The sacred undulations of the Ganges welcome me as I sit in the boat; thoughts seem to pass like flowing water. River peaceful Benares, city replete with antiquity.

Cacophony of the Ganges flowing near the Ghat. Crumbling against ever-bluer sky; I ran through the street, up the short incline through narrow alleys, I arrived at the ghat...the steps down to the river, a place where people of the riverine bathe, wash clothes utensils, gossip, pray; a place of arrival, departure, of welcome and farewell.

I meet a sannyasin[24]. He met the Pope and said he was 'kissing his hand like this!' a gesture so bizarre, so over the top, I'm not sure the Pope approved, nor his bodyguards.

The boatman does let me disembark for a ransom of 600 rupees. How else could I have had the privilege of a boat all to myself?

From the ghat to an alleyway, where I am introduced to a faqueer, a strange fellow who reads palms. It is a low-ceilinged, single-storey building, with rush matting on the floor, embroidered fabrics. The air is thick with joss sticks. The faqueer has a dark, pointed beard.

An intelligent and insightful astrologer. There is a sonorous Tibetan singing bowl beside him, and a few tomes of Vedic astrological manuals, even a picture of Pope John Paul II.

'You are a romantic, moody boy, in your dealings with others. You say what you think and often think before you say it, and at times you speak when you might better refrain, and refrain when you might better speak.

'You are a spiritual pilgrim, my brother soul, a Brahmin in a former life, with the secret power of the Lotus, who gives the new colours and echoes, over the play of water on lapping pools of infinity, and azure skies, full of star questions and prophecies; turquoise deeps and indigo dreams. You seem to have a lot of troubles, and these are troubles from old life times, reverberating through time. Please guard the use of your power!

'You are a very independent-minded; a wayfarer. The next decade will be very unsettled for you. Know your problems are of life-times past, and that problems will come from others.' He takes my hand enthusiastically, and investigates the lines of my palm with rapt interest.

'Let me see: the solutions speak in the darkest peaks of soul searching, when you go down, seek the smoother slopes, and fix yourself to plateaus to get rest. Here you will receive more prana[25], and there what you are you will be; this is what you are!' He sighs deeply.

'Please my dear friend, you must release your past through prayer. You will be free one day, there is no fixed path, it is a road without a compass, and yet you are guided. There is a light within. There is the abyss and precipices, shore limits of visible horizons, such is life. Like in the desert, the circular flashing of the sphere, thunder, destroys the ego, the false self, the person that you are is beneath the rubble there.

'You will go far, and you have a deep imagination, and inspiration, a well that gives. Your quest is your destination, you can be assured you are always on your path, though you must get back up again and keep trying.

'Even if you don't know where you are, reach out to where you belong, here within your own heart. Those miles less distant are to be found there, those inviting calls to go deeper, to return home, to yourself, are in there.'

He points at my heart. 'There are songs with which we resonate. Take time, you will reach your space. You must go far to find the river of your destiny, my friend. But you will get to where you belong. You will have three jobs, the last being the most rewarding.

Oh and please do not marry an older woman. And alcohol is very bad for you.' I've given him my date of birth so he can figure things out using his

astrological calculations, and I also give him the dates of birth of my immediate family.

'Your mother is a good lady, but very strict and self-controlled. I caught her saddest mood, perhaps they have coloured your own in childhood?

'Your father is a cursed man. I fear much in his case. You must tell him the right things and pray for him.'

The robed astrologer sounds the sonorous dish, a Tibetan singing bowl, and places it upon my crown, as the vibration sounds to infinity.

'Avoid alcohol, a little tobacco is fine. You are the lucky man of longevity. It is very good to smile; it releases a good vibration.

'I see maybe one relationship, but my dear friend, I am so sorry, many heart breaks. There seems to be no end to your recovery. Everything will be well, in your next life, you live in a Holy City as a Holy Man.'

He wished me well on my journey. And concluded with a prayer, and gave me two talismans to help heal my father relationship. He concluded with a prayer:

'Infinite, eternal and universal Trinity, the divine maintenance and direction. OM! O Earth, O Air, O Heavens. OM. Let us meditate on the supreme splendour of the Divine Sun, and may his light enlighten us all.'

Dying Hindus hope for a worthy death. Here is smell of burning flesh. A shoulder bone rolls off a fire. It is carried away by a dog. There is no separation of life and death. The Dashashwamedh ghat, place of 'ten horse-sacrifices'[26]. The merit of this sacrifice continues to attend all who bathe here in the sacred river.

Let me explain the legend of this ghat. Shiva, dispossessed of his Benares Varanasi, had the idea to regain it by challenging the incumbent king, with quite an impossible ritual challenge: the performance of ten simultaneous horse-sacrifices.

However, the king was quite punctilious. He faultlessly performed all ten *awamedha* and thereby attained untold merit and favour. A power we don't see, is invisible, yet it moves everything. Varanasi is where the Varuna and Assi emerge into the Ganges.

All the postcards I've sent and requests for donations direct from the destitute. The boat takes me upstream. The current is strong, impossible effort. Somehow we manage. Nothing is impossible here. Against a mighty current the oarsman fights. Close to the ghat step, he pulls us along the bank edge, the boatswain cries, 'More effort!' In the boat, we float on strong currents of monsoon rain. Swollen River. I reflect on my experienced in India so far, from a ritual bath to cricket game, temple blessing to a hand and neck massage.

He pulls the boat against the current, pulling alongside the ghat. The boats in front of us attempt the same. However, each boat in front has groups of western tourists.

Our boat is light, just me, the oarsman and boatswain. I enjoy the spectacle of tourist boats being swept backwards, dramatically, downstream, fast. The river Ganges, swelled with monsoon waters, is almost dispatching them far from the Ghats.

I survey at great speed the distance we cover upstream. Then like a sling shot, the sheer force generated, accumulates such a release charge on the prow, now launches out all energy, great hydro-flow supply, launches them downstream. Some boats lose their oars once the boatmen's strength cannot compete with the current and he lets go of the ghat. In the blinking of an eye, they are increasingly like specks vanishing downstream.

We alight at Manikarinka[27] Ghat; being the oldest, most sacred. I realise it is the 'burning ghat' where firewood is weighed by dying geriatrics, purchased with their last rupees. Here I witness a funeral rite before turning from the smouldering pyre.

I see behind the light that shines upon Holy Ganga, sun setting, light refracted on water's edge. My footsteps surrender to water as I bounce from stone ghat plank to riverman's boat.

Deep response to India's beauty; natural simplicities.

I watch from a distance, scenes passing through train windows, idealistic reveries, springing from spiritual needs; coping with physical frustrations, limitations.

Slowly flowing amid strict topographical observation.

I feel the love of the poet for this majestic country. I feel my life in intense fleeting moments. Life as a river; this river of life.

With all its travails, depths, hopeful darkness, heights of humble glory, flowing endlessly, on river's edge. Now dawn light enfolds dark's retreat, pushing it away with equal and constant force, but it always returns.

Perhaps those deceptive tributaries do what matter most? They bring you back with greater perseverance to re-join the river and reach your destiny.

Those whirls, eddies, currents, rapids, come suddenly, so you appreciate the calming flow, when it resumes, until at river's end, you open, emerging into that expanding vastness of ocean.

I feel a peculiar harmony with Banyans that soothe, birds that are always there for you, and other animals. Their vastness and elemental mystery is not entirely tarrying, since I found that I was part of a greater whole: that I am that; part of that, and so I feel a tremendous unconscious connection with the spirit of the Earth.

That I am that I am that, and I know, so long as I acknowledge it, which I can't help but know, no turning back from that revelation, that I am that, that I am inextricably linked to Her, that I am, and protected by Her, that I am.

She sustains me as I am sustained by her. That I am. There comes a time when the rubber meets the road; You pass your test and get behind the wheel, navigate with speed and skill. I had to decide where I wanted to go in India. Was I going to follow through with this India decision as I promised myself.

There was such vast, unambitious, still serene, beauty in the river, in nature's undistorted peace. I compared it with my tormented, petty, unstable lack of peace inside. The river bank was not so settled. The currents do what they do.

The noise of the river was great. The day seemed entirely unreal, the night was dreamlike, remote...and I sat smoking on the balcony, by a tree in which monkeys played. Truly here in the Kingdom of the Night – so much attuned to eternity and unity. England seemed so much more finite, fractured. A detached world at the highest reach of the branch of the tree of life, whose roots dig deep into the Indian ocean. The two are almost complementary opposites. India is imagination and inspiration; England is pragmatism. At home, I am forever inspired by India. India is sensitivity, idealism, peace; England is masculine, divided, boring, somehow more constrained, and fixed in time: less spiritual.

India is free, nothing fixed, childlike, female-spirited, full of wise silences and *solitudes*.

India is where an Englishman may turn to for comfort, to her womb for re-birth. In the Mother's waters to bathe and see eternity reflected in Her.

Sunset Ganges, Benares

Backstreet, Benares

The City of Victory and the Taj Mahal

Fatehpur Sikri is a 24 mile taxi drive from Agra. It is the remains of a ruined city, scattered over dry rock ridge. The Imperial Palace is a vast complex with mosque. The road getting there is a train of trucks, camel carts, rickety buses, crazed road-crossing monkeys. Saras cranes preen themselves on irrigation runnel edge; mud brick villages, old men relaxing on charpoy beds[1]. Chai poured, bicycles repaired, chillies fried, women in billowing saris leading goats to fields on flat plains. Crenelated walls rear out of camel thorn. Taxi stops at the main old gate of the city, by which you enter; exit.

I climb up 'better view' battlements; guide accosted, I see Buland Darwaza[2], great arched gateway of victory. Mosque, with framed Arabic calligraphy on its arch: 'Jesus, Son of Mary (on whom be peace) said: "The World is a bridge, pass over it, but build no houses upon it. He who hopes for a day may hope for eternity; but the world endures for an hour. Spend it in prayer, for the rest is unseen."'[3]

Akbar[4], the Great Emperor, Sufi mystic, feels all existence as one. Manifestation of reality is Divine Revelation. Love of God, one's brethren, more important than narrow religious ritual. The Hindu and Muslim elements fuse in latticed screens, sharp *chajja*[5] eves, *chatrri* like umbrellas, pavilions; decorative sculpture.

Marvel at this philosophical laboratory of great, simple metaphysics. *Diwan-i-Khas*[6]: hall of private audience, intact, covered with inter-laced designs. "The pursuit of reason and the rejection of traditionalism, brilliantly patient, above the need of argument. If tradition were proper, the prophets would merely have followed their own elders (and not come with new messages)."[7]

The Jewel House of Justice[8], meted out, where Akbar was weighed at the beginning of the Persian new year. Ruddy sandstone rises artful; staged composition of Mughal architecture; dramatic, assured in style, in scale & outline. Magnificent *Jama Masjid*[9], Capital of the Mughal Empire (1571-1585), when Sikri was but a village: home to a Sufi mystic, Shaikh Salim Chishti of Sikri, who Emperor Akba sought for intercession. He was concerned with succession, aged 26. Although not for want of brides (besides his Hindu, Muslim and Christian wives, there were the 254 in the harem).

He was still without an heir, for reassurance foretold he would have three sons. *Jama Masjid* is a beautiful mosque, containing elements of Persian and Hindu design. Fatephur Sikri was a veritable bazaar of disputing divines, and Akbar presided over their heated debates with the relish he usually reserved for elephant fights.

Such inquisitiveness as the Hindi columns and Muslim cupolas demonstrate, directed popular fervour from 'Bhakti' and 'Sufi' devotionals towards a Supreme Transcendent; which subsumed both the Allah of Islam and the Brahman of Hinduism. The faith would satisfy the needs of his realm. Fatephur contains the finest elements of this achievement. *Diwan-I-Am*[10]. I am at the hall of the public audiences.

This is a large Pachisti courtyard, to the right *Ankh Michdi*[11], surrounded by cloisters. The *pachisi*[12] courtyard is set out like a gigantic game board. It is said that Akbar played the game *pachisi* here, using slave girls as pieces. To the right there is a panoramic view, stretching into the sands. A minaret called the Deer Minaret[13] stands in the foreground, beside a courtyard used for visiting merchants. The minarets were erected over the grave of Akbar's elephant. Great stone tusks protrude from the 21 meter tower from which Akbar is said to have shot game. Below it, stone rings, to secure elephants for trampling criminals. Sufism– called *tasawuuf*[14] in Arabic– refers to a spiritual path. It is the art of awakening to a spiritual consciousness by complete surrender to the Divine Essence, and is referred to as 'to die before you die.' The syncretic identity of the Sufis is such that it embraces people from all religions and walks of life– Hindu, Muslim, Christian, King, or Poor.[15]

The word is also traced to the word 'Suffa'[16] or bench, because the early 45 practitioners used to occupy the bench at the entrance to the Prophet's mosque at Medina. They sat on those benches offering incessant prayers and fasting. They were called *Ashab-e-Suffa*[17], or the People of the Bench. The bench area is visible to this day in the Prophet's chamber in that mosque. They also became known as *Al-fuqara*[18] which is the plural of the word *faqir* or the poor. The Persian equivalent of *faqir* is dervish. *Safa* also means purity, and Sufis are called *Auliya Allah*, or the friends of Allah.

'There is only the Creator and his creations and one should not differentiate between the creations. To serve the creator, one should serve the creation,' says Haji Syed Salman Chishti, Gaddi Nashin of Dargah Ajmer Sharif[19]. The founding principles of Sufism as laid down by Khwaza Mui'in-ud-Din Chishti[20]: 'River-like Generosity, Sun-like Bounty and Earth-like Hospitality.'

The essence of Sufism is purification of the heart through constant self-observation. Sufism is more demanding and requires deeper understanding than merely discharging customary religious obligations. The Sufi's path to awakening is based on the three concepts of Iman, Islam and Ihsan. Iman refers to the faith in the heart, Islam is complete submission to the Divine Will, Ihsan refers to worshipping God as if you saw Him, leading a spiritual life and killing one's ego. One's journey from the external world to the inner soul is similarly defined by three stages.[21] The juxtaposition of negation and affirmation in the same sentence, can be seen in 'there is no divinity' (negation) followed by 'except God' (affirmation).

The same concept is often conveyed as follows: 'There is no guide except The Guide', 'there is no truth except The Truth' etc. Emperor Akbar was a devout follower of both Shaykh Salim Chishti and Khwajah Mu'in-ud-Din Chishti of Ajmer. Akbar had taken a vow that if he managed to capture Chittor, he would walk on foot from Agra to Ajmer to thank God. After his dream was achieved in 1568, he continued the practice of visiting Ajmer on foot as an annual pilgrimage for almost ten years, until 1579.

'The world is a bridge. Pass over it, but do not build your dwelling there.' Nietzsche must have been influenced by this when he wrote: 'Man is a bridge; not a goal: a way to new dawns.'[22]

The Taj Mahal: face of eternity. Jahan was heartbroken, commissioned a testament to Love, 1643 (during a transit of Venus), completed a wonder of the world. Rabindranath thought it 'a tear on the face of eternity'. Indeed, it was, but grafted over a more ancient Hindu temple preceding it. There is laughing blossom, sunny proclamation, pure white esteem, genial glow of contentment, infused with this fanned desire, which consumes me with its power. Through the ivory gate, through which most dreams pass, I catch a glimpse of eternity on an orchid's dew drop.

The River Varuna has become quite polluted. Here all oppression is covered in extravagance. All colours and monuments distract from the darkness of the broken-hearted, through whom God commissions services to Beauty. I thwart an attempt to be sold a marble elephant, ignore pleas for purchasing a leather whip. I do not need a Moghul sword from the Wallah.

My steps are not determined by observant sahibs, my foresight, blind as it may be, by the heat, or the fetid moat, or passing train. Something remains for me to decipher from the post card booklets I bought for 10 rupees. It surpasses the colossal double walls of my expectation; the circumference of this fort recedes into my own desire to be elsewhere. Near the red fortifications, 496 years on from the great earthquake of 1505, sprawl the beggarly unfortunates who always pass my way, holding out a smile and a resignation, as if to say that hope is a timeless piece of art, not confinable to any century, or a living mausoleum; where sacrifice is an acceptance of fate, and fate an acceptance of handicap. From Agra's orient land I floated like a butterfly through lucid air, enamoured of a fragrance, of delight. I could see the beauty of Taj Mahal, from the rear prospect, alongside the Varuna river.

Thereafter, I return by taxi to Agra, and visit the Red Fort. However, after Fatepur Sikri and Taj Mahal, I am quite overwhelmed by a third mega monument. From there I get a cycle rickshaw to the station. In the waiting room I meet a Hare Krishna monk who gives me a copy of the Bhagavad Gita, and recommends going to Kanyakamuri, where he says the energies are very pure and will be very good for me.An unfortunate backdrop (if rather proud of me) to view it from here. According to the rules one must pay $20 for entry (Indian Government Tourism minister). I do not pay to see the wonder of the World, but go around the back. No picture of the divine garden, in front of the monument of Love; I read of Akbar's grandson, Shah Jahan, who bequeathed North India this splendid monument; Mumtaz Mahal, Shah Jahan's second wife. When she died in 1631, Shah Jahan knew the depth of stories, how they turn smooth and rub on the heart. Imprisoned by grief, with no consoling ghosts, bearing with old age, though his virgin daughter Jahanara dressed the cracked marble. I pose for pictures, three young girls with their father. One is very shy.

Author at the Taj Mahal

{ 18 }

Ashoka's Pillar

At Sarnath there is a 34m Gupta Stupa, the spot where the Buddha preached the famous sermon of the 'middle way' to Nirvana after he reached enlightenment at Bodhgaya. Deer are still to be seen here, where the Buddha gave the Sermon in the Deer Park. The pillared picture here dates from around 500 AD. It is a shrine that stands over 20m high. Ashoka-the great Buddhist Emperor.

A Sadhu at Sarnath, 60km from Varanasi, holding a trimurti[1] He comes out of his cave, observes me keenly as I pass by, with a blessing: NAMASKAR. There is no life for one who has come under poverty, it seems. All depends on wealth or else life falls apart. He seems to say a lot just by his smile, and his welcome; what calls me out to enjoy the indifferent spectacle of life. Existence is as old as the rocks here. Having renounced the world, he is happy gazing at the dying world.

He seems to be content with his austere existence. Maybe he feels the same pain and joy as I do. Is he not someone else?Is he not myself also? What is this self of ours? Not this petty ego, but that which binds us all together? The sun sets on the water's edge, footsteps bounce on the wooden bridge. Higher levels of thought are spirit united with Cosmos.

I watch from the train window: countryside, fleeting scenes, course of the river, sunshine all about, light clouds gathering. There on edge of the river is darkness; tributaries that lead me back to the river of destiny; past whirlpool, strong currents, rapids. I long for calm sailing to the ocean; the harmony of shades meeting the wave. Silvery water glistens in the sun's reflection. I arrive at the ghat, and ascend to the river path; past people selling clothes, utensils. Ah, the evil of gossip; those who seek to destroy. I recognise the glance on a train through shaded glasses; bruised legs, and insinuations of hate and envy.

A Sanyasi hums mantras to rouse him from slumber, and recommends one for low esteem. There is a vast unambitious serene beauty on the river, in nature's undistorted peace. There is that satisfaction that hides itself behind black glasses.

Once the mind is befriended, and overcome. Siddhartha settled under a tree at Buddha Gaya. At the age of 35 he isolated the nature of suffering and transience, formulating his scheme to overcome it, so, he attained Enlightenment here. As the enlightened one, he hastened to Varanasi,and so, it was here at Sarnath in the Deer Park that he pronounced his message to five erstwhile companions, the First Sermon. In the nearby museum there is a most sublime Buddha. This is the earliest Buddha image found, dating from 9th century. Siddhartha Gautama had forsaken security of a settled, civilised life for the uncertainties of the outcast. Austerities, unavoidable, the noise of the river, unreal day, the night like a dream, the screeching of monkeys, fractured, detached, out of reach of the roots that reach down into the Indian ocean.

England seems to be politely cruel, puritanically pragmatic, made ugly by utilitarianism. India seems idealistic, peaceful, freer, nothing fixed. Spirit of silence and solitude, comfort in return for distraction, a womb and waters to bathe, glimpses of eternity. When Brahma collected the sweat of Vishnu's feet, when he was touched by two members of the Trimmurthi, the Ganga was created and became very Holy. Kapila, the penitent sage, who was falsely accused of stealing the horse which Indra took (she was jealous of King Sagar, who sent his 60,000 sons to search for the horse); with one glance Kapila burnt to death all the sons. Cremated corpses, livestock carcases, raw sewage, water waste from factories. $33 to address the overwhelming problem, dense human population belt, one in 12 of the world lives in its catchment area; an incredible concentration of population.

IV

Dravidia

{ 19 }

The Road to Madras

Epic 48-hour train journey during which I absorb the formidable dialectical apparatus of Schopenhauer's 'Welt als Wille und Vorstellung'; an older man on the 1st-class bunk next to me asks for a blow job. I refuse. He asks me why, with an air of disappointment. I cannot think of anything more punishing than to cite its illegality in India, were we to be caught.

He replies, 'but this is India!'

I am not sure what to make of the remark, except the paradox of it is not lost on me. The ease with which he asks this surprises me, as one of my own age or younger, is too ashamed to make such a request, without subtle overtures, and still then, mostly hiding from being honest. I admire his honesty, and feel flattered; to accept, if only he were attractive enough. Still the feeling of knowing his intent, has me back in my bunk, ensuring the blue veil is drawn across, and that he didn't see where I was returning to as I passed him.

I had read most of Nietzsche's work in England before my trip to India, and during it I was reading more. 'Go your ways! And let people go theirs!', 'See to it that no parasite clings to you', 'Everything of today is falling, decaying', 'Are not music and words rainbows and bridges between things seemingly eternally separated?', 'Let where you are going, not where you come from, henceforth be your honour!'

On the train, I read the entire 'The world as Will and Representation.' 'It is us he inhabits, not the underworld, nor the stars in the sky. The spirit who lives in us makes those.' 'The inner nature of phenomena is something that remains secret', 'the subject perceives and constructs forms of phenomenon entirely out of itself (independent of an object)', 'knowing requires a knower and a known'; and quoting Plato, 'Timaeus': 'What is that which always is, and has no becoming? And what is that which is always becoming, and never is?' I ponder these riddles with enthusiasm, enthralled by the rhetorical paradox.

In former days, it was called Madras, where the British established Fort Saint George, one of the first places for the East India Company. Down the southern line, I go, to the Port of Madras. On the platform, there is a crowd of youth, each shouting over the other, for money, or donations to their pen fund; a sergeant canes them left to right, to disperse the gathering. I'm amazed at how wild they go for me, as though I am an earlier version of Jusitn Beiber. I dash into the municipality, founded by James II, in 1686, and encounter Marina Beach and my first view of the Bay of Bengal.

Massulah boats and fishermen arranging nets, scattered along the coastline, as the surf vigorously laps the beach. A coconut palm tree near Fort St George catches my eye, also called the tree of life because Indians use all parts of the tree; it seems to reflect the blue of the bay.

I admire Chennai's southern palms, but decide to travel on a Hindi bus tour from the station. We stop at the snake museum. There is a bus parked beside us with deaf children visiting this zoo. I decide to leave the bus tour,

and go instead to the nearby International Headquarters of the Theosophical Society.[1]

Wisdom underlying all religions stripped of accretions, superstitions. Philosophy of life, intelligible, demonstrable: justice and love guide the cosmos, aid unfoldment of the latent spiritual nature in the human being, independence of spirit. Truth as a prize to be striven for, not as a dogma to be imposed by authority. Individual understanding and intuition more than mere acceptance of traditional ideas; knowledge and experience, not assertion; truth sought by study, reflection, meditation, service, purity of life and devotion to high endeavour.[2]

All religion is an expression of Divine Wisdom, adapted to the needs of a time and place. Condemnation, and evangelism, have no place in true religion. Thus, earnest tolerance to all, even the intolerant, not as a privilege they bestow, but as duty to perform. To remove ignorance, not punish it; peace and Truth their aim.

Abandoning completely materialistic philosophy hitherto held; mere belief that discounts half of the reality.[3] Annie Bessant says, apply the light of Theosophy to the various fields of human activity: religious, social, economic, political, etc. The Theosophical Order of Service, and The Sons of India, in 1908. The Headquarters at Adyar were enlarged by the purchase of Blavatsky and Olcott Gardens. The Great Banyan tree Adyar Aala maram, or the Adyar Bodhi tree, in the middle of the Theosophical Society Campus; estimated to be second largest banyan tree in India; hence the world, around 450 years old. 40,000 square feet of ground occupied by the tree and its offshoots Curious Emblem encodes profound concepts about human beings and the universe; a vast evolutionary process embracing the whole of nature, physical and spiritual.

'With study a serious enquirer may study and contemplate the deepest mysteries of existence. Thus, our motto:

"There is no Religion Higher than Truth".' Truth is the quest of every Theosophist, reflects the light of the one eternal and spiritual Wisdom. In the centre of the two interlaced triangles is what is known as the Ankh (or the Crux Ansata): circle surmounting the Tau Cross (the type of cross which follows the shape of the letter 'T').

Patience and dedication, hope and honesty. Look at your mirrors, examine where the truth lies, see the lies, and respond accordingly. Be willing to see the past be gone, for a window of the New Day to Be Opened. Believe in yourself and in the God. Peace comes even when all seems to be falling apart. Joy dawns, when before, I was sad. Kind to animals; I see them as tests—mirrors of God—you know. I am humbled by such creatures. Human beings are truly a work of Godly Art.Within me lies the Treasure, within me is the Key. The Gatekeeper says I have been the key. That I am the Ankh.Rising from a modest start into infinity and Rising more equally on each side, in balance, obeying the master. Who takes me into this lesson of balancing the He and She within, to know now you are Free. Both sides equal, healing from the pain. This journey of resurrection, out of the ancient knowledge where I am saved, to ascend.

The Ankh is an Egyptian symbol of great antiquity and it portrays the resurrection of the spirit out of its encasement of matter, otherwise expressed as the triumph of life over death, of spirit over matter, of good over evil. This concept of the 'Resurrection' is found in all the great religions. The Interlaced Triangles: these are often called the Double Triangle, viewed by the Jewish Kabalists as the Seal of Solomon and also known as Sri Yantra and Satkona Chakram in the Indian tradition.

They are surrounded by a serpent. This combination of the triangle and the surrounding serpent symbolises the created universe, through which creation is limited in time and space. The Triangles, looked at separately, symbolise the three facets of the manifestation which is known as the Trinity in various religions, and personified in Christianity as Father, Son and Holy Ghost, and in Hinduism as Shiva, Vishnu, and Brahma.

The darker of the two triangles, which is downward- pointing, and the lighter triangle, which is upward-pointing, symbolize respectively the descent of the life of Spirit into matter and the ascent of that life out of matter into Spirit, the perpetual opposition between the light and dark forces in nature and in man. The Serpent has always been a Wisdom symbol. Hindus call their wise men 'Nagas' (meaning serpent). Christ adjured His disciples to be as 'wise as serpents.' What is known as the Uraeus (or sacred Cobra) seen on forehead of a Pharaoh of Egypt, denoted his initiation into the sacred rites, where knowledge was gained of the hidden Wisdom.

The serpent swallows its tail, represents the 'circle of the universe', the endlessness of the cyclic process of manifestation. The Swastika: Form of the cross, Fiery Cross, with arms of whirling flame revolving (clockwise) to represent the tremendous energies of nature, incessantly creating and dissolving the forms through which the evolutionary process takes place.

In religions which recognise three aspects of Deity, the Swastika is associated with the third aspect, the Third Person of the Trinity, who is the Creator: Brahma in Hinduism and the Holy Ghost in Christianity. Mention Ledbeeter! The Aum Surmounting the emblem is the sacred word Om of Hinduism in Sanskrit characters, the three letters representing the Trinity.

There is also the idea of the creative Word or Logos sounding throughout, and sustaining, the universe. In the Prologue of the Gospel according to John, in the Holy Bible, we read: 'In the beginning was the Word, and the Word was with God, and the Word was God'. The emblem as a whole symbolises the Absolute, God, both transcendent and immanent.

God transcendent– that is, in and beyond creation– (the sacred word AUM) overshadows the cycle of manifestation (serpent), energized by divine activity (Swastika); and within this field of manifestation the linked triangles of spirit and matter enshrine the symbol of immortality (the Ankh), God immanent – that is, indwelling in all created forms.

After viewing the temple, and banyan, and walking in the grounds, seeing an avenue of trees. Beneath each tree is a stone with a country inscribed on it. I was told each tree had been planted with the soil of the respective nations. In the bookshop, an Indian lady told me not to eat fish, and to save the fish, for they need protecting.

I notice there is no Cross of Jesus Christ of Nazareth, since it cannot be inclusive of the ankh, that would be a gross diminution, and elevation of the witchcraft of the Chaldeans. I suspect, in a sense, Theosophy was a reaction for disaffected Christians. No doubt very clever people, however susceptible to their own hubris, as Blavatsky clearly was.

There are things are aren't meant to know, that is forbidden, clearly the Cross of Christ is not compatible with that in the truest sense. There is no religion higher than truth, And there is no Truth Higher than God, might be the qualifying statement required. Neither do I feel Anthroposophy, which Steiner made in the West as a break away from the Eastern origin of theosophical occultism.

{ 20 }

Mamallapuram

Mamallapuram[1], the famous centre of Pallava art and architecture, is situated on the coast of Tamil Nadu. It's about 34 miles further south of Chennai[2] by taxi.

Here I encounter the Elephant rocks, perhaps perfect examples of Nature imitating art. They look to my eyes like the behinds of two large greys. The shore temple is fenced off, but equally impressive; the spire rises, and there is a shrine to Shiva. It faces west to capture the sunset. Was made in the middle of the 7th Century AD.[3]

There is a rock, enormous, called Krishna's Butter ball. I have found the most noble stone in this land. It is precariously balanced on the sandstone embankment, an improbable sight; seeming as though it could topple over at an elephant's trunk's push. When the British Archaeological Survey discovered and excavated this site, they attempted to move the rock with two elephants, but could not shift it an inch to topple it, and roll it down the hill.

I stand posing for the camera with a group of school children who I hail, and who all wave. Now I'm Sisyphus, perchance, Indiana Jones. I'm bemused by the black smudges between Parvarti's thighs, Shiva's feminine aspect; blackened by centuries of eager, thumbing devotee hands, rubbing for fortune and glory. I meditate in a rock temple, like an ascetic at his penances, the teaching Buddha, the mudra of fearlessness. The sculpture student who is conducting this tour for me takes a photo as I sit. He introduces me to his friend who is tall and handsome.

The Cosmic Shiva. Shiva, destroyer of the world, necessary for creation, the god of cosmic dance. He comes into my world, and dances across it: a brief interlude. God of the black hole. I cheer myself on to give myself the energy to continue my path, validating myself, observing my steps. I feel power in the cycle of observation, moving forward with this topsy-turvy energy, to see how far I get. I do not stop. I knew the world before you, but now I see things like that other world. My mind moves towards the target. I see myself outside myself through your judgment, yet your invitation to broader ideas is like a sledge hammer.

To keep moving, the more certain I become of this movement, out of my heart to this intention, the stability of travelling. Moving through what I could never have expected, on the path of achieving it. I kept moving. In those days, I did not know what was ahead and looked behind to support me with the fuel of forward movement.

What was the end goal? I came very far in India. Over my head, you break down my ground. I fall, lost and dazed. What master plan do you have for life and the dance? In the Lion Throne (*Dharamaraja Mandapam*), the oldest here, I see a shrine to Shiva and Vishnu, at the highest point of the hill, and the baby elephant carved from stone, which the apprentice sculpture student strokes.

Wandering near to the sea, there is a tree, where the man and woman are married physically to the tree with a red thread, and then to themselves, an ancient Indian custom practised to this day. I'd like to be married to a tree, in this way my union might be rooted to in the earth and grow to a mighty oak reaching into the sky. I swing on a vine between a tree, near to the marriage tree.

Scenes from the *Puranas*, depicted on the *mandapam*, show the goddess Durga. (What would come of it, that evil eye in the box? Maybe it takes their souls, like the first cameras did. Perhaps this one steals a person's shade; makes him vulnerable? I see shadows and reflections, stolen pictures, toxic atmosphere, an omen of death in a dream reflected, beneath the surface, as a dear soul perishes after being defiled.

These events are part of me, and they are a danger foreseen. How will I make use of them? Will they overwhelm me? Send me insane?) These dark auguries have a vital influence over me here. If the greatest threat to my conditioned and narrow view, born of limitation in England, is travel, is it any wonder real engagement with the passing stream of illusion is a package tour of self-assertion and honesty, rather than blind self-delusion?

I can ill afford such a journey, yet maybe it gives me this life as a punishing conjunction of learnings that remain from many lives, all presented in this particularly dynamic one? A demon rises in the air, looking, I was warned: 'Beware lest they take your shadow.'

Spring breathes a song, into blossoming flowers. My body is just so many memories. A wounded child lives inside of me. I must meet him to heal. A *Ratha* is a chariot. One of the five *Rathas* that is a sculptured temple in the style of a chariot; carved from solid rock. There are amazing examples of this in the Pallava style. The sun wheels of fire are symbols of spiritual attainment.

The Pallavas, whose origins are uncertain, endowed Mamallapuran[2] with its greatness during the 8th Century. Deriving their name from the champions of Mahabharata (the Indian epic embodying the essence of the Indian Cultural Heritage, an absorbing tale of a feud between two branches of a single Indian ruling family that culminates in a vast, cataclysmic battle).

The *Arjuna Ratha* is dedicated to Shiva and Indra (the rain god), depicted on the outer walls. One can just see the *Dharmaraja Ratha*, which is the tallest of the Chariots, to the right. It has a Shiva and Parvarti combination, symbolising the true equality between men and women.

The *Panchantantras* carved on the face of a huge rock, 30 meters by 12 meters. There are 153 semi-divine creatures here, animals and deities. Arjuna is making penance to Shiva, to secure a weapon that will destroy all his opponents. Pillared pavilion, from front of the *mandapam* (temple), ancient stone cut to KRISHNA. He who protects his kinsfolk from the wrath of Indra, the rain god.

A sadhu stands outside a *mandapam*, bearing the three-pronged fork, and reminds me of a retired Captain, who is following the spiritual life, receiving alms.

Arjuna's Penance

Kanyakumari

Kanyakumari[1] has been a great centre for art and religion for centuries. It was also an area of great trade and commerce. Kanyakumari is a coastal town in the state of Tamil Nadu on India's southern tip. Jutting into the Laccadive Sea, the town was known as Cape Comorin during British rule, and is popular for watching sunrise and sunset over the ocean. It's also a noted pilgrimage site. The confluence of the Arabian Sea, Bay of Bengal and the Indian Ocean at the temple The Bagavathi Amman Temple is dedicated to a manifestation of the consort of Shiva, Parvarti.[2]

The author of *Periplus of the Erythraean[3] Sea* has written about the prevalence of the propitiation of the deity Kanyakumari in the extreme southern part of India: "There is another place called Comori and a harbour, hither come those men who wish to consecrate themselves for the rest of their lives, and bath and dwell in celibacy and women also do the same; for it is told that a goddess once dwelt here and bathed."

Our Lady of Ransom Church is a centre of Indian Catholicism[4]. It is Gothic, white, with 12 towers which symbolise the 12 disciples of Jesus Christ. There are gigantic statues of St. Thomas and St. Francis Xavier placed on the main tower.

When entering to the church I see the beautiful statue of Mother Mary, which is a pleasing counterpoint, in the middle of the main altar. Clearly it is from Rome and clad in a sai. There is a little Cross on the altar. There are beautiful paintings of St. Matthew, St. Mark, St. Luke, St. John, are exquisite on the main altar. The colorful light patterns thrown by the stained glass windows on side of the church gives a rainbow appearance inside the church, reminding me somewhat of the effect in the ancient coloured glass at Mehrangarh Fort Jodpur.

It has a statue of Mother Mary made during 16th century and was brought from Rome to Kanniyakumari. There is an ornate golden and the statue of Mother Mary is placed in the centre of the altar and venerated by the name of *Alangara matha*. The statue of St. Joseph and St. Francis Xavier are on right side and left side respectively. There are wooden carvings depicting the coronation of Mary as queen of heaven and earth. Intricately carved depictions of angels playing the musical instruments like violin, flute and drums in the upper and side adorn the altar. Jesus Christ inviting his disciples for ministries and forgiving Mary Magdalene are depicted in the side of the altar. Outside there is a huge ship's mast.[5]

After wandering through the narrow streets of the old part of the town, and eyeing a blue fluted character standing on a lotus behind a white-washed wall, I decided to buy this curious feminine man with a peacock feather in his hat; painted as he is on a screen. It is nice to find an image of Him, since I had met a Krishna devotee in Agra who advised me come here. Innocent, if exotic, as it may seem, I am no longer in the habit of having foreign idols in the house![6]

I walk past the market stalls of the city walls. I visit Bhagvaty Amman Temple[7]. I am told it is one of the 108 *Shakti Peetha* in Hindu mythology. It is therefore one of the major Hindu temples across India and is mentioned in almost all the ancient Hindu scriptures. I have not seen a temple like it.

What is most unique it its proximity to the sea, and the subterranean temple vault accessible by descending below the level of the sea into what feels entering a cave hewn of pure rock. Behind the temple precinct, which has a sort of cage around it, there are holes where the temple snake appears when the bell is rung.

The location Kanyakumari, i.e. the southern tip of India has been held sacred by Hindus' as it is the confluence of three seas. Offering *Pitru Tarpan* and bathing in the sea in the Kanyakumari beach is considered holy because it the convergence of many important *Theerthams*[8]. There are a total of 11 *theerthams* associated with the temple in the ocean surrounding Kanyakumari.

Kanyakamuri (or Cape Comorin) is the 'Land's End' of India, where two seas and an ocean meet; the Bay of Bengal, the Arabian Sea, and the Indian
Ocean.

I look out to a small island off the Cormandel Coast. The Thiruvalluvar Statue is a 133 feet (40.6 m) tall stone sculpture of the Tamil poet and philosopher Tiruvalluvar, author of the Thirukkural, who is possibly one of the greatest Tamil poets in India. Thiruvalluvar Statue was unveiled on the 1st of January 2000. The pedestal of the statue is artistically designed and is decorated with 10 elephants that signify the various directions.

Adjacent to Thiruvalluvar Statue is a rock island. The sea is too choppy to get a boat there today, and the rocks are lashed by huge waves. Swami Vivekananda, an Indian Hindu monk, was chief disciple of the 19th-century Indian mystic Ramakrishna. He was a key figure in the introduction of the Indian philosophies of Vedanta and Yoga to the West. Vivekananda meditated here at this rock island, in 1892, before he set out to become one of India's most important spiritual crusaders, developing a synthesis between the tenets of Hinduism and the concepts of social justice.

He is said to have attained enlightenment on the rock. According to local legends, it was on this rock that the Goddess Kumari performed austerity. A mile distant on the mountain road, a dust cloud clears, beside a rishi; the river flows.

On Kanyakumari beach there is a dilapidated temple. It is a cloudy, unattractive day, and I experience little but shadows, grey dark pools of water on the beaches. Across the peninsula, a monument to Vivekananda[9]. To think he swam to it, and sat there, surrounded by the sea, and meditated there; reflecting on the state of affairs in India; the thought of the poverty of the masses in his country made him miserable. He said: 'Unless casteism is rooted out, there will be no salvation for my countrymen.' He then went to the West to teach the spiritual values of India; his intention being to return to India and awaken his countrymen.

I read the Bhagavad Gita the Krishna monk gave me at Agra station: the Spirit of the Great Congress of the Ocean and Sea is here.

I'm intrigued by the Colonial history of Cape Comorin.[10]

*　　*　　*

Immanent and within, consciousness, basic life force, giving rise to this world, power over mankind, creates the awesome world from that diamond in the inner sky.

Do you see the light of new intention; light circulating. Some shades revealed, others concealed, all at different frequencies, into images at the back of the head. Vision, reflections of reality, of the creative soul; spirit-matter-clear-

ance for manifestation. Sacred circle surrounds glorious light rays at the place of cleaning purification. All that is two-sided, at war with itself, unifies here. This pure sphere is infinitely wide, sparkling starlight, inwardly picturing new things in one's world, where outward emerging it gives of itself, all treasures coming now into being.

{ 22 }

Maudrai

Layer upon layer of transitions; of cultures, of languages, of climate. In the stream of change upon change, the deeper you read in the play, the more you see into illusion. Salvation is a glimpse of purest joy into his sea-blue eyes; the wheel spins constantly like a monkey in the mind. Waking is better to grasp, than thinking out of a place of pain and apathy. You laugh and dance through life; laughing at one's foibles and shadows. No need to feel that fear, the veil of light and peace brings countless fields of colours, more hopeful interactions.

Do you ever see the true handiwork of the hub, of the spoke, of the axle, of the generator of the wheel of life? It is inside you, spinning at your centres. You are a spoke set in motion; the road flickers past. Will the veil fall at the last breath? Will you see? From dream shadows running, nothing wakes you except Light, guiding you, nothing chases you like time; then it synchronises. Illusion is not unreal regarding what is, what we live as something that does exist for us, as reality dreamt alive, against the fabric of perceptions and inner process, that which is dreamt for us, the scene we feel through of that reality, with the complexes revivifying Light exposes after deeper dream still.

We are given this life to run for real, and while travelling soberly, we can forget our little-selves, and what is not for us, and then you see there are decisions, choices; what will you do? Now there is no way we can run to prove the real feeling of our waking dream is peace. Guaranteed by God. When I was on the ground, afflicted in my mind, persecuted by fearful phantoms, post-pinned, derided, shamed, spoken at, delusions fastened me to the wall. My fire dimmed; hidden, stolen, as thieves threw dirt and stones at me. It was a cold, cruel calculation: to leave me with no fire left, just the embers glowing. I tried so many times to relight it, but I was without skill or ambition.

I left like a dandelion clock plucked of seed; shaken, shifted, moved. I clung to places where I was torn, shredded, with just enough integrity to bear me through the storms. The life fire of my passion dims, is but a pile of glowing embers. It has tried many times, to breathe itself to life. Fire yet glows in the depths of me, so low, struggling through this wounding of my body, carries me within, though weighing downwards:

I will be swathed in light, live and be well; calling on that diamond light from the Throne of Grace, from above in the Highest Heaven, to heart's intention, and feel that soothing, delicate breeze of the Spirit; fire ignite me. I will rise from this present darkness, from the refiners fire, I will ascend on His healing wings, from the ash that wickedness, jealously and hate tried to bury me in. From this bewildering world's furnace-forge, from that outrageous spinning wheel of karmic resolution, my new creations, visions and dreams shall spring forth, truly my own through God's Glory, & no one-else's.

I will journey myself and be a free-form man of God– content. Ancient writings have their barriers, language, culture, our society does not have the words to express the nuance. Poetry is the language of the Gods, it can speak from a time when spiritual knowledge enjoyed a position of respect and prominence in the Golden Age.[1]

Is life not a dream? Then I will be awake in peace, this life, as first blossom flowers, white light rising through roots, into the warm glowing belly of sun. You watch it before you enjoy it, yet do not hold onto it, for all things pass away, somethings cannot be touched, only observed admiringly. I have travelled across the length and breadth of

India. Consorted with beggars, thieves, Maharajas, Gurus, yogis, sad-hus; there is wealth, spirituality, poverty, corruption.

*   *   *

If you see that life as one big paradox, dream, then dream of life, as life becomes a dream, if dream, your reality be peace, as you dream it, for it is all a dream. It is all a massive hoax. For me it is play after play of desires. And every time you embrace fear you can enjoy. Every time you enjoy you fear losing it, when you get wealth, there are plenty to take it, when you are esteemed, there are many to despise, and you long for beauty and fear old age, you want fit in, but fear the square holes and death: everything you do is fear! Will you be fearless? How much will you suffer?Will you die or renounce? Ah, what you could have if you would remember the truth of who you are, not the truth of others.

When I settled down to learn the lesson, there was a short time and space where I fell silent, and listened to what could be heard; to be pu-rified by those lessons. I began surrendering life in greater simplicity to priorities of service and contemplation. Maybe I would no longer be that seeker who sees, but still likes to seek. At the current level of un-derstanding, like refining a foreign poem into a more familiar tongue, I find words that contain some semblance of approximation to the original vision. I bring my child within, my mood or feeling, and re-alise it is not possible to leap above the current place of awareness, af-ter my hard experience of life there is the fullness of secrets guarded; to be revealed?

I must be ready to receive, to understand, just as I must have that capacity for comprehension in my heart and mind. I have worked for twelve long years, labouring at my disciplines, and my writing; sacri-ficing my life to this end, and no one believed I did any work. My ef-forts went unseen. Lonely in my life, I did not experience requited love.

Rejection and listlessness was my bread.

This was the discipline required of me, to know the meaning and value of what I had been holding onto, as life passed me by. Knowing undone to be free from all bondage. And my guru saw before me a shining light, a purified vessel ready to accept and hold the truth. He looked into my eyes and spoke: 'Tat Tvan Asi'[2]

With 'thou art that' throbbing in every particle of my being, I ascended to the spiritual knowledge of my master: 'There was enough humility to admit that my interpretation of the text was not yet fully accurate or complete. Not in my own language or any other.'

*   *   *

It was a dramatic taxi drive all the way up the road. There was no train-line to serve the route. It was the longest taxi ride I've ever taken. I doubt I could afford to cover such distances by taxi in England. The taxi proceeds right up the long road between the Eastern and Western Ghats. Looking back, I'm unsure why I didn't go to *arichal munnai*; I've heard its as amazing as Kanyakamuri. What struck me something as absolutely fascinating was Rama's Bridge[3], a natural land bridge all the way to Sri Lanka (until the great cyclone of 1480 submerged large tracts of it). I had hoped in some way to traverse it, and enter Sri Lanka to see the cricket in Kandy. This did not transpire in the allotted time, and the impulse carried me north to Darjeeling, by indirection.

The man in the temple city of Madurai, at that canteen told me he wanted the £2 coin produced by the Royal Mint commemorating Princess Diana. He said it in such a way as if he expected me to have one, since I was English. The Sri Meenakshi temple was in the middle of the old town, a riotously baroque example of Dravidian[4] architecture. The gopurams[5] covered from top to bottom with a profusion of multi-coloured images of gods, goddesses, animals and mythic figures.

{ 23 }

Banglore

On the way to Banglore I met a *Bibisaheb*[1]. She wore a red Chadar. Her husband greeted me with a *saalaam*, bowing his head and touching his brow with his right hand. It was now the second month of the two monsoon months. There were yatra's in the train. A travelling troupe, this pair, presenting song and speech. They invited me back to their home when we arrived in Banglore. She said it was important to pray to God every day. I took leave of them to explore downtown Banglore, with its music shops and pizza restaurants, all very westernised.

Her husband mentioned that Churchill[2] had stayed in Banglore before WWI. He walks me to the station.

I board the train to Mumbai. In the newspapers there is talk of a 200 rupee bounty (a month's wages), to anyone who can catch a holy cow. Rickshaw wallahs, bus drivers, *chai* boys are reported to be armed with sticks and staves chasing the placid cows around the markets and down major roads; hustling for quick money. India is changing, apparently soon all the cows, lounging on dual carriageways, blocking roads, occupying parking spaces will be gone. People are arming themselves with lassos and tranquiliser guns. How perfectly American India is becoming!

The East is West of Bethlehem. No time for Bombay hustling in my heart's house. That's my room. I came on here weary from the East-ern hills. Somewhere West, lost a man dusts him-self down as a calf lifts him up to the sky, and licks his shirt, and tells him, 'We are Holy Cows, you must not get rid of us, we make your city holy, and you honour us. Do not forget us in your bid for progress or you will be lost.'

So From Banglore to Bombay, the town of boiled beans to the Buan Bahia: another day in a train, the view of the countryside of Maharashtra, en route to Aurangabad. I sleep in the bunk during the night wearing the silk pyjamas that were made for me in Jaisalmer.

The memory of the old sky line is sparkling in the sunset, as we speed to the end of the line; to Mumbai (Bombay) from Madurai: The City that was once known to the Greeks as *Megasthenes*.

{ 24 }

Aurangabad: The Ajanta Caves

Hidden away in the hills of Northwest India, some 200 miles from the busy streets of Mumbai, emerge a magnificent jewel of art and religion: the Ajanta Caves.

Ceiling decoration emphasises the meditational experience of caves. According to the Madhyamika school of Buddhism, 'everything must be dropped and given up unto the Absolute'[1]. That one must surrender everything to the Supreme, in total trust. It is said emptiness alone remains before salvation is gained. One is empty and one may be filled with life anew.[2] The caves are an iconic focus for Nirvana[3], of attaining the immortal sphere, being removed from death. These things cannot be said in words alone, and in architecture there is hopeful approximation. Caves seem perfect for this.

Yet in the caves one feels one must be careful not to offend the gods. There are things that cannot be said in the cave. Even the absolute carrying an image of earth is possessed of the human words; symbols? Of that realm, only accessible by mystical ascent. The sublime ornamented columns have fine sculptures. I stand in the cool peace. Here is a wonderful celebration of life free from passions and ideas. I feel intense involvement with the cave and the art work. I feel myself sublimated before the ephemeral and evanescent masterpiece.

Here the tedium and deadening effect of the slobby, rigidifying weight of the modern world evaporates before the spiritual atmosphere I sense here. It is cool. My once peevish brain is tutored in subconscious, calming meditation; presence of higher vibrations across centuries of meditations. The very space radiates OM Shanti[4]. I am enveloped by sumptuous visions of form and colour, ceaselessly vibrating. Can you succeed in projecting the totality of austere monasticism, as though it were an Abbey? In the cold dark stone that hones inner compassion, there are Bodhisattvas[5] in cave shrines, watching me.

If the purpose of a painting is to sharpen our perception of the transcendent, then this place is suggestive of states of consciousness achieved through deep breathing, meditation and ecstatic vision. The aesthetics are inseparable from the discipline of seeking Oneness, the witnessing consciousness. The cave sanctuaries are transcending a luminous representation of *Maya*[6]. It is a creative illusion that reflects the macrocosmic dream: 'Beauty and truth are one, just as life is one.'[7] The solitude of the caves clears my mind, just as any recluse who strives to enhance his consciousness discovers. These are monuments of accomplished mystical purpose here, hewn from sheer rock.

The ancient landscape: its diction and syntax are pictographically austere. I reach the secluded location of the magnificent caves, excavated on a perpendicular rock face rising from the curving Waghora river[8]; it speaks to me this way, endlessly archaic; anachronisms and accents out of thick jungle that has now dispersed into desert, these past two hundred years.

The most evident antiquity I have seen. Either side of the advent of Christ, from 200 B.C. to 650 A.D. Carved into the horse-shoe shaped rock. The stone appeared to the ancients— they did not paint it on the outside but chiselled in hardest stone– the sacred work of becoming and overcoming, and transcending.

These are welcome in a land of sugar-sweet refreshment and *chai wallahs*. These are no abstract sculptures of shadows; the sunlight shines from the mouth of the cave, but the interiors are vast– I wonder how they could ever have carved all this by hand? This very hard rock.

'A stone is frozen sound', says Pythagoras. How could they be cut from 70ft high granite cliffs 2,000 years ago? Chiselled. Well, it took them four hundred years to do it. All interior space and details, sculptures carved from the same piece of stone; the mountain itself. One face facing west, east and south in the position of the rising sun. And *stupas*. Cave 18 is for the winter solstice when it filters through the cave and illuminates the *stupa*.[9] Cave 26 does the same in the summer solstice.[10]

I explore the niches, alcoves, carved out of rock, see the *Jadicas*[11], and there is grace, nobility and serenity of Buddha. There was a place for the monks, and the *chaitya*[12] hall for prayer. A place far from the civilised world, where you could sit in caves and meditate. There are seven shrines made in the name of Buddha. There is a remarkable *Vajrapani Boddhisatva*[13] painted on the interiors. Other caves are devoted to Vishwakarma[14], the patron saint of architecture. To think this was first seen again by a British tiger-hunting party.

I am so impressed by the cave paintings. I decise to make a derivative drawing on 19th of a 1st century BC to 5th century A.D. Ajanta Cave 2 painting, called the Miracle of Sravasti.

Furthermore, there is an inscription from Cave 26 that comes to mind: 'A man continues to enjoy himself in paradise, as long as his memory is green in this world.' A memorial in the jungle that will endure as long as the sun and moon shine in the sky.

After getting a taxi to Aurangabad, I decamp outside the airport. I meet a delightful Indian fellow who is very handsome and we get on like a house on fire. He poses for a picture with me. I am sad to leave him. Inside the small airport, I wait to be called for a baggage check, when presenting my passport. What I realise is that I am breaking the top rule of travel here: Never travel with ganja. I realise the man in Varanasi at the bus station had given me six pieces of the stuff wrapped in newspaper. And me being a charitable fool had helped him buy his bus fare to Kathmandu by buying it. The damn stuff was still in my ruck-sack; bizarrely, I've folded one into my boating shoe; the sole had conveniently worn it away and ground it to merest powder. As an armed guard ushers me to the security desk for a bag check…

I suddenly announce my failure to pay the taxi driver, and flee out down the airport driveway to the nice taxi man; I had good reason to be pleased to see again. After that palaver, I get the flight from Aurangabad to Bombay, reading the India Survey of the Environment. And in the mandate of the lord of creation, we are sons and daughters of the universe, embodied here on earth, and we have an obligation that is to love our family, and friends, and partners, and to undertake the all-pervasive care of the world around us.

Human consciousness impels us to probe the transcendent part of our nature. This is a unique part of our experience. In Christ consciousness there is total peace. What then flows from Heaven's highest throne, down to Earth? Involves me in that continuous light presence. What sacred source, renewing light of your re-birth? Vicious wounds healed as scars, without absence, how may we know presence? Operative love, felt in music, poetry, through beauty's grace, adds infinite value to our lives, from above, exposing our self-centredness, hardened face of the man who belittles potential's fate, to transform. Even though they deny heaven on earth, we remain part of that totality, though denied, the truth shows through it. Certainties bring order to chaos, but order is inherently chaotic. Our field, 72 degrees out of the full 360 degrees. What we prefer to see, determines life alone in a small scale of degrees.

When we form a trinity with Heaven and Earth, we are not subjects who perceive objects, a man looking at a landscape for example. This is an artificial barrier that the thinking brain constructs, it is blindness, a self-created stumbling block.

It restricts our true vision and undermines our human capacity to experience nature from within. We are beings in sympathetic accord with nature. To the extent that we are nature. I eat my dinner of vegetables, the peppers and the rice that's left; I see it as living, even though it's cooked. Even the rain water dries on the tarmac, takes the form of a rainbow that scans the tracks of the hills as I pass by: When I move the candle, light follows me. For what are these things without me experiencing or seeing them? Then I know that nature lives within me, and I in it.

The sound of nature, listen here; Heaven, inner voice and music, walking delight, harmonies, feeling in outer seeing, from inner peace. I suspend my sensory perceptions and my conceptual means of studying landscape in a scientific way; embody nature in my sensitivity and allow nature to embrace me in its affinity.

I know that I am not separate from nature but intrinsically part of it. It is me and I am it. We must unlearn much to see Nature truly. To participate in the internal landscape, the resonance of vital forces in nature. This inner transformation, for which nature is a healing part, is necessary. Thomas Traherne, the music of Vaughn Williams, the life and example of St Francis Assisi, the social commentary of John Ruskin and Gandhi; all point us to some useful truths. To harmonise our own feelings, and thoughts for the inter- flowering spirit, we must make ourselves worthy of this relationship again. It is a strange task indeed *to translate us back into Nature*, as Nietzsche says, for there is a basic and eternal text of *homo natura* that we must be return to, after so many long accretions. Euro-fascist solutions will not help us, we are not passive children to be told by the deep state or proud politicians, but must face responsibility and stand and be vocal for true accountability. For the shadows reflect on the waters, and beneath them, we are destroying our life's blood, by this impersonal, pervasive force, like a dragon's claw, we create in our collective economic domination. Now I see these things as vain abstractions. Perhaps no change may come until, by some invisible sleight of hand, man's spirit evolves into an apprehension of oneness. Only healing oneself, becoming whole, facing one's shadow. Connecting with the earth. Recycling one's negative feelings, dropping them down into the earth. Inviting the new to rise through the roots of one's feet; connecting with the diamond light of God from above, lemniscating the energies like that old Sadhu advised me on the road to Shimla.

To attain to a full view of Heaven, we must dance, there are those who stand on the woodland glade, and follow the new principle of co-operation; others more pioneering preach the gospel of co-creation. We are all brothers and sisters of the nature world, of Mother Earth. To reach to Heaven is to invite the Spirit to come and help us with our upward task. Dinosaurs will wish to retrain the old way, the ego way, the illusion and the destruction, and the shadows on the wall to deceive us. If we approach them knowing this, then it is possible to fight unilateral forces and prevail. This is a united effort for the sake of global peace and environmental integrity.

Dangerous and dark visions now seek to destroy the earth. Embittered, defeated, one seeks inner refuge in the stillness and silence of the All That Is within. Quietly meditating, praying, helping to heal the wounds of the relationship with [Mother] Earth and [Father] Heaven. Just as the adult seeks to parent the hurt child within. It is possible to bring the impossible to creation. Only doubts and fears can divert us from this task.

And so we hope and trust, and dedicate our lives to serving, and giving our self in selfless service, and that takes a personal, psychological and spiritual turning around; a rebirth, a personal transformation. Gandhi says *one must be the change one wishes to see in the world*. And indeed, one must find love and relationship to cleave the necessary light into that dark rock. Chipping away at it with much discipline and perseverance. The natural forces of the Divine Light are here to consecrate an ever-blossoming relationship of man and beast and nature. The brother has gone beyond the wall of the monastery where his life was formed to God, and now he reaches the cell where his ultimate liberation beckons, where he must fight from dawn till dusk against the empty husks of despair, and will give all his life to God's repair. With help against principalities and powers, there will be the evil watchful eyes to ward away, but he will stand on the firm rock temple, and make combat in the desert heat, with armour and weapons of God, so no man may beat the one who lives in Christ's victory, and sacrifices to the good of his friends. It remains unchanged and unchangeable, throughout existence.

Ajanta Cave 2 painting, Miracle of Sravasti

V

West Bengal

{ 25 }

Calcutta

I did not think like a tourist, I entered into the world where the real people are, and engaged with them, rich and poor. Instead of escaping the toils of life, I gained a profound experience of its meaning. The road was flanked by heavy grass, the flatness of slums, poverty, destitution. The capital of West Bengal...Kolkata, as they call it... one-time capital of India, and the second city of the British Empire. Designed for 2 million, the population is 12.5 million.

Nowhere in my life had I experienced such a high concentration of people as here in India's cultural capital...I had landed late at night at Calcutta Airport, met a curious businessman, who said he was a marine engineer, and had studied at the University of Hull during Mrs T's era, 1980s England, and asked me had I heard of Shantiniketan?

I had not but he advised me to go there, one of his favourite places in all India. He was very curious about me, what was I reading? *Up from Eden*? Ken Wilber? Fascinating. You remind me of a sort of Pink Floyd politician!' He added, 'Have you read any Jeffrey Archer?'

The next morning I woke in the airport restroom, a huge upper floor in the airport building, like say the duty-free section of Heathrow, except there were camp beds in rows like it was turned over to sleeping quarters for soldiers. Only people used this to sleep, once they got a ticket for a matter of rupees. And I woke up and saw the muscular bicep of the young south-east Asian man beside me. Perhaps he is from Myanmar? Or Nagaland?

I got in a taxi from the airport into town. There appeared no rules of the road. An anarchic procession of bicycles. Muddling along, yet there was order in chaos, near misses, honking of horn, a language of presence on the bustling road, to avoid accident or incident. Do they use their mirrors, I wondered? It was like driving blind, relying on mere sound for positioning. The beautiful Indian girl, finding bananas for her love night, her lips like cherries, her cheeks red.

Wandering cows, goats, camel-drawn carts, absent-minded pedestrians, trucks carrying heavy loads; Ambassador taxis that had seen better days, young men showering on the street with soap. Driving with a smile. Joss sticks burn in the taxi from an air vent, turned towards me; I get out and explore the Museum. And try a hand-pulled rickshaw for a short distance.

The Kalighat in Calcutta I was unable to visit; surrounded by Hawkers, impossible. The *Kadamab*, whose yellow-orange flowers are in bloom during monsoon. The police man brandishes a lath, there was a group of *Bauls*, from a wandering religious sect; they sing beautiful songs while high on *ganjika* beside a marmelos tree. It is from its hard-shelled fruit that a delicious 'sherbert' can be made. Passing the Sal trees that grow in the dry climate, the Sephalis with their small white flowers on orange coloured stalks...

There is a man in a *gamcha*, a scarf worn around his waist as a *lungi*. He is chewing Pan, the leaf of the betel-pepper plant. Shell lime and spices added to the taste. There was a Madhabi, with its pink or red flowers. I ate Mohanhog for breakfast, a sort of porridge made by boiling cornflower in milk. I was greeted with *Namaskar*, accompanied by the folding of hands in a prayer-like position. The branches of this trees extend downward and upward, nourished by the three modes of material nature. The twigs are the objects of the senses. This tree also has roots going down, and these are bound to the fruited actions of human society.

The branches of the banyan tree spread in all directions. In the lower parts, there are variegated manifestations of living entities: human beings, animals, horses, dogs. These are on the lower branches, whereas the upper parts are higher forms of living entities: the demigods, *Gandharvas* and many other higher species of life. As a tree is nourished by water, the tree is nourished by three modes of material nature. Where the modes appear greater in quantity, the different species of life are manifested accordingly.

The tips of the branches are the senses: ears, nose, eyes, attached to the enjoyment of different sense objects. The subsidiary roots are attachments and aversions, by-products of suffering and sense enjoyments. The tendency towards piety and impiety develop from these roots. Living entities are conditioned by my eternal fragmental parts. Due to conditioned life, they are struggling very hard with the six senses, which include the mind.

Every individual soul has his own personal individuality and independence. By the misuse of that independence one becomes a conditioned soul. Shackled by the false ego, the mind is the chief agent driving man in this material existence. When the mind is in the mode of passion it is troublesome. When the mind is in ignorance it goes to the lower species.

I then walk to the Albert and Victoria memorial[1], standing impressed by the edifice of Empire in stark white stone, two lions guarding it. And then I get a less environmentally friendly means of transport that lets me out near the Kali temple[2]. I refuse to go in, afraid of death? I drink coca cola on a bench. I realise that to create one must destroy. Creativity is organised chaos. Here is vibrant compression; decisively wrought. I let them know how I feel, and gently, a new dawn light falls and spirit goes before me, as I cross the Hooghly river[3] to Howrah[4], ahead.

Victoria Memorial, Kolkata

{ 26 }

Shantiniketan

The first-class carriage on the Shantiniketan[1] Express. The on-board entertainments: two men in costume playing a Sarod.[2] It eases the time it takes to get to the peaceful town; home to the Visvabharati University, founded by Rabindranath Tagore[3] I check into the retiring room at Bolpur train station that still has original Anglo-Indian furniture; a mosquito net four-poster. I then hail a rick-saw wallah. He is young, about my age, speaks little English. He peddles on with me as passenger, along a sandy road, towards Shantiniketan. He waits for me as I visit the museum. I learn about Tagore. As a child he was confined to his room. He stressed the vital importance of our relationship with Nature.

There are several interesting quotes from Tagore written on the museum displays:

'In the modern world the fight is going on between the living spirit of the people and the methods of the nation building organ.' 'It is like the struggle that began in Central Asia, between cultivated areas of man's habitation and the continually encroaching desert sands, till the human region of life and beauty is choked out of existence. Where the spread of higher ideas of humanity is not held to be important, the hardening method is national efficiency, gains a certain strength, and for some limited period of time, at least, it proudly asserts itself as the fittest to survive.' 'Human civilisation does not lie in the isolation of independence, but in the inter-dependence of individuals as well as nations.'

'To bring the distant near, and make a brother of a stranger.' 'Desire to see everything that there is, round the bend of the red road rolling away, from the village, across the river, beyond the hills, and over the blue waters of the ocean.' 'How little I know of this world; deeds of men, cities, rivers, mountains, arid wastes, unknown creatures, acquainted– The Great Earth, and I know only a niche.' 'Entreat a lady– if one exists– and finally after a long painful ascent-become a man.' 'If you want to grasp eternity, it has to be in spiritual, and not human form.'

'The mysteries and phenomena of India: the only appropriate complement to the ordeal.' 'My whole attention would be drawn to the shadows under the bayan tree. Some of its aerial roots had formed a dark complication of coils. It seemed as if into their mysterious region some old-world dream land had escaped the divine vigilance and lingered on: "with tangled roots hanging down, from your branches, O Ancient Banyan tree, you stand still day and night, like an ascetic at his penances. Do you remember...?"'

'To call our inner garden a garden is to say a deal too much...a citron tree, a couple of plum trees, of different varieties, and a row of coconut trees, a paved circle, the cracks of which various grasses and weeds have invaded...the flowering plants, which refuse to die of neglect. Nonetheless, I suspect that Adams' Garden of Eden could hardly have been better adorned, for he and his Paradise were alike naked. Our inner garden was my paradise, I well remember, how in the early autumn dawn I would run there as soon as I was awake.'

'The terraced hill-sides were all aflame with the beauty of harvest crops. My eyes had no rest the livelong day, so great was my fear lest anything should escape them.' 'Great forest trees clustering closer, underneath their shade, or waterfall trickling out, babblings its way over the black moss covered rocks.'

'Why, oh why had I to leave such spots behind? As dusk came, as the stars blazed out wonderfully, through the clear mountain atmosphere. Into this wilderness I venture alone.' 'The banks of the Ganges welcomed me into its lap like a friend of former birth. Every day there was the ebb and flow of the Ganga. The various gait of so many different boats. The Ganges freed me from all bondage and my mind, whenever it listed, could embark on the boats gaily sailing alone, and sail away to lands not named in any geography.' 'Through the deep silence of this illimitable whiteness we few human creatures walked along with our shadows, without a warning. When we reached home, my sleep had lost itself something still deeper.'

'The Ganges again. Again these ineffable days and nights, languid with joy, sad with longing, attuned to the plaintive babbling of the river along the cool shade of its wooden banks. Here it felt indeed like home, and in these I recognised the ministrations of a Mother.'

'I found the world bathed in a wonderful radiance, with waves of beauty and joy swelling on every side.' 'The hero hermit who breaks ties with the world in an attempt to subdue human nature, assuming the infinite is something extraneous to all worldly things. At last a young girl wins his affection and restores him to the human world. In foreswearing the world and then accepting it once more, the hero discovers the infinite in the finite.'

'The all-pervading pressure of worldly existence compensates itself by balancing life against death, and thus it does not crush us. The terrible weight of an unopposed life-force has not to be endured by man.'

'I feel like a pedagogue of uncertain prospects, struggling with my intensely thinking mind, seeking development. I see a world that recognises only legality, dead formulas in place of life, custom and routine; in the place of wise activity, that also requires discipline, structure of a spiritual sort. God put into my head the desire to travel here. I could not put that into anyone else's head. It is like a light has blinded me here, and made me dumb.'

Here, Tagore speaks of regarding the whole man, not superficial qualities as paramount: to respect intelligence, not cleverness. To respect vision, inner cultivation, not outer riches. I feel my whole education is stunted, and deformed, that my spirit has been bowed down and enslaved by rules and conventions, the validity of which no one seeks to question; unrealised first principles. I feel that independent-minded young men, if they stand out, court secret admiration for doing what others have no courage for. Yet to submit oneself to the collective pressure, and play out a facile game, is the path of least resistance.

Those who stand out of the group and speak out, are inevitably crushed, but one's life and spirit is immortal, a reminder to the morose mantras of the mortal, that there is more to life than what I knew back home! Maybe that is why I am travelling alone, and have no contemporary English companion with me, for this very reason? Parental control; it would be too dangerous to the conventional lines in which they are inculcated like Pavlovian dogs. Yet it has been my path to visit this land; make some sense of the impression and experience. Those who are unwilling to listen to the truth, turn, without realising it, to unconscious defences, to hate, jealousy, and denigration against *l'esprit libre*.[4]

It is very irksome when defects, vitriol arise from one's peers, even family members. It is almost as if society requires divided and emotionally dishonest men. To heal the pitiful bondages and delusions so as to be healthy and free. Those contortions of mind, blockages of emotion, that deflect the light by which we seek shine in the world what is holy and true.

From the waters of narcissus' death spot, I look into the spaces behind me, dark place, seen only through the reflection in the shield mirror, so that I do not turn to stone by Medusa's snake head writhing at me. I do not wish to be vanquished by the realisation of my own darkness than anyone else's hideousness; so long as I recognise what is mine in myself. Having been slow to return to myself, to become as in all things,

I have endured much suffering. And now there seems to be no sorrow, no troubling happening, now that I have beheld my own unity, as though in a vision. Spring's livelier changes are beautiful, lifting one's mind to love, and to be free to walk those Eastern paths again. I see beauty is a grace which moves the soul to love, that knowledge of lesser beauty, leads one to higher spiritual beauties. A hazy freshness rises, imbuing my better self with life's awful beauty.

As I walk across the lawn from the museum, towards the Uttarayan complex, a multi-coloured snake dashes across my path. I freeze with fear, unable to determine if It is red on black or black on red, which determines whether its venom would be fatal. Fortunately, it seems as frightened as me, and shows this by its considerable dash in the opposite direction! Now I am in the art gallery within Tagore's former residence.

I wish I was studying here and not back at Reading, England. However, I suspect the snake has done much to ensure that I do not come here to study. Quite a few seminars at the university are conducted in the open air under 'teel' trees or in the mango grove. From the evergreen, feather branches of the *Jhau* appears a multi-colored snake! Fear strikes me still. The great Tagore, who as a child was not allowed to leave the confines of his room, stressed the vital importance of humanity's relationship with nature. This is seen in the Banyans of ages past used as umbrellas for lectures and seminars. It is in nature we rest with art. The university is a testament to Tagore's genius and social vision.

* * *

Brahminhood[5] does not depend on birth, but on character. The rules of caste prescribe the duties to society a man has to fulfil whatever his lot may be. The functions in society depend on the capacities. After a man realises the full warmth and glow of human and familial affection, be it through brotherhood, relationship, marriage, parenthood, he is called to free himself from attachment to house and family so that he might realise his/her dignity as a citizen of the universe.Without a spiritual brotherhood. Possessions, without caste, nationality, enjoined to preach in the spirit, of the joy of The Gospel, of love and service. The ambassadors of God on earth, witnessing to the Beauty of holiness, the power of humility. The joy of poverty and freedom of service. The true Sannyasin is he who with self-control and spiritual vision, suffers for mankind. The labour of life is laid upon us to purify us from egoism, and social institutions are devices to help the growth of the soul. The desire for posterity, possessions, worldly prosperity, is to be relinquished, has to have no power or authority of any kind.

Your mind is devout, haunted by dreams of imperishable beauty, echoes of unceasing music. You live so intimately with the ideal, that you are persuaded of its reality. To me it may be a dream, yet it is a dream in which you live, and thus it is more real than the reality I have ignored. I see the severe training of body and soul that is prescribed to you. To remain pure from passion, despite, lust and resentment. You were a living martyrdom; made more difficult than ever killing yourself. Such a death is all too easy. It is life that is taxing. You gave up your home and society to escape the social bonds. You were not against home and society because you suffered shipwreck early in life. It is society and family that has brought disgrace on its own institution! It lacks compassion, and has become grossly acquisitive, through abuse, through materialistic interpretations of its obligations and duties, in the formation of character, in the rearing of future citizens.

Even so, mere judgment of the mind is an illusion. One that is not conducive to peace. However, for true realisation it is necessary. The brute craves impulsively, under tyranny of lust and greed, he is fascinated only with satisfying his cravings, acquiring the latest trappings of commercial culture.

What are the true desires? One is only a true artist if one craves beautiful things, then is it possible one can crave false desires, and in craving the flesh, become an adulterer? Wherein lies truth? In the great festival of life, I am beset with severe thinking, my life is made harder by this, my mind seeks atonement. To be energised, to be disinterested, to be in solitude, to seek privately within myself. This world lures me to sin, but are not these sinful things the pathways to Divine Bliss? I seek the sublunary. I do not care what others chose to think of me, or do, I go about my work as a soldier goes to battle, if there are any consequences to my actions, it is my intention that is pure. I seek ecstasy.

I must perform my works, not live in dream, illusion or false asceticism. I cannot retire prematurely from this world. I cannot allow myself to despair of this world. I seek what is within me, communion with my heart, to be intoxicated with the knowing of these affirmations, to love and enjoy life. To appreciate creation for all it gives, all that is universal, in the field, from which I am a focus. This gives me ever renewing strength, the possibility to flourish while yet I live.

'Only performing works one should desire to live a hundred years.' *Isa Upanishad*, ii.

You pierce behind the veil of illusion, realise The Divine Presence in this world of human society, growing on the earth. You did not shrink from the torturing the brute that bred you. Like the hunted hare, you feel no silly sentimentalism for the chase, for the pursuers. Those who held you captive in their false moralism.

You sought the purity of food to give you strength. Instead they served you slops and called it just desserts. This was necessary for the purity of your mind. Your control of your passions was spontaneous. Each day, wandering mendicant, purifying yourself from all earthly taint, becoming fit for your spiritual home; fast approaching with that unexpected, timely termination. Each day was exacting concentration. Contemplation. How you cleansed your mind. Each day you retired from the world, when your duties to society were fulfilled; duties you self-created to match your dignity, despite the alienation and near-universal rejection you experienced: the trampling of love you saw about you; maintaining your integrity as a free-spirited human being.

Your life was one of love and righteousness, wherein you turned your eyes inwards, keeping yourself free from the temptations of this world. You were finally able to transcend yourself, receive the gift of freedom from the narrowness of selfish individuality, when you worked more because you cooperated with the greater plan, as a virtuous man, despite the opposition, which was vicious...Restraint, liberality and mercy were your virtues. They did not come easy, as your ego mind was hard to tame, after years of living on the borderline.

Death and renewal of life is eternal. No dream, but a successive process. It is the power to build again, in the rubble of the things from the past, destroyed. With acumen, thoughts rejected, courageously knowing through lacerative pain, more than was previously assumed as true; beliefs torn and steamed off the board of confirmation, as hypostasis, enlightened by expansive homecoming.

Words of thoughts of expressions; access gained, to the red chamber in that dream, where homeless, one recognises estrangement from a fallen world of strangers, where small sensations gather together, like the time you leapt into the river's current, floating on that wind of apprehension to prove your worth, that you resembled a dolphin. After you had delineated all that hard wiring in your brain, associations of shapes, lines, shadows, desires, interests, hopes, obsessions; illusions fixated, delusions, recompense from the pursuing truth that dogged your youth.

Or the glint of the mirror light in the carpet, that indicated you were about to withdraw into the labyrinthine pipe dream, pursued by the pink elephant vision, leading you into the realm of none-sense. In trance you gave free reign to your true self, accessing deep mystical thoughts under the great moon, watched by gargoyles, recovering memories emanating from your dreams.

When you pondered the existence of the improbable, since it simultaneously postulated the premise of all probabilities.

When your mind, spontaneously perceptive, connections in the meaningfulness of unrelated phenomena, like the crumpled pillow that looked like the marble head in the style of Michelangelo; the time you said I felt to you like a sculptor.

There was a power in our love, beyond good and evil, light and darkness, whose aspect guided us to a reconciliation between ourselves and all that was buried. In the measure of our days together, we inhabited our own dimension, in a stream of infinite energy, in harmony with whatever event was completed in the moment; whatever spark of persona played out in our wildest drama.

And when the kingfisher came on that unthinkable thought, which entered me like a bird unsolicited, out of the blue, I felt a spirit searching for enlightenment and emancipation from the fleeting world, to impinge so sharply in my imagination that your extreme monopoly of my life, for itself, came in that titanic overthrowing, bequeathing me such lament, that your communications with me in vision, dream, or sign came as star lights to stir my sleeping soul awake, and rescue it from the slough of despond. You brought what was too painful to comfort me, only for the disturbance to break, and enrich me: helping me realise a pattern of greater significance.

In one departure, one return, all that was ever In between you and I, was downward into those cataclysmic depths like that of Orpheus or Dante wandering through the dark streets of the City of Diss. Ours was a journey of exile, a walkabout to the great escape from bondage, where eagles dared, that bridge too far. Outward bound, only to return again, again, across the ocean, inwards from where we left, from where we began, in succession, to see that place for the first time, as it always ever was. Each time, wearing us out, until we could see how really impoverished what we collectively felt had become.

In the face of the vast edifice, and the one-eyed Titan, all that was unrealised went out of life and time, into a sensual enjoyment of the immediate; swinging from one pole to the next in tyrannic partiality, from the primitive to the civilised, from the foolish to the wise, the stars reflecting in the river projecting a part of ourselves we knew when we saw each other, eye to eye, on the white cotton shroud, lying on the floor, under the oak beams on those late spring afternoons.

Whatever change we sought, was made within, according to its own twisted logic, after tormenting silences, undone by vibrant persistence, to keep returning for the higher feeling, that came from blind loyalty to the journey's remembrance of the spirit's venturing, with small and great uncertainties, and foolish excitations, confused in my heart's expectations, and your heart's usage, rare mortal who saw into the reality of things, despite what abuse you suffered; it only altered you beyond all appearances.

Having touched the flame, you become divine; as I immediately descend back to black, when the shadow came to me in dreams, hiding all my anti-social wishes, and the thick pungent wafts from that sacred pipe, and forced infusions, quickening the blood, vast, heady inhalations, that purified those visions as poetry, in long, bloody, sober, thirsting, punishing journey's across blistering, masochistic landscapes, through all those crowds of bitter, spitting men and women, gnashing fit of morality, whose virtue becomes outraged, while their own elopements pass notice. I am an unfortunate man, the whipping-boy; ruined and heart-broken. Is not all life pathetic and futile now?

Omnis festinatio en parte diaboli est. As so frequently, the root of it was a lack of love, to those who love and honour themselves, to be peaceful, though unpeaceful, to the trained appearance of peace, knowing nothing but fear, learning how to be bold, the illusions created by intoxication, reckless indulgence, passions burst in unparalleled cataclysm, like a wild mare on heat, carousing with concupiscence; how to accept the illusion without losing one's way?

Concordia cresscimus; de generatione et corruptione. Another impressive tour of duty, another tally on the scoreboard. Uncontrollable desires, sincerity, passivity, Himalayan synergy, creation, life, death, Shiva, Parvati, India, England, imagination, thought, hallucination, tragedy, beauty, feeling, dawn, hope.

*   *   *

At Bolpurtrain station there are four boys who board the train; they sweep up rubbish. They are what we might call 'The Railway Presentation Team'. I call them the railway boys;

I don't think anyone pays them, unless they present their found plastic bottles. This was their job and their life, and they enjoyed nothing more than receiving baksheesh for their hard and happy work. They had pride, and adopted their station.

Shantiniketan, that peaceful place, in the 1st-class retiring room at the Victorian railway. He appeared like a phantom, I felt his approach, stirring my heart. Did he appear to sully my soul at its moment of victory? I do not know, I can only ask. Could such a sweet smell come from such an ulcer? A boy, smoking tobacco, hand-rolled shag, a youthful beard, soft sweeping shadow, arousing sympathy, rubbing my leg with fresh sprigs, then joy, no brittle twigs of birching this early in Spring; some soreness surely to come, perhaps in summer. My secret joy. Your smooth soft climbing stems reach upwards, seeking the light from abstract redbrick walls, senseless sight, yet familiar, how do you derive any joy from me, except when you quiver?

Oh, how you bloom; your truest petals? They are ulcerous. A fragrance feigns divinity. I see a clematis vitallbus shooting into the sky. A bright premature encounter?

What intoxicating scent. Will your flower last to late autumn? If I then left you another month, you would surely die. Clematis vitalba Charming Clematis. Dhanwali, Santai, Charki, Garol, Wantah, a vigorous climber, distinguished clusters of many small cream-colored fragrant flowers, spreading petals. Petals ovate-oblong, woolly-haired beneath. The numerous stamen filaments are hairless. Leaves are compound with usually 5 leaflets. Leaflets are 3-8 cm long, ovate-lanceshaped, long-pointed, strongly toothed or lobed, hairy beneath. Charming Clematis is found in the Himalayas, 600-2400 meters. Flowering: July September. I ascend the foothills of the Himalayas, 600-2400 meters above sea-level; experience your sweet flower in late August.

{ 27 }

Darjeeling

The higher we climb, the more I feel we are moving upwards into the branches of the Bodhi tree. Here in Darjeeling one senses kensho-satori, the dropping away of 'self', as a realisable ideal.

Darjeeling, maybe here I will have a foretaste of 'the Great Death'. I have seen familiar shapes here as in England. Not just the lines of cottages, this is after all a British-built hill station. Darjeeling comes from Dorje, the Tibetan word for vajra. Do-rje means noble stone; Do = stone and rje = noble or prince. It embodies not only the brilliance of refracted or reflected illumination, but it also symbolises the impervious and fixed solidity of the point of power around which all else turns – the axis mundi or hub of the world. A dorje, then, is like the diamond, though an inadequate symbol for it. I'm told a lama founded a monastery that once stood on Observatory hill. Dorje Ling, Land of the Thunderbolt, or Land of the Vajra Diamond; the Land of the Sacred Stone. Roads are steep, narrow and winding.

The normal route from NJP to Darjeeling is via Siliguri, Sukna, Simulbari, then by Rohini road up to Kurseong and then Hill Cart Road (NH55) to Darjeeling. Up to Kurseong the road condition is good. This was my haphazard and reluctant way of discovering India; just as I sincerely wished, so as to be vividly transported in this culture, so foreign from my own that it would be the rarest gift I could experience in this life.

Ah! What an epiphany in the rapturous mountains, where life here must be seen and felt to be believed. How I slipped into this life here, through happenstance, hilarious, heart-breaking, and thoroughly unexpected. We pick up clothes immediately, as it is cool. Darkness has descended, the hill is light-adorned; flickering. Sky black, some starlight, rare in monsoon. The chill of the Himalayan Darjeeling Station, from where we thought of taking a toy train to Ghoom, the second highest railway station in the world. Marked as a part of world heritage, the Darjeeling Himalayan Railways offers 'joy rides' in their blue toy trains. We decided to hop into one. The train on the railway tracks built literally on the motor road would inevitably remind one of Rajesh Khanna and Sharmila Tagore of Aradhana. What surprisingly came as a package with the joy ride was a tour into the lives of the people of Darjeeling.

The train hopped past the houses, so close that you could actually extend your hand to pick a bougainvillea from their garden and smell the smoke whizzing out of the kettles in the road-side tea stalls. Chaiwallah grins, glad-eyed children wave. There are those who say Darjeeling is not worth a visit anymore, still those who come annually. They are the ones who say that Darjeeling is the place. It was afternoon, but the sun was lost somewhere. Past St. Andrew's Church, the mall road took a turn to lead us along pathways clad in mystery. Cloud-mist gliding past like smoke past British Raj bungalows with open-squatted windows. The zoo and the mountaineering institute. Past quaint shrubbery, pansies, foxgloves, rhododendrons everywhere.

At the Hot Stimulating Cafe we take a chai, and Bob Marley all over its walls, which seems apt as I am playing Bob Marley *Buffalo Solider* on my Walkman, and Cochil enjoys it so much that he is singing it. Some say that Darjeeling has lost its charm. We walk across the mall in the twilight, with tourists crowding the curio shops beside Nathmulls', charmed place of poetry. The night is clear, snow on Kanchenjunga, celestial apparition against the dark Himalayan sky. The calling was clear! I may be healed by surrendering to what I truly long to know. Life, you endure, always changing, demanding ways I move where life is: learning to flow with persistent tides, as death's spectre draws back another blow, to move one within one's living awakening. Breath into my dying embers, one last gasp, a wind to raise my sorrows in one more passion-flame, releasing all that dimmed the light within, my charnel of ash. The light you alone protect as a seal within my unvindicable heart.

There are mountain mists, sacred, a map of the future at the end of the world where one rises beyond the dialectic and into the presence of another, the allusion to convention, the distant mysteries of that bewildering space, fog dense, the foothills like the Dhular Dhar. There seems a suppression of the feminine side of nature in all religion. I wish the heavens would clear so that the profundity of Kachendzongkha might reveal itself to the anxious seeker. Why do you hide from me? There is no road up the mountain in Darjeeling. The Queen of the hills takes its name from the Sikkimese 'Dorje ling', literally, 'place of the thunderbolt.'[1]

The namesake is not easy to understand as I view nothing but the enveloping curtain of Cloud; it is monsoon season. Darjeeling and its surrounding tea plantations are nurtured by mentation, where prayers written on the four aethers flutter away to distant lands. Durga Parvatti. Prayer, wind and whistle; flutter of affliction, carries healing requests. Here earth meets heaven; hills are emerald, lush.

Rich, yielding soul meets sky. Lake, deep depths, more than any one tread without drowning, are set amid towering mountains, where magical mists, like divine dragons, rise from forests. Herein lies this former British Hill Station, established in 1840, at an altitude of 2,134m. Ah! Darjeeling! I Wish the Heavens would clear. The profundity of Kanchendzohgkha. Pull back your cloudy dressing to reveal your majesty. The very thought excites me up the foothill road, to meet you. Oh! Queen of the Hills! The place of the Thunderbolt. Thronged peaks, and rounded buttresses appear wrapped in snow; unchanging summit. The snows have been lying there, in their pale beauty, for tens of centuries.

At that tremendous height of 29,000 feet, no storms, no rains, can ever come to wash away the snow, though fall it may. From time, to time, on the smoother, less precipitous slopes, the frozen masses must remain unchanged forever. And hope, human thoughts and action, can disperse the smog, though mountain snow retreats as things heat up. The Himalayan mountaineering institute. I walk there with Cochil from the guest house. We learn it was established following the successful ascent of Mount Everest by Sir Edmund Hillary, and the late Tenzig Norgay, 29th May 1953. Climb from peak to peak, their motto, and a useful one in life. To caper above the valley of shadows and run along to the summit. To dare abyss-fall, with pick in hand, makin one's ascension, courageous, through endurance with the opening up to the Light; and on again to the next mountain challenge.

Momentary snow-clad mountain view; a pensive pose on the balcony of the hill cart road. Disappointingly cloudy this morning. I must return here out of Monsoon season. If only it would break and scatter, and I could see the clarity of an unclouded range; clouds have hitherto obscured that mighty view. I'm told I'd be enshrouded with a cloak of invisibility. I pitch my eye high, enough to see the longed-for peaks, by a rift in the cloud; that hallowed, unmissable glimpse. I watch dark dim mass, unveiled for seconds amid changing clouds. I look up higher, awestruck. The vast snow-peaks rise from mantling clouds; clear window suddenly swept by a strong East Wind.

Observatory point. Cages containing snow leopards. There is a telescope donated to the people of Darjeeling in the 1930s by Adolf Hitler, who was much impressed by the dark tendencies of esoteric Tibetan Buddhism. We walk back through the streets, from HMI. Linked together by our impromptu friendship, wearing corduroys, blue roll necks, and he holding my index finger in the grip of his hand. This raises a few eyebrows from passing westerners. We descend in a hired jeep, down the mountains to the foothills onto the vast plains with tea fields, beside a man who trades tea, and holds out his hand and encourages me to smell the taste of it, being of rare and pure pure quality, he says. Along the platform, back at Shantiniketan, the train stops. Cochil[2] jumps out. I say a very sad farewell before the train proceeds onwards to Calcutta. A beautiful man wearing a pink-red silk garment walks through, playing a guitar with animal fur drum; he has large soulful eyes, a double neckless around his muscular, lean neck; black hair glows radiant in artificial light. He is playing what looks like a Kora, but it is presumably of Bengali manufacture. Moved by his fleeting appearance, I see he is accompanied an older man dressed in orange,[3] playing a hand drum. At one stop to the next, sadly, then to take the night sleeper, and thence to Delhi from Howarth.

VI

Delhi

{ 28 }

Old Delhi

Back to where I began. Many paths lead me back here.

Delhi is the meeting place for the alluvial plain of the Jumna valley and the last outlying ridges of the Rajputana Hills. Its northern part is monotonous dry lowlands. Along the verge of the river- some 10 miles in width, fringing the bank, marks the western limit of the ancient bed of the main channel.

As the river approaches the city of Delhi, however, this lowland region rapidly contracts in width, terminating about a mile above the town, where an offshoot of the Mewat[1] Hills abuts the water's edge in a wide stony plateau.

The range to which this northernmost outlier belongs may be considered as a prolongation of the Aravalli[2] system. Ten miles south of the city, the range divides into two branches, one of which, turning sharply to the south-west, re-enters the borders of Gurgaon[3] ; while the other continues its northerly course as a narrow ridge of sandstone, and, passing to the west of Delhi, finally loses itself in the valley of the Jumna.[4]

The land here is never more than the lowland at its base ; while its surface consists of barren rock, too destitute of water for the possibility of cultivation, even in the few rare patches of level soil.

The Jumna, before reaching the borders of Delhi, has drained its waters for the two older canals which it feeds, and only forms a narrow stream, The rest is drafted off into the Agra Canal.

From the earliest period of Aryan colonization in India, the point where the central hills first abut upon the Jumna seems to have formed the site for one great metropolis after another. The whole country, for some 10 or 12 miles around the modern Delhi, and particularly in the south and south-east, is covered with the debris of ruined cities.

The Mahabharata vaguely enshrines the memory of this primitive settlement, and tells how the five Pa'ndavas, leading an Aryan host from Hastinapur[5] upon the Ganges, expelled or subdued the savage Nagas[6], the aboriginal inhabitants ; how, having cleared their land of forest, they founded the stronghold of Indraprastha[7], which grew into a great kingdom; and how at last, as the Aryan race became strong enough for discord, they turned their arms against their own kinsmen, the Kauravas[8], whom they overthrew in a great war, the central theme of the Hindu *Iliad*.

In the middle of the 1st century B.C., the name of Delhi makes its earliest appearance in tradition or history; and thenceforth the annals of the District become identical with those of the whole Upper Indian Empire. Passing in succession under the rule of Hindus, Pathans, Mughals, and Marathas, Delhi came at length into the hands of the British, after Lord Lake's victories in 1803.[9]

The tract then ceded to the Company included a considerable strip to the west of the Jumna, both north and south of the Mughal capital.

The modern city of Delhi or Shahjahanabad abuts on the right bank of the river Jumna, and is enclosed on three sides by a lofty wall of solid stone, constructed by the Emperor Shah Jahan, and subsequently strengthened by the English.

The eastern side, where the city extends to the river bank, has no wall; but the high bank is faced with masonry. The circuit of the wall is 5 miles. It has ten gates, of which the principal are the Kashmir and

Mori gates on the north ; the Kabul and Lahore gates on the east ; and the Ajmere and Delhi gates on the south.[10]

The Imperial palace, now known as 'the fort,' is situated in the east of the city, and abuts directly on the river. It is surrounded on three sides by an imposing wall of red sandstone, with small round towers, and a gateway on the west and south.

The architectural glories of Delhi are famous.

It is impossible in passing to to attempt an adequate description of them. They have been treated in Fergusson's *History of Indian and Eastern Architecture* (1876).[11]

The palace of Shah Jahan— now the Red Fort[12]— perhaps less picturesque and sober in tone than that of Agra, has the advantage of being built on a more uniform plan, and by the most magnificent of the Royal builders of India. It forms a parallelogram, measuring 1600 feet east and west by 3200 north and south, exclusive of the gateways. Passing the deeply-recessed portal, a vaulted hall is entered, rising two storeys, 375 feet long, like the nave of a gigantic Gothic cathedral—"the noblest entrance," says Mr. Fergusson, "to any existing palace."

Omitting all mention of the music hall and smaller holdings, or fountains, however beautiful, the celebrated *Diwan-i-Khas* or Private Audience Hall forms, "if not the most beautiful, certainly the most ornamented of all Jahan's buildings." It overhangs the river, and nothing can exceed the delicacy of its inlaid work or the poetry of its design. It is round the roof of this hall that the inscription by Persian poet Amir Khusrow:

> If heaven can be on the face of the earth,
> It is this, it is this, it is this.

Which may safely be rendered into the sober English assertion, that no palace now existing in the world possesses an apartment of such unique elegance. The whole of the area between the central range of buildings to the south, measuring about 1000 feet each way, was occupied, says Mr. Fergusson, by the harem and private apartments of the palace, covering, consequently, more than twice the area of the Escurial[13], or, in fact, of any palace in Europe.

"According to the native plan I possess (which I see no reason for distrusting), it contained three garden courts, and about thirteen or fourteen other courts, arranged some for State, some for convenience; but what they were like we have no means of knowing. Not a vestige of them now remains....Of the public parts of the palace, all that now exists is the entrance hall, the *Naubat Khana*[14], the *Diwan-i-Aam*[15], *Diwan-i-Khas*[16], and the The *Hira Mahal*[17] —and one or two small pavilions. These are the gems of the palace, it is true; but without the courts and corridors connecting them they lose all their meaning, and more than half their beauty. Being now situated in the middle of a British barrack-yard, they look like precious stones torn from their setting in some exquisite piece of oriental jewellers work and set at random in a bed of the commonest plaster."

I return to New Delhi, Rajev's hotel, where I seem to always return to as my adopted home. And where Rajev lets me deposit my burgeoning assortment of handicrafts and books. I then walk from New Delhi train station to Connaught Place[18]. The contrast from old to new Delhi couldn't be more stark.

Glass towers, luxury goods, lifestyle fads, absorbed from the West, the desire for wealth, abundance, cashing in, prayers to Lakshmi[19], fat Hindu businessmen, in stark contrast to their slim brethren; a third of the world's software developers are reported to be here. Outside the economic circle, the rural poor, the holy men who wander. The suckling babies and their emaciated mothers, vegetable carts lined up at night with rows of beatific, childish faces asleep with clouds of mosquitoes, feasting upon uncovered bodies.

A man taking a shit on the pavement. I walk on the road, and give coins to the poor; flanked by heavy grass, I approach the main bazaar in New Delhi, Pahraganj[20]. Braving the muddled streets, in great heat, at slow pace, through alley ways, choking in dust, rupees, orphans plead with me. The aroma of spices, cheap Indian tobacco, drums, rickshaws rattle down the road tooting their horns, warning: they'll run you down; I jump behind a Holy Cow.[21]

{ 29 }

Jama Masqid

Masjid-i-Jahan Numa[1] is the great mosque of Old Delhi. Jahan means 'world' and 'numa' means visible. Imagine: once there was nothing here. Now look how minarets camouflage the sunset. Do you hear the call to prayer? It leaves me unwinding scrolls of legend until I reach the first brick they brought here. How the prayers rose, brick by brick.

A little to the south of the Chandni Chauk is the Jama Masjid, or 'great mosque,' standing out boldly from a small rocky rising ground. Begun by Shah Jahan in the fourth year of his reign, and completed in the tenth, it still remains one of the finest buildings of its kind in India.[2]

The front courtyard, 450 feet square, surrounded by a cloister open on both sides, is paved with granite inlaid with marble, and commands a view of the whole city. The mosque itself, a splendid structure forming an oblong 26 feet in length, is approached by a magnificent flight of stone steps.

Three domes of white marble rise from its roof, with two tall and graceful minarets at the corners in front. The interior of the mosque is paved throughout with white marble, and the walls and roof are lined with the same material.

When I arrive I am not permitted entry owing to the evening call to prayer.[3]

{ 30 }

Jama Masjid of Delhi

{ 31 }

Chandni Chowk

Dusty bazaars, hawker-throng-frenzy, revolting brass peacock shoe-horns, Jodhpuri suits, tourist saris, camp: everyone seeming cheerful in the face of budding hardships, friendliness met with filth, overcrowding. Invited for a game of cricket, exotic fabrics, certainly eye-catching, constant demands to check the sahib's wares, auto-rickshaws, flocks of animals on the road, oil tankers, on-coming and overtaking buses, shiny expanses of tar, pink Rajasthan and elephants, motionless mind sees motion, shadow, changeless change, reflections, particles of dust, the shoe polisher, the Delhi shoe shine.

Let me explain. A boy came up to me and pulled on my arm. I looked down and could see him pointing at a shit on my boating shoe. 'How did that get there?' I exclaimed. Here sir, he replied. Come with me. We walk beneath the portico of Connaught Place. He has his wooden shoe shine box with him, which he opens so that it becomes a footrest, with polish and brushes. 'I do not want my shoe shined by you, you obviously put the shit there!' Behind a pillar is an elderly shoe shine man. I ask him to polish my shoe. This he does for 14 rupees. The shoe is far cleaner than it has been since I bought it.

The slipper maker, the Dhoti maker, the tranquil yogic mind, the population rate, 17 million a year, rich and poor toiling, boiling, beseeching inspection of wares, Parsi, Hindi, general picturesqueness, shallow projecting balconies with highly insecure appearances, the cool, evening, the cool dishabilllé of white flowering muslin, Humayum's tomb, Mughal architecture, 16th-century, the old mosque of Delhi, the statue of Gandhi leading his nation to independence, the uncertain future, the non-industrial village life, people passing, never at ease, others secure in meditative rest, where are you not given to belong?

Passing streets, filled with bustling people, fancy dress shop for Hindu festival goers, a tiger and monkey suit; I look with amazement at this paraphernalia, the extra-special appearance over the generality of bazaars, 'the manifest air of well-to-do-ism prevailing here'. 'Singh and Sons' jewellers, garland and incense stalls, an abundance of fresh fruit, from the familiar to the exotic, mango and melon thirst-quenchers, pakoras, samosas, bhajas, vivid spices, a transfusion of smells, perfume, admixture of sewer stench, pretentious buildings in point of decorative art, cornices and walls raised in rich arabesque stuccoed relief, floral designs in pigment, houses and shops stretching in heterogeneous character, contents disguise this discrepancy, neatly clothed with turbaned owners outside. The gold-embroidered slippers, the Sunjit exports, shopkeepers, Kashmiri pashminas, tat, pashmina emporia, everything for the obsessed multi-buyer: bed spreads, shawls, sandalwood,prayer beads, 5 rupee each gems, sapphires, silver rings, fossils, books, marble Sivalings, Ganesh bathroom tiles, single silk cover cushions, tiger painted toy chests, 6-foot carved wooden Buddhas, ornate pea-cock throne chairs, sweets, travel guides, stone-carved chillums; that pervasive, energetic display of rugs.

I crossed the sacred tapestries of the bazaar, encouraged to think that in passing so far I had seen such weird and wonderful sights. Now sweet incense fragrance imbued my exhaustion. Mind with an upward ascent, elusive, pushes beyond my unholy abstinence, from what would make me whole.

Homeless, depressed, delinquently shadowing the rickshaw from afar, as I pass a bear suit costume for use at a Hindu festival[1]. I see a golden Trimuratri; shaft, spear and sword. Mantras of the Siddhas hum in my ear. I reflect on the deer park; ethereal light, glows bright, greenly in calm waters, sparkling then; a script, could be Tibetan, as seen on scrolls in Tibetan monasteries, unfurls in fifth dimensional real time implicit from the third unto the fourth. A secret code that the inner masters pass through the ages, hidden from the mass, hidden, to be spared from the uncomprehending; invisible. I intuit the presence of assurance, despite the prevalence of those ushered by dark, blind men. Did anyone question them? The controllers? It may be bold, but the strong are told there's an end, for a friend who looks no further.

Now, stop those thoughts Lord, and help me move over, to the other side of this story. May a peacock drawn light-chariot, carry me over treacherous waters to completion, for I have sadly digressed...

Chandni Chowk is the main street of the old city of Delhi (Shahjahanabad). Chandni Chowk, literally means *moonlight square* and derives its name from the fact that originally, a canal ran down the centre of the street with pools at major intersections which would reflect moonlight. Perhaps that is what I am picking up in my disembodied reverie?

Today, the stream is gone and Chandni Chowk is an extremely busy road. Perhaps I have disassociated for a reason, recoiling at the chaos before me. I pass shops, schools, residences, places of worship, old and new along this weird and wonderful road. I glide past the Queen's gardens, Town Hall, library; high clock tower and Church of St. James[2] in a dream in the back of a very adept and swift rikshawallah.

I have worshipped at the feet of a fool who was to meet me discreetly, if not meekly, in that long-winded hunt. I am restless. I see, but I'm slow to hear. Him I loved, but briefly saved. The cave from where I glimpsed compassion, shimmers as an enlightened thought, in my heart space, where a diamond in the distressing darkness suddenly shone, as a gift from my Eternal Friend.

May Spring come soon, so I may roam, and fast encounter that sphere of positive intention, where back space programmes of the past indoctrination spin in negative relation to my new a future that moves beyond what is now past. Once overthrown, the black moon, supplanted, as thick tar, recycled in the earth fire. Once that spun behind me, fastened to like invisible head straps, I am free to enter that eternal real, eternally grounded to the eternal Mother, whose bosom is beneath me; centred to quartz that vibrates at an ever-increasing pulse-clock, moving the hands of a new time into my being from the clock face of my heart.

The bazaar naturally appears a place to wonder at. The wise man wanders through the bazaar invisibly. *Bazaar* is Persian and means market, even though it implies the bizarre. Can the wise man be a wizard in the market place? I wonder, as the rikshaw *razes* down Chandi chowk. Items line the bazaar stalls, silk saris, jewellery and gold. No limits, unconditional freedom here. It all began with me, and what I was greedy to absorb. I brought my attention to India, and India returned to me parts of myself, that went unacknowledged in England.

There I felt all was well with me, and the world. It fostered unconditional love, for myself, and what I felt was good about me. Whereas England and Amsterdam had ways of reminding me what was wrong. It was the place I felt confident and healthy, as though this was my home, where I felt welcome and respected.

I walked in my own direction, stepped into a different world, that made me grateful to be alive and be me. I loved myself enough to go there, on that strange impulse. I loved the people I met and they loved me. I was grateful for who I am, all my experiences led me to India it seemed, and even after India, I could not forget. And despite that this all happened in no more than three months one summer in my twenty-first year; memories and insights.

I have matured within me. To where I am now as I write this, and where I was then when I travelled there, I see far more than the passage of fifteen long years. There would always be a part of my soul that is forever Indian. Homeward-bound, England. Eight-hour flight home, during which I read a lot of *Bhagavad Gita* the Krishna monk gave me in Agra (for want of anything more fundamental concerning spirit, human existence).

Two English boys sat on opposite isle, maybe an expat's, or chief exec.'s or diplomat's children, returning to boarding school in England? The centre of London appears after vast tracts of suburbia, as we turn to descent, Heathrow: below, small houses in neatly arranged lanes and cul-de-sacs, then tower blocks of metropolis. I spy the milk-man scooting down the street at 4am. It's 10th September; the world is about to change for the worse again. Morning light of new day in England breaks. We circled the City; Thames, serpentine, sparkling, and Palace of Westminster, wherein the Commons once held the keys to Calcutta. Touchdown.

*   *   *

Then, Heathrow express, Euston. After purchasing my ticket I am penniless. I arrive at Stafford, bus to Woodseaves, home again. House is empty. I let myself in. A car pulls onto the drive. I hide in the large kitchen cupboard. My mum, brothers, enter the house. Once I hear them in the kitchen. I leap from cupboard, to surprise them. Clearly shocked, if not disturbed, at seeing me this way. My Indian Narnia jest seems lost on them.

*   *   *

A week has passed, post-travel exhaustion. I rest another week, then return to Wantage Hall, greeted by the clematis in late flower, traveller's joy, just before the onset of an English autumn, armed with anecdotes of my Indian travels at breakfast, lunch, dinner, and breakfast, lunch, dinner, and on and on unto the bar evenings.

And all this adjusting to university life again, with lectures, essays, tutorials, I feel even more out of alignment with myself. I feel a constant longing for India. I plan return voyages, perhaps including Sri Lanka, the land of the Thunder Dragon. Mondays I go for a buffet at the Katmandu Kitchen on Southampton road. It is hard to be in England after India. Cinzano, Cobra, port, vodka, whisky.

Anything to dull the senses to the present depression, the feeling of grief, immense frustration then tsunamis of feeling breaking over everything. By the new year, unreasonableness of acknowledging life isn't easy boils the pain and anger within, infects my life insidiously. Shame, suffering, difficult childhood, early scars undermining present confidence, early experiences of adult cruelty. India distracted me from all this pain.

But the well remains the same; fragments chafe layers of wounding, gone progressively gammy. Deep rhythm of Indian exposure, Intense, fresh melodies of encounter maturing—generous, strange manners and difficult dialects: whose detail gave excitement, unspoken assurance, whose pitch was on the edge of unsuppressed desire and feeling, flowering amid the complexity, my banal life now as a philosophy student.

My summer in India gave me space, to get away from the expected keys, then big amalgams of expressiveness and rigour, passions distracted me, memories, reprieve from unsatisfactory university life where I strikingly drank myself to sleep most nights, to block out the pain and the unity of following from India, in harmony, wrapped around being away to India for a few months, open and friendly with the people I met, happy and honoured, full of the romance of that encounter, when an Englishman and an Indian meet, their tendency to dream together in conversation.

Here then is the poetry that complements the two. The East is East and the West is West, and when the two come together exciting things happen. Banyans instead of oaks, peasants in robes, Itinerant men, who we haven't had part of our society since the middle ages. House or temple of unaccustomed form—the slightest peculiarity in manners—even the hall marks of a different religion—all contribute to the impression of novelty in which consists the excitement of foreign travel. The proof is in those keener perceptions of the beauties of English scenery after I return from abroad.

My certain feeling of the centuries of progress, and industrialisation, and how that has divided our lives along ordered paths, where to urinate on a pavement, heaven's forbid, would incur, if caught, the intolerance of the law. I institute comparisons; and the manners here are no longer the sole medium, but one of various media through which I view the world, now I'm nestled within the home shores.

More keenly, perhaps, I feel how ignorant I am of my own country, unless I had crossed the seas before I could become acquainted with home. I wanted to admire the romance of the Ganges— the sublimity of Darjeeling— the beauty of the Ajanta and the Thar Desert— before I could tell what is the rank of the Severn, in picturesque character, among the rivers of World.

{ 32 }

The End

This 'original' cultural experience, still less touristic; no spurious or merely repetitive experience, bearing testimony to frustrated expectations. Perhaps my work lacks the authenticity and integrity of an insider's experience: I did not expect to write an India book, being unacquainted with its language and manners, having lived 21 years under an English sky.

However, I feel moved to note down the valuable and interesting details of the people; nothing that a stranger could not as well have told; and I cannot but lament that I had not said more of the common life, and habits, and peculiarities of Indians, and less of the scenery and sights of India.

My travels in India opened my view of its temples, the people, their pursuits, proclivities and modes of life. This book was written, for the most part, amid the scenes which it attempts to describe, with the gestation of the intervening years. It was begun in Delhi; and the parts relative to the journey to Darjeeling were composed from my observations in those places I recorded in my travel journal, and others I vividly recall. I give an authentic, if occasionally mystified experience of the peculiarities of my Indian journey.

A prying, voyeuristic look behind the scenes of India, in the regions of India. My desire was to flee dull repetitions of home, school and university life, so as to be vicariously immersed in the intimate spaces of

India. I already felt alienated from my own past and sought to appropriate something of the East; the ancient site, the various landscapes of desert, mountain and river; it was whimsical, Romantic travel, by which I aimed to vanquish the *spectre of belatedness*. I wanted to go with the illusion of discovery, to be immersed in the local, by sustaining singular rejection of anything of too Western. This desire for local colour was not uncomplicated, yet it became a major *topos* for me to be deployed variedly and enthusiastically in order to sustain my imaginative geography; so to be a participant-observer in the culture of India.

After my return to England, I had enough space for comparative portraits of East and West, India and England, and for the exploration of borderline between the two. I carried within me my own subjective utterances about the India that I experienced. The sound of my emotional ties with India helped me greatly to identify with the place, and initiate my own intercultural literary travelogue. Thus, in my retrospective appraisal of India, I felt back then I was almost Anglo-Indian, even if the qualification departs from the standard dictionary meaning.

I wished to pen a literary account of an Englishman in India[1], who has a passion for that real taste for the exotic, esoteric & beautiful; and being well versed and receptive to India, he aspired to impart the knowledge He had acquired in the Subcontinent to my compatriots. This account is entirely my effort to describe India to the reader. Not as a mere tourist viewed her, but rather to pull back the veil, and describe those contradictions, which reign in Indian society as I experienced them. Taken *cum grano salis*[2]; to dwell upon my own experiences, and give elaborate explanations, where necessary, in footnotes, to give such a view of manners as may delight the reader.

I sought to dive beyond and describe more of what only one of a few friends might have heard as anecdote, about my time there, behind the scenes of that colourful land. The extreme ease with which I got on with Indians, the zest of their lives, my openness to them transcended fellow feeling, to admission; initiated me into the very *arcana* of India. So as to create an unsealed book. Having dwelt there some time, I dwelt upon the forms of life belonging to the India I undertook to describe.

I was more traveller than resident, since I did not stay in one place more than three days. I did, however, gain some insight into the inner operations and doings of community life. Perhaps there were a few of those inaccessible and impenetrable experiences to which outsiders are usually barred.

So I felt honoured that my entry to that exclusive region was occasionally granted. I felt my nationality had something to do with it, or the imaginative form an Englishman assumes, in the minds of foreigners. I used common rhetorical strategies in travel writing, assigning to places an aura of mystery and intrigue. I felt attached to Indian culture, the crossing of the cultural divide seemed easy. Subsequent to more formal introductions, I felt initiation into the realm of *arcana*; Slowly merging myself with this 'other' India.

In the context of my poetic practices, I wished to ascertain my experience of India, and to reinforce my identification with Indians, my strong feeling of a shared past, by complying with the country's written and unwritten cultural codes and social customs. It is true that I also went to places where *devas* would fear to tread[3]. What a land of resounding contradictions, its comprehensive fabric of the most ancient surviving culture on the planet, and its beauty, the lack of separation here between life and death:

India and I agreed very well. For India has always been the Eastern light of my West; the greenest land of my imagination. It has not disappointed me;

Though, perhaps, it has that effect upon others. But I have been familiar with its temples and caves too long to dislike it. I was favourably impressed by some aspects of Hindu Religion, particularly aesthetic. India is the most actively spiritual land I know. Here mass pilgrimages are still enacted. People in India never have enough of religion. My acceptance and, indeed, my idolisation of India, convinced me that that some part, of my past life, or indeed actual blood, was Indian. I received much admiration and sympathy from my Indian acquaintances, and, on the other hand, strong suspicion and alarm on the part of the Westerners I met.

It is for all these reasons that throughout my time in India, I sought to differentiate my experience from that of the majority of Western travellers or expatriates, who were looked upon as foreigners, and myself as one who had managed to enter into the spirit of the country and its people. I could not help but compare my own experience with that of tourists, since I often received a high degree of intimacy with Indian society.

I suspect I know a thing or two of India, but what do Englishmen know these days of Indians beyond those curry houses? I have lived in the heart of their houses, in parts of India freshest and least influenced by strangers– have seen and become *pars magna fui*[4] a portion of their life, and hopes, and fears, and I almost felt at home. I saw men and things as they are, intensely, in all their crudeness. I could not entirely root out the bitterness I sometimes felt about my own home.

I knew and understood the Indian way of life– not least because I mixed with people from all social ranks, from the Maharaja to the untouchable– but my own relationship with India was deep and significant. My bond to India was arresting in its implications. Being implanted with near total, unreserved immersion in the Indian element, as well as all the inspiration. I drew from it. My representations of India are the fruit of my careful observation and knowledge of their society; faithful depictions of the real, the authentic: my attempt to see things as I really experienced them, to explain the peculiarity of the Indian character to the un-Indianised.

This account is my genuine cultural experience, as well as my comprehensive and authoritative opinion. Through it I express my complex feelings of alienation from my own country, as well as a lightning tour within Indian society. I was resentful as I left England, for it seemed I was welcomed with open arms in India, and allowed to be myself, and be playful. Leaving England for a summer holiday, I could not entirely exorcise my aversion and sullenness towards our little island. India was born of my desire to distance myself from England, a country I do not like especially, nor where I ever seem to be much liked?

However, it was not possible to completely unmoor myself from my English education, and the institutions that formed me and with a year remaining at university I was inevitably to return home after it. I remained a detached observer and a critic in another culture. The difficulties that beset my mission were delicate, and no very graceful task, except to experience the literature and manners of a nation so dissimilar to our own, that it requires an attention and impartiality hard to sustain.

I sought to be less ignorant of the language and customs of the people amongst whom I travelled, defer my judgement, and carefully examine whatever new information came to me. Such a culture as that cannot be readily or easily known and understood. My pessimism and alienation towards Indian-ness, fuelled, on the one hand, by the emotional instability caused by my turbulent relationships.

I realised that the more I entered into Indian-ness, the more of a foreigner I felt. My sense of self was never a strong one owing to whatever accidents of childhood, so I did feel somewhat an invention: fluid, multiple, relative, and in places my identity as an Englishman in India was intentional, especially in harping back to former times. I was most comfortable in those places that retain their old Raj era charm. In India I loved the feeling of mobility and my avoidance of being fixed—epitomised by my distancing and self-involvement as regards my relationship to India. This did not annul my propensity to create an illusion of unity and containment, nor did it efface the uneasy relations of power that connect me with other places and peoples, which become the object of my identifications.

My affiliations were ways of belonging and my fantasy of incorporation and natural attachment to India resulted in identity building through processes of inclusion, commitment, involvement, merging.

The amalgamation through which these identifications of mine arose was partly constructed in the imagination.

However, this immersion in difference was very real and grounded in time- and space-bound actions with real, material effects. I lived in the places I imagine, and my direct experience of India enriched my poetry with first-hand observations, yet it naturally complicated my identification process.

My poetics of Indian acculturation showcase my effort to 'go native' and enter dynamically the domestic, social, and political spaces of my adopted country. Nonetheless, much as I sought to practise and prescribe acculturation and translation in the broadest sense of the word, my writing is consistently sensitive to questions which revolve around the impossibility, discontents, risks or pitfalls of acculturation.

My inoculation into the Indian milieu had been successful; I had, in the end, remained a foreign body in the target organism. No one can attempt, with impunity, to graft themselves on foreign skin; the habits of one's childhood cling on, and I seek in vain for sympathy from those who have travelled in life on quite a different road from that which I have followed. I cannot claim to sustain authority as a privileged insider to the India of my travelogue, in the land of carved stone temples, of my whimsical rambles in India.

Home?

Footnotes

Chapter 1 - The Journey Begins

1. **Monsoon,** the term was first used in English in British India and neighbouring countries to refer to the big seasonal winds blowing from the Bay of Bengal and Arabian Sea in the southwest bringing heavy rainfall to the area. The etymology of the word monsoon is not wholly certain. The English monsoon came from Portuguese monção, ultimately from Arabic mawsim ("season"), "perhaps partly via early modern Dutch monson." (monsoon, n. OED, Oxford University Press). The southwestern summer monsoons occur from July through September. The Thar Desert and adjoining areas of the northern and central Indian subcontinent heat up considerably during the hot summers. This causes a low pressure area over the northern and central Indian subcontinent. To fill this void, the moisture-laden winds from the Indian Ocean rush into the subcontinent. These winds, rich in moisture, are drawn towards the Himalayas. The Himalayas act like a high wall, blocking the winds from passing into Central Asia, and forcing them to rise. As the clouds rise, their temperature drops, and precipitation occurs. The southwest monsoon begins around the beginning of June and fade away by the end of September. The moisture-laden winds on reaching the southernmost point of the Indian Peninsula, due to its topography, become divided into two parts: the Arabian Sea Branch and the Bay of Bengal Branch. The Arabian Sea Branch of the Southwest Monsoon first hits the Western Ghats of the coastal state of Kerala, India, thus making this area the first state in India to receive rain from the Southwest Monsoon. This branch of the mon-

soon moves northwards along the Western Ghats (Konkan and Goa) with precipitation on coastal areas, west of the Western Ghats. The Bay of Bengal Branch of Southwest Monsoon flows over the Bay of Bengal heading towards North-East India and Bengal, picking up more moisture from the Bay of Bengal. The winds arrive at the Eastern Himalayas with large amounts of rain. Mawsynram, situated on the southern slopes of the Khasi Hills in Meghalaya, India, is one of the wettest places on Earth. After the arrival at the Eastern Himalayas, the winds turns towards the west, travelling over the Indo-Gangetic Plain at a rate of roughly 1–2 weeks per state, pouring rain all along its way. June 1 is regarded as the date of onset of the monsoon in India, as indicated by the arrival of the monsoon in the southernmost state of Kerala. The monsoon accounts for nearly 80% of the rainfall in India.

2. **McLeod Ganj,** is a suburb of Dharamshala in Kangra district of Himachal Pradesh, India. It is known as "Little Lhasa" because of its large population of Tibetans. The Tibetan government-in-exile is headquartered in McLeod Ganj. McLeod Ganj was named after Sir Donald Friell McLeod, a Lieutenant Governor of Punjab; the suffix ganj is a common Persian word used for "neighbourhood" (The Imperial Gazetteer of India, VOL. XI COONDAPOOR TO EDWARDESABAD, p. 301.)

3. "What the moral? Who rides may read.
   When the night is thick and the tracks are blind
   A friend at a pinch is a friend, indeed,
   But a fool to wait for the laggard behind.
   Down to Gehenna or up to the Throne,
   He travelsthe **fastest**who **travels alone.**" - **Rudyard Kipling, The Winners**
   ("The Story of the Gadsbys"), Published in Volume 2 of the Indian Railway Library in 1888 as "L'Envoi" to The Story of the Gadsbys.

4. **Nagas** are various ethnic groups native to the northeastern India.

5. For an excellent book on one of the great moral adventures of our time, attempting to break from orthodox political and economic institutions, read the creation a new community: *Auroville: Dream and Reality* gives a view from the inside of the remarkable experiment in communal and intentional living. "Until we Dream of Life and **Life becomes a Dream**..."— Stevie Wonder.

Chapter 2 - A Dicey Start in Delhi

1. Why not focus on the **86,400** seconds in a day? Perhaps the seconds can slip away fairly easily. There is a saying in Tibet: "If you take care of the minutes, the years will take care of themselves." Each minute is full of possibility.

2. **Sir James George Frazer** originally set out to discover the origins of one ancient custom in Classical Rome- the plucking of **the Golden Bough** from a tree in the sacred grove of Diana, and the murderous succession of the priesthood there- and was led by his investigations into a twenty-five year study of primitive customs, superstitions, magic and myth throughout the world. The monumental thirteen-volume work which resulted has been a rich source of anthropological material and a literary masterpiece for more than half a century. Both the wealth of his illustrative material and the broad sweep of his argument can be appreciated even in the abridged version of a thousand pages.

3. **Chai** (lit. 'mixed-spice tea') is a tea beverage made by boiling black tea in milk and water with a mixture of aromatic herbs and spices. Originating in India, it is traditionally prepared as a decoction of green cardamom pods, cinnamon sticks, ground cloves, ground ginger, and black peppercorn together with black tea leaves, retail versions include tea bags for infusion, instant powdered mixtures, and concentrates. The term "chai" originated from the Hindi word "chai", which was derived from the Chinese word for tea, *cha*.

4. **The Raj**, The British Raj (literally, "rule" in Sanskrit and Hindi) was the rule by the British Crown primarily on the Indian subcontinent from 1858 to 1947. The rule is also called Crown rule in India, or direct rule in India. The region under British control was commonly called India in contemporaneous usage, and included areas directly administered by the United Kingdom, which were collectively called British India, and areas ruled by indigenous rulers, but under British tutelage or paramountcy, called the princely states. The region was sometimes called the Indian Empire, though not officially.

5. A **bazaar** is a permanently enclosed marketplace or street where goods and services are exchanged or sold. The term bazaar originates from the Persian word bāzār, from Middle Persian wāzār, from Old Persian vāčar, from Proto-Indo-Iranian "wahā-čarana". The term, *bazaar*, spread from Persia into India, and Arabia and ultimately throughout the Middle East. Europeans often saw Orientals as the opposite of Western civilisation; the peoples could be threatening- they were "despotic, static and irrational whereas Europe was viewed as democratic, dynamic and rational." (Nanda, S. and Warms, E.L., Cultural Anthropology, Cengage Learning, 2010, p. 330). At the same time, the Orient was seen as exotic, mysterious, a place of fables and beauty. This fascination with the other gave rise to a genre of painting known as Orientalism. A proliferation of both Oriental fiction and travel writing occurred during the early modern period. Edwin Lord Weeks was a notable American example of a 19th-century artist and author in the Orientalism genre. His parents were wealthy tea and spice merchants who were able to fund his travels and interest in painting. In 1895 Weeks wrote and illustrated a book of travels titled "From the Black Sea through Persia and India".

6. **Pareidolia** derives from the Greek para (παρά, 'beside, alongside, instead [of]') and eidōlon (εἴδωλον "image, form, shape"). The German word Pareidolie used in articles by Karl Ludwig Kahlbaum— for example in his 1866 paper "Die Sinnesdelierien" ("On Delusion of the Senses"). When Kahlbaum's paper was re-

viewed the following year (1867) in The Journal of Mental Science, Volume 13, "Pareidolie" was translated as pareidolia: "...partial hallucination, perception of secondary images, or pareidolia." Sibbald, M.D. "Report on the Progress of Psychological Medicine; German Psychological Literature", The Journal of Mental Science, Volume 13. 1867. p. 238 { 299 }.

7. Charu or cāru, is a word derived from Sanskrit that refers to something beautiful, graceful and pure in a spiritual sense. The word also means "one who is radiant and graceful" and is often used in the Ramayana for praising Lord Rama. **Charus** in Sanskrit means "Dear; beloved; charming". Apparently, smoking this type of hashish is a beloved 'sacrament' of many a Sadhu (religious mendicant) *connoisseur*.

8. In the Indian subcontinent the corruption **'chowk'** is often used in place of souk.

Chapter 3 - Amritsar

1. Commonly known as **the Golden Temple**. This important Sikh shrine attracts more visitors than the Taj Mahal with more than 100,000 visitors on weekdays alone and is the most popular destination for non-resident Indians (NRI) in the whole of India.

2. The **Katras** are self-styled residential units that provided unique defence system during attacks on the city.

3. **Harmandir Sahib**, meaning "abode of God" (Punjabi) or Darbār Sahib, meaning "exalted court" is a gurdwara located in the city of Amritsar, Punjab, India. It is the preeminent spiritual site of Sikhism.

4. **Shabad** means sound, Guru means teacher or knowledge that transforms you. The simplest meaning of Shabad Guru is a special sound that is a teacher. The Shabad Guru employs the Naad, totally balanced universal sound, to remove the constrictions and distortions of the ego.

1. **The Mahābhārata,** Sanskrit: Mahābhāratam) is one of the two major Sanskrit epics of ancient India, the other being the Rāmāyaṇa. It narrates the struggle between two groups of cousins in the Kurukshetra War and the fates of the Kaurava and the Pāṇḍava princes and their successors. It also contains philosophical and devotional material, such as a discussion of the four "goals of life" or puruṣārtha (12.161). Among the principal works and stories in the Mahābhārata are the Bhagavad Gita, the story of Damayanti, the story of Savitri and Satyavan, the story of Kacha and Devyani, the story of Ṛṣyasringa and an abbreviated version of the Rāmāyaṇa, often considered as works in their own right. The Mahābhārata is the longest epic poem known and has been described as "the longest poem ever written". Its longest version consists of over 100,000 śloka or over 200,000 individual verse lines (each shloka is a couplet), and long prose passages. At about 1.8 million words in total, the Mahābhārata is roughly ten times the length of the Iliad and the Odyssey combined, or about four times the length of the Rāmāyaṇa. W. J. Johnson has compared the importance of the Mahābhārata in the context of world civilization to that of the Bible, the Quran, the works of Homer, Greek drama, or the works of William Shakespeare. Within the Indian tradition it is sometimes called the fifth Veda.

2. **The Jallianwala Bagh**. Memorial to the Amritsar massacre (13 April 1919). A crowd of nonviolent protesters and pilgrims, mistaken for rebels and shot by troops of the British Indian Army under General Dyer's command. The momentum it gained for Independence culminated thirty years later. Many people died in stampedes or jumped into a deep solitary well to escape the shooting. 120 bodies were removed from the well. Many more died during the night as curfew was in place. It was among the most monstrous outrages of the British Empire. At the time, the Bengali Poet, Rabindranath Tagore, renounced his Knighthood

in symbolic protest. General Dyer's actions were considered very un-British. Subsequently, he greatly injured the image of British rule in India.

3. **Dhaula Dhar,** Mountain range in Kangra, Kully and Chamba. McLeod Ganj is situated above Dharmsala that lies on a spur of the Dhaola Dhar, 16 miles northeast of Kangra, in the midst of wild and picturesque scenery. It originally formed a subsidiary cantonment for the troops stationed at Kangra, and was first occupied as a station in 1849, when a site was required for a cantonment to accommodate a Native regiment which was being raised in the District. A site was found on the slopes of the Dhaola Dhar, in a plot of waste land, upon which stood an old Hindu resthouse, or dharmsala, whence the name adopted for the new cantonment. The civil authorities, following the example of the regimental officers, and attracted by the advantages of climate and scenery, built themselves houses in the neighbourhood of the cantonment ; and in 1855 the new station was formally recognized as the head-quarters of the District.

4. Lieutenant Governor of the Punjab. There was once a garrison here. **Sir Donald Friell McLeod** KCSI CB (6 May 1810 – 28 November 1872) was an Anglo-Indian civil servant who served as Lieutenant Governor of the Punjab between 1865 and 1870. He was one of the founders of Lahore Oriental College, now part of the Punjab University, and is generally remembered as a philanthropic administrator and promoter of education, of both Oriental studies by Europeans, and European literature studies in India.

5. **The Kālacakra** (Sanskrit), is a term used in Vajrayana Buddhism that means wheel of time or "time-cycles".

6. In sanskrit, **Mand-ala** means 'container of life'.

7. **A kora** is a pilgrim's circuit, in a clockwise direction of the central chapel of the official residence of HH Dalai Lama, rather like in the Jokhang Temple in Lhasa.

8. **Trimūrti**. Sanskrit, "three forms" is the trinity of supreme divinity in Hinduism: Creation, maintenance, and destruction/transformation; personified as Brahmā, Viṣṇu, and Śiva. Shaivites

hold that, Shiva performs five actions- creation, preservation, dissolution, concealing grace, and revealing grace.

Chapter 5 - The Parvati Valley: The Hot Springs of Manikaran

1. A metaphor for Depression. See: 'The black dog upon his back', a terrifying nursery metaphor, Johnson writes, in response to a letter from Boswell: '...what will you do to keep away the black dog that worries you at home?' A black dog has walked over him. Horace tells us that the sight of a black dog with its pups was an unlucky omen. See: E. Cobham Brewer, Brewer's Dictionary of Phrase and Fable (Philadelphia: Henry Altemus Company, 1898), DOG.
2. The etymology of the word **Dhuni** is connected with the Sanskrit root dhvan, to dun or to din. Sayana explains it by bending or shaking, and Theodor Benfey, too, translates it by to shatter. "Like a river, a dhuni is always changing. Each dhuni also has its own personality that is as much subject to moods as a person. The glow of the dhuni is both a receiver and a transmitter, and like a screen on which Rorschach-like images are projected, it delivers a code" (see: Autobiography of a Sadhu: A Journey Into Mystic India by Rampuri. Inner Traditions / Bear & Co, 22 Feb 2010. p. 54).
3. **Pulga** is situated 9498 feet above sea level (2895m). The long path to the remote village takes one through mountain pastures and forests. Pulga is half way between Manikaran and the hot springs of Khirganga. It is accessible by foot on the uphill Parbati River mountain path. The snake incident inadvertently sabotaged my attempt to head further into the mountain range and experience the Khirganga hot mineral water springs and their therapeutic qualities, where I'm told water heat distance is much reduced than that of Manikaran. The hot springs are only 5km from Pulga.
4. **Wallah**. Indian suffix indicating a person involved in some kind of activity, where they hail from or what they wear (Topiwala).

For example: Dabbawala, lunch box deliverer, Auto-walla, driver of an auto rickshaw, Chaiwala, a boy or young man who serves tea. Chai wallahs are everywhere in India.

5. **Dal** is a term in the Indian subcontinent for dried, split pulses. The term is also used for various soups prepared from these pulses.

Chapter 6 - The Road to Mandi

1. **8th February, 1998.**
2. **Truth, consciousness, bliss.** epithet and description for the subjective experience of the ultimate, unchanging reality in Hinduism called Brahman.
3. **Avadhuti** is the all-vibrating subtle central channel within the body, running from the base of the spine to the crown of the head. It is androgynous. It represents, inter alia, the element of space.
4. **Padma** ("lotus") is a symbol of spontaneous generation (Svāyambhu). It grows in mud but rises in immaculate purity to the surface and opens to the sun - the evolution begins in the mire of Samsāra but rises to full enlightenment and purity. The closed lotus symbolizes potential and the open lotus — actualization.
5. **Sri Rama**, Rāma or Srī Rāmachandra) is the seventh avatar of the Hindu God Vishnu.
6. **Asuras** ("life of the spiritual world" or "departed spirits") are described in Indian texts as powerful superhuman demigods or demons with good or bad qualities. The presence of a Deva Deva (Sanskrit, "heavenly, divine, anything of excellence") can be detected by those humans who have opened the "Divine eye" (divyacakṣus).
7. **Daya** ("Compassion").
8. **A devotional hymn** associated with Aditya or the mobile Sun God (Surya) and was recited by the sage Agastya to Rāma on the battlefield before fighting the demon king Rāvana. Vālmīki

is celebrated as the harbinger- poet in Sanskrit literature, who compiled this hymn.

9. From Sanskrit *kama* meaning "love, desire" *akshi* meaning "eye". This is the name of a Hindu fertility goddess. She is considered to be an incarnation of Parvati.

10. Someone who practices **tapas**, or "deep meditation, effort to achieve self-realization, sometimes involving solitude, hermitism or asceticism". It is derived from the word root tap which depending on context means "heat" from fire or weather, or blaze, burn, shine, penance, pain, suffering, mortification.

11. **Mūlādhāra**, "root support" or Root chakra. The primary chakras according to Hindu tantrism: Sahasrāra, "thousand-petaled", Crown chakra. or Ājñā, "command", Third-eye chakra, heart chakra, solar plexus chakra, sacral chakra.

12. He could be mixing two sounds RAAA and OMMM to give RAAAAMM or RAM. This mantra is apparently good for removing karmas stored in the Third Chakra. Chanting RAAAMM is reputed to stir the pot of Karmas in the body at the solar plexus chakra. His circling around his head, might signify the circulation of energies pertaining to this mantra. It is written that the Third Eye Chakra is the centre of the inner Guru. "This is the only place that resolves, destroys, demolishes and eradicates the Karma." See: Dr Pillai www.pillaicentre.org or preferrably, John Main, Laurence Freeman, Bede Griffiths, OSB, MARANATHA https://wccm.org/

13. **Silvio Berlusconi,** an Italian media tycoon and politician who served as Prime Minister of Italy in four governments the second of which was 11 June 2001 – 17 May 2006.

14. The electronic version of a printed book (e-book). In 2001, Microsoft and Amazon started working together to sell **e-books** that could be purchased on Amazon and using Microsoft software downloaded to PCs and handhelds.

15. **Gibraltar Cottage**, Knightley, Staffordshire.

16. "His forest fleece the Wrekin heaves", XXXI. "On Wenlock Edge the wood's in trouble..." by A. E. Housman (1859-1936), **A Shropshire Lad.**

17. **Shaktism** is a Goddess-centric tradition of Hinduism. Shaktism (Śāktaṃ, lit., "doctrine of energy, power, the Goddess") is a major tradition of Hinduism, wherein the metaphysical reality is considered feminine and the Devi (goddess) is supreme.
18. **Kālī** also known as Kālikā, is a Hindu goddess.

Chapter 7 - Shimla: The Vieeregal Lodge

1. **Ewoks** are a fictional race of small, mammaloid bipeds that appear in the StarWars universe. The Ewoks are named after the Miwok, a Native American tribe, indigenous to the Redwood forest in which the Endor scenes were filmed for Return of the Jedi, near Nicasio, California. An Ewokese language was created for the films by Return of the Jedi's sound designer Ben Burtt. On the commentary track for the DVD of Return of the Jedi, Burtt explains that the language is based on Kalmyk, a language spoken by the Kalmyk people of Russia.
2. **Sherpa** (Nepali) is a language spoken in Nepal and Sikkim mainly by the Sherpa community. Sherpa is a Tibetan word meaning "eastern people", from shar "east" and pa "people".
3. **Bronkhorst**, Johannes, author of 'The Two Traditions of Meditation In Ancient India', Motilal Banarsidass Publishers, 1986. However, this Bronkhorst was a Dutch window cleaner, printer and activist in the Provo protest movement, Amsterdam NL (1946-2007).
4. Also at several tourist places in India, **foreigners are charged** almost 100% more for an entrance ticket or camera than Indians.
5. Had I arrived six days before, It would be on the day **Lord Dufferin** moved in, Had I arrived six days before, 113 years ago.
6. *Aedificare magna est non facile*. Latin, 'Nothing great is easy to build'.
7. **Lord Ian Basil Gawaine Hamilton-Temple-Blackwood** (4 November 1870 – 3 July 1917), known as Lord Basil Temple Blackwood, was a British lawyer, civil servant and book illustrator. His illustrations were credited only to 'B.T.B.' Whilst at Oxford,

he became friends with Hilaire Belloc, with whom he would enjoy long walks and canoeing trips. See: Hilaire Belloc: A Biography, A N Wilson, Hamish Hamilton Ltd 1984 (p.51) & Blackwood's. His amusing pen and ink sketches illustrate: The Bad Child's Book of Beasts (1896), The Modern Traveller (1898), A Moral Alphabet (1899), More Peers (1900), Cautionary Tales for Children (1907) and More Beasts for Worse Children (1910). In his introduction to the Cautionary Tales, Belloc describes Blackwood's drawings as "...the nicest things you ever saw".

8. She challenges traditional assumptions about **the role of women in colonial life.**

9. **Lord Curzon** had an obsession for accuracy in heraldry. Lord Curzon collected several armorial devices and altered decorations from Messer's Maple & Co. London. See: Splendours of the Raj: British Architecture in India, 1660-1947 Hardcover – May, 1985 by Philip Davies.

10. **Mount Jakko**, 2,450 m, is the highest peak in Shimla.

11. Now the capital of the state of Himachal Pradesh, **Shimla was the summer Capital of the Raj** from 1864 onwards. Perched 7,000 feet in the foot hills of the Himalayas, here it was the temporary capital of the rulers of 1/5 of the population of the world. It began as an 'English Convalescent Station', it developed into a popular resort with British residents of India (1820s), as it also became the summer capital when the Governor-General began to take his administration with him to the hills to escape the intense heat of Calcutta 1300 miles away.

12. **Shimla** first began as a sanatorium, where invalids from the plains would recuperate once Major Sir William Lloyd built the first house. Simla: Past and Present by Edward I Buck. Published by The Times Press, Bombay (1925)

13. **Lord Combermere's** ADC, Captain Mundy, spoke of the rooms which were primitive: "I soon grew tired of these four-footed Pindarees, became callous to their nocturnal orgies and kept a cat." Journal of a Tour in India by Godfrey Charles Mundy. Chapter IV, p. 115 'The Climate of Simla': Published Published by John Murray (1858).

14. **Shimla cricket ground** laid out in 1847. Chail CricketGround (44km from Shimla) was established later in 1893, but Bhupinder Singh Maharaja of Patiala made Chail as his summer capital when the ground was developed. The ground is located at 2444 meters above sea level, that makes it the highest cricket ground in the world. Annandale racecourse is nr. the Ridge, is on a spur of land, close to Vidhan Sabha, Shimla. Annandale is 4km out of Shimla centre, at 6117 feet above sea level, on a patch of table ground ¾ mile circumference. Captain Charles Pratt Kennedy, who was the first British explorer in the valley, named it after his childhood sweet-heart Anna. Lord Dufferin's Military Secretary, Lord William Beresford, had it extended to include a cricked and polo ground, by cutting a big part of the hill. Apart from races it was used for fetes, birthdays, army tattoos, races, dog shows, gymkhanas and flower shows. The annual polo tournament was held at Annadale until it was moved to Calcutta. It is now a heliport for military mountain rescue/disaster relief and parades.

15. **Splendours of the Raj**: British Architecture in India, 1660-1947. Author, Philip Davies. Edition, illustrated, reprint. Publisher, Penguin Books, 1987.

16. As **Rudyard Kipling** had put it in his poem Public Waste. First published in the Civil and Military Gazette, March 9th, 1886.

17. Private Secretary to the Viceroy resided at **Observatory House**, the Lieutenant Governor of Punjab lived at Barnes Court, the Commander-in-Chief residence at Snowdon, with oak chimney pieces and walnut staircases. http://hpshimla.nic.in/sml_heritage.htm Himachal Pradesh Government -Tourism Portal.

18. **Christ Church, Shimla**, is the second oldest church in North India, after St John's Church in Meerut. Built in the neo-Gothic style in 1857 to serve the largely Anglican British community in what was formerly called Simla, Christ Church is situated on The Ridge. It stands out as one of the prominent landmarks of Shimla and its silhouette is visible for miles around the vicinity of Shimla city. Christ Church is one of the enduring legacies of the British Raj. Christ Church was designed by Colonel J. T.

Boileau in 1844, and the church was consecrated after 1857. The clock adorning Christ Church was donated by Colonel Dumbleton in 1860. The porch was added in 1873.

19. **Ian Stillman** is a deaf British aid worker from Reading, Berkshire, England, in the United Kingdom, whose imprisonment and subsequent release from prison in India garnered media attention. He founded the Nambikkai Foundation (a charitable trust providing vocational training for adult deaf in South India.). According to the BBC, Stillman, "a deaf charity worker who has lived in India for nearly 30 years, was arrested (in 2001) after cannabis was found in a taxi he had hired." See: "Fury as deaf charity worker jailed", 25 June 2001, BBC. Stillman's attorney's claimed that Stillman, who is deaf and well known in India for his charitable work with the deaf, was the victim of "a gross miscarriage of justice." Stephen Jakobi of the advocacy organisation Fair Trials International told the press that "It is the most horrific case I've ever seen of an innocent man being done down by law." The United Kingdom Council on Deafness collected tens of thousands of signatures on a petition to the Indian government asking for Stillman's release. He was released following successful intervention by Prime Minister Tony Blair and the Foreign Secretary. See: "Dream trip that turned into an Indian jail nightmare", 8 January 2003, The Guardian.

20. According to experts, **many people die** due to lack of minor surgeries (The Times of India. Oct 21, 2015).

21. 'Green forest abode of the Gods'. The name **Haryana** has been derived from the Sanskrit words Hari (the Hindu god Vishnu) and ayana (home), meaning "the Abode of God". However, some scholars believe the name comes from a compound of the words Hari (Sanskrit Harit, "green") and Aranya (forest).

22. It cost over £1 million and was designed by **H.S. Harington**, the chief engineer of the Kalka-Shimla railway.

23. Mike's Railway History - http://mikes.railhistory. railfan.net/ r019.html

24. *Vivace* [It.]: Lively, brisk. Scherzo [It.]: Playful, jokingly; a playful or joking musical form. Capriccio [It.]: Capricious, capriciously,

at the players' pleasure; also a musical form in a light style. Adagio [It.]: Slow tempo. Sotto [It: Under, below. Sotto Voce [It.]: Undertone, subdued. Misterioso [It.]: Mysterious. Pesante [It.]: Weighty, emphasized. Lacrimoso [It.]: Tearfully, maudlin. Empfindsamkeit [Ger.]: Sensitiveness, sentimentality. Eilend [Ger.]: Hurrying. Ein Heldenleben [Ger.]: "A Heroic Life. Ein-Wenig [Ger.]: A little. "Elegy" (French: élégie) may denote a type of musical work, usually of a sad or sombre nature. See: Glossary of Music Terms by For all of its pervasiveness, however, the 'elegy' remains remarkably ill-defined: sometimes used as a catch-all to denominate texts of a somber or pessimistic tone, sometimes as a marker for textual monumentalizing, and sometimes strictly as a sign of a lament for the dead. Weisman, Karen, ed. (2012). "Book: The Oxford Handbook of the Elegy". Oxford Index. Oxford University Press. & Oxford Dictionary of Musical Terms (Oxford Quick Reference) – 5 Dec 2002 by Alison Latham.

25. Read: At times the god-head reveals Himself through people. For me, at that time, it was two-handsome young Viking looking students. Praise be the spirit that brings out the very best in courage, understanding, generosity, empathy, clarity and intimacy. Difficult to woo bi-curious straight men, if one is emotionally incontinent. In people with whom one feels assured to be accepting of oneself, one could make it easier for them; there is a passing understanding, unspoken, as though they themselves wanted it as much as you. Ah, to mix it up! The hallowed moment when together they unpeel the accretions of conditioning unto the wild straights of honesty and abandon to impulses otherwise tightly controlled. See: "From Sex to Super Consciousness" by Osho.

26. **Friedrich Nietzsche**, *Ecce Homo*: How One Becomes What One Is. Ecce homo: Wie man wird, was man ist. Written in 1888 and not published until 1908

27. **The Dhauladhar range** (lit. The White Range) is a southern branch of the main Outer Himalayan chain of mountains. It rises from the Indian plains to the north of Kangra and Mandi.

Dharamsala, the headquarters of Kangra district, lies on its southern spur in above the Kangra Valley, which divides it from Chamba. The Imperial Gazetteer of India, v. 11, p. 287.

28. **Goenka**, S.N. (2000). The Discourse Summaries: Talks from a Ten-day Course in Vipassana Meditation. Pariyatti Publishing.

29. In the **Rigveda**, where a rājan is a ruler, see the dāśarājñá, the "battle of ten kings".

Chapter 8 - Rishikesh

1. **The Beatles** first met the Maharishi in London in August 1967 and then attended a seminar in Bangor, Wales. Wanting to learn more, they kept in contact with the Maharishi and decided to spend time with him at his teaching centre located near Rishikesh, in 'the Valley of the Saints' at the foothills of the Himalayas, in the summer of 1969.

2. A large, colourless **diamond** that was found near Guntur in Andhra Pradesh, c. 13th Century. Koh-i-Noor acquired a reputation within the British royal family for bringing bad luck to any man who wears it. Queen Victoria came into possession of it after the British conquest of the Punjab in 1849. Since arriving in the country, it has only ever been worn by female members of the family. Kenneth J. Mears; Simon Thurley; Claire Murphy (1994). The Crown Jewels. Historic Royal Palaces Agency. p. 27

3. **Dragon Flies**. *Meganeura* is a genus of extinct insects from the Carboniferous period (approximately 300 million years ago), which resembled and are related to the presentday dragonflies. With wingspans of up to 65 cm (25.6 in). While on the hammock outside the room, an enormous dark green dragonfly flew at me. It was around 8inches long – and came at me like a heat seeking missile but was making the noise of a mini-helicopter. My experience of this 8in-Jurassicsized- beast was distressing. Dragonflies, which have existed on Earth for 325million years.

1. Also spelled **Hardwar** is an ancient city and municipality in the Haridwar district of Uttarakhand, India. The River Ganga, after flowing for 253 kilometres (157 mi) from its source at Gaumukh at the edge of the Gangotri Glacier, enters the Indo-Gangetic Plains of North India for the first time at Haridwar, which gave the city its ancient name, Gangadwára.

2. **River worship** ceremony.

3. **Ghat**. The steps leading down to the river. Kar Ki Pauri Ghat means (Hindi) 'Footstep of the God'.

4. "The Geological Evidences of the Antiquity of Man, with Remarks on Theories of the Origin of Species by Variation" by **Charles Lyell**, 'The North American Review' Vol. 97, No. 201 (Oct., 1863), pp. 451-483.

5. **Pooja** is as an act of showing reverence to the almighty through invocations, prayers (like mantras, holy chants), rituals, etc. Praising the God through Poojas helps to establish a spiritual connection between the deity and the devotee. The combination of right timings, right offerings and right sounds are decisive for invoking archetypal beings through a pooja. Through our group of trained Vedic specialists we organize timely rituals to gain from the ruling energies of the day. There are different poojas for specific purposes.

6. **The Ganges** is considered a Goddess who was originally living in Heaven. Saint Bhagirath long meditated to give liberation to his ancestors (reduced to ashes due to the curse of the sage Kapil). The gods blessed Bhagirath with Ganga. Lord Shiva held Ganga to reduce her mighty flow. When Ganga flows on the mortal remains of the ancestors of Bhagirath they receive Moksha (Liberation from the cycle of death and rebirth). Following the same tradition, Hindu people today offer the remains of their dead relatives (after bunring the body) to the river Ganga, expecting moksha for them. In the name of Saint Bhagirath, the river Ganga is known as Bhagirathi at the source and receives its

name 'Ganga' when it meets the Alaknanda River at Devprayag. For centuries, people consider the river Ganga as a Holy River and it is part of their life, where they come to get Moksha for their relatives who have passed away and to remove their sins. The Ganga Aarti is kind of thanks giving to the river Ganga.

7. **Aarti** also spelled arti, arati, arathi, aarthi (ārtī) is a Hindu religious ritual of worship, a part of puja, in which light from wicks soaked in ghee (purified butter) or camphor is offered to one or more deities. Aartis also refer to the songs sung in praise of the deity, when lamps are being offered.

8. **Raja Bharthari**, or "Sant" Bharthari, is the hero of many folk stories in North India. He was the ruler of Ujjain in the 1st century BC, He was so much immersed in romance and sex, that he wrote 100 stanzas on 'the art of romance and sex', now famously called 'Shrungara Shataka'. All the stanzas are on sensuality and sexual pleasure. King Bhartruhari was obsessed with his youngest wife Pingala, she was beautiful and charming. Once the King's brother complained to the King about the affair of the Queen with King's charioteer and advised him to banish her for the sake of the kingdom. The King was too obsessed with her to heed his brother's advice, in fact when the Queen heard of this from her sources, she manipulated the king and banished his brother from the kingdom. One day a yogi came to his court and presented the king with an apple, which he said would bless one with 'youth and longevity' on eating (stories say that the ascetic got the apple as a boon from the gods and that the apple was from the Kalpavruksha- 'wish fulfilling tree'). The king wanted queen Pingala to have the apple, so that she would always look young for him. Queen Pingala gave the apple to the charioteer. She wanted him to be young and strong. The charioteer was in love with a prostitute, he gave her the apple to eat. The prostitute thought 'it would be better if someone deserving ate this', she always liked the king, he was noble and pious, his long living also meant the peace and stability of her kingdom, so she took the apple to the king and give it to him. King Bhartuhari was surprised to see the apple with her, and enquired how she got it.

She told him how she got it from the charioteer, king sent men to bring the charioteer, he told the king that he got it from the queen, and confessed of his affair with the queen. Bhartruhari realized the fleeting nature of the pleasure from worldly objects, he wrote a poem about the incident which changed him in his Niti Shataka. (100 stanzas on Moral conduct). "(She) whom on I contemplate, is not passionate for me, she loves another; / that whom she loves, loves another; / One whom he loves, loves another. / Refuse (disdain to) that woman, that man, Cupid, me." Deep Vairagya (dispassion) arose in him, he gave up the desire for his wife, realizing his mistake he brought his brother back and crowned him, renouncing the world he lived rest of his life as an ascetic. Bhartruhari wrote Niti-Shataka and Vairagya Shataka during his later years. See: 'Vikram and The Vampire' by Sir Richard Francis Burton, 1870. He is sometimes identified with Bhartṛhari, a Sanskrit writer of influential texts: the Vākyapadīya (on grammar and linguistic philosophy), that discusses logical problems such as the liar paradox and a paradox of unnameability or unsignfiability, which has become known as Bhartrhari's paradox; and the Śatakatraya, a work of Sanskrit poetry, comprising three collections of about 100 stanzas each.

9. The term originates from the Sanskrit term **pandit** (paṇḍitá), meaning "knowledge owner". It refers to someone who is erudite in various subjects and who conducts religious ceremonies and offers counsel to the king and usually referred to a person from the Hindu Brahmin caste but may also refer to the Siddhas, Siddhars, Naths, Ascetics, Sadhus, or Yogis. From at least the early 19th century, a Pundit of the Supreme Court in Colonial India was an officer of the judiciary who advised British judges on questions of Hindu law. In Anglo-Indian use, pundit also referred to a native of India who was trained and employed by the British to survey inaccessible regions beyond the British frontier.

10. **Palki** is a litter or a class of wheel-less vehicle; type of human-powered transport, for the transport of persons or idols

11. **A Sanskrit Poem** written by Pundit Jagannath. Pundit Jagannath was Sanskrit scholar and poet born in 1590. For complete Ganga Lahari Stotram in Sanskrit with English translation. Om Jai Gange Mata, Maiya Jai Gange Mata / Jo Nar Tumko Dhyata, Manvanchhit Phal Pata / Om Jai Gange Mata, Maiya Jai Gange Mata / Om praise to Mother Ganga, / Maa Gange hail to you; / Anyone who worships you, / will get fulfilled all his wishes, / hail to you, Maa Gange./ Chandra Si Jyoti Tumhari, / Jal Nirmal Aata Sharan Pade Jo Teri, / So Nar Tar Jata / Om Jai Gange Mata, Maiya Jai Gange Mata / Your aura is like the moon's light, /your sacred water is always pure; /The one who takes shelter in you, /will cross all world's trouble, Maa Gange hail to you./ Putr Sagar Ke Tare, Sab Jag Ko Gyata / Krupa Drishti Ho Tumhari, Tribhuvan Sukh Data / Om Jai Gange Mata, Maiya Jai Gange Mata/ Everyone knows that, You have liberated / the sons of Sagar and if anyone / has your blessing he will get pleasure of / all three worlds (Heaven, hell and earth). / Maa Gange hail to you. /Ek Baar Jo Prani, Sharan Teri Aata / Yam Ki Traas Mitakar, Param Gati Pata / Om Jai Gange Mata, Maiya Jai Gange Mata / Having once come into your protection,/ you release them from harassment of death / forever through liberation of death / and rebirth. Maa Gange hail to you. / Aarti Matu Tumhari, Jo Nar Nit Gata / Sevak Wahi Sahaj Mein, Mukti Ko Pata/ Om Jai Gange Mata, Maiya Jai Gange Mata./ Whomever sings your praise, worships you with lights. / Your servant, your devotee will easily reach liberation, / hail to you Maa Gange.

12. **Shloka** (meaning "song", from the root śru, "hear") is the pre-eminent Vedic poetic meter or verse form The shloka structure is embedded in the Bhagavad Gita, the Mahabharata, the Ramayana, the Puranas, Smritis and scientific treatises of Hinduism such as Sushruta Samhita and Charaka Samhita. The traditional view is that this form of verse was involuntarily composed by Valmiki in grief, the author of the Ramayana, on seeing a hunter shoot down one of two birds in love. See Arnold, Edward Vernon (1905) 'Vedic Metre in its historical development', CUP.

13. Sometimes spelt phonetically as **pooja** or poojah, it may honour or celebrate the presence of special guest(s), or their memories after they pass away. The word pūjā (Devanagari: ????) comes from Sanskrit, and means reverence, honour, homage, adoration, and worship. A Pooja is performed with the help of a local priest (or pundit). It is necessary to give donations to priest after this Pooja. Those unwilling to give money for a Pooja might avoid pundits if they are asking you for a ganga Pooja, or something like that. One could try to avoid any kind of activity which causes pollution in the holy river ganga or nature; especially plastic.

PART II: Rajputana

Chapter 10 - Udaipur

1. **Brahma Kumaris** teaches a form of meditation that focuses on identity as souls (as opposed to bodies). They believe that all souls are intrinsically good and that God is the source of all goodness. The university teaches to transcend labels associated with the body, such as race, nationality, religion, and gender, and aspires to establish a global culture based on what they call "soul-consciousness". Melton, J. Gordon; Baumann, Martin (2010). Religions of the World. A Comprehensive Encyclopedia of Beliefs and Practices. ABCCLEO, LLC. pp. 383–384.
2. **Ranakpur** is widely known for its marble Jain temple, said to be the most spectacular of the Jain temples. There is also a small Sun temple which is managed by the Udaipur royal family trust. is dedicated to Tirthankara Adinatha. Local legend has it that Dharma Shah, a local Jain businessperson, started construction of the temple in the 15th century following a divine vision. The temple honors Adinath, the first Tirthankar of the present half-cycle (avasarpiṇī) according to Jain cosmology. Kumar, Sehdev (2001). A Thousand Petalled Lotus: Jain Temples of Rajasthan, p. 96.

3. During the famous Indian **Sepoy Mutiny in 1857** several European families fled from Nimach and used the island as an asylum, offered to them by Maharana Swaroop Singh. To protect his guests, the Rana destroyed all the town's boats so that the rebels could not reach the island.

4. **India by Pierre Loti** [i.e. Julien Viaud]; translated from the French by George A. F. Inman ; edited by Robert Harborough Sherard. (New York : Duffield, [n.d.]), by Pierre Loti.

5. **Rajput** (from Sanskrit raja-putra, "son of a king" is a member of the patrilineal clans of the Indian subcontinent. They rose to prominence from the late 6th century AD and continued to dominate many regions of central and northern India until the 20th century. Encyclopaedia Britannica. 27 November 2010.

6. Second World War (apparently air force **slang**): of unknown origin. An elephant with a raised trunk is a symbol of good fortune in South Asia.

7. There were many recognitions of similarity. They say the travellers are 'gyptian because when they left the East, journeying west, they carried with them the ancient wisdom of India. So that these people from the East, stopping in the land of the Pharo, before reaching Bucharest, and the rest, were able to prophesy the future, and bless strangers like brothers, for a fee. They whispered to their horses and rode bare-back; used cards of wisdom. They originated in northwest regions of the Indian subcontinent and left sometime between the 6th and 11th century to work in Middle Eastern courts of their own volition, or as slaves. A small number of nomadic groups were cut off from their return to the subcontinent by conflicts and moved west, eventually settling in Europe, Turkey and North Africa via Iran. Kenrick, Donald (2007). Historical Dictionary of the Gypsies (Romanies) (2nd ed.). Scarecrow Press. p. 126 & p. 189.

1. The exact date of origin is not known, but legend associates **Lord Brahma** with its creation.

2. may be derived from word **'Pushkarni'** means- lake. It may be derived from word Pushp which means flower, and Kar means hand.

3. **Yoni** (Sanskrit: "womb", "uterus", "vagina", "vulva", "abode", or "source") is a stylised representation of female genitalia representing the goddess Shakti in Hinduism. Within Shaivism, the sect dedicated to the god Shiva, the yoni symbolises his consort. The male counterpart of the yoni is the lingam. Their union represents the eternal process of creation and regeneration, the union of male and female principles, and all existence. Legend has it that the lake was consecrated to Lord Brahma, the creator of the universe when a lotus dropped from his hand into the vale and a lake emerged in that place. The Temple of Brahma is the most important temple in Pushkar, dedicated to Lord Brahma, one of the holy trinity of Hinduism. In fact, it is the only Hindu shrine in the world where Lord Brahma is worshipped. The temple enshrines a life-size idol of Lord Brahma.

4. **Vāmana Purāṇa** is a medieval era Sanskrit text and one of the eighteen major Puranas of Hinduism. It is a text with the character of a Purana. Prahlāda is Sanskrit meaning filled with joy. Prahlāda is a figure in Vedic literature, a saintly boy known for his piety and bhakti to Lord Vishnu.

5. The word **Chakra**derives from the Sanskrit word meaning "wheel," as well as "circle" and "cycle". It's described by many as a spinning wheel of light [citation needed]. Of the 88,000 chakras within the human body, seven are considered of principle importance and are referred to as the "major chakras"; Whirling

vortexes of energy located over the main endocrine glands –the innumerable marmas where

flesh, veins, arteries, tendons, bones and joints meet, as seats of prana or subtle energy.

6. **The three doshas**—Vata, Pitta, and Kapha—are derived from the five elements. Also known as mind-body types, the doshas express unique blends of physical, emotional, and mental characteristics. In Ayurveda, health is defined as the dynamic state of balance between mind, body, and environment. You can achieve and maintain a vibrant and joyful state of health by identifying your mind-body type and creating a lifestyle that supports your unique nature. I am Kapha-Pitta according to the Chorpa Cenre. "Kapha is such a strong structural element that it lends its thick, heavier physique to two-dosha types, even when it is not the predominant of the two doshas. As a Pitta-Kapha, you may have Pitta's intense manner and Kapha's solid body. You are more muscular than Pitta-Vatas and may even be quite bulky. This is a particularly good body type for athletes since it combines Pitta's drive and energy with Kapha's endurance. You may find it hard to miss a meal. The combination of a strong Pitta digestion and Kapha's stability generally fosters excellent physical health. Your personality demonstrates Kapha stability and Pitta force, complete with a tendency towards anger and criticism that is far different from the serenity of a pure Kapha. You can keep this tendency in check with mind-body practices that "cool" the mind and balance the body, including meditation, optimal nutrition, and spending time in nature.

7. *Somnia sunt surculos Rerum*, L.. Dreams are the seeds of things. "Trust in dreams, for in them is hidden the gate to Eternity." See: Khalil Gibran. Dreams are like seeds underground, when they germinate into reality, in their search for for the Light. Finem omnia bona or Omnia Bona Sunt Quae Bonum Finem Habeant. All's well that ends well. All good things do come to an end, and there is yet more time of the 3 months in this idyllic Country. "To come to an end" is an English idiom; if you want a corresponding Latin idiom, you could say omnia bona capient finem,

literally "all good things will grasp the end" but meaning the same as the English equivalent. (This is in the future tense because Romans tend to be much more particular about tenses than English speakers; all things will sooner or later come to an end, not that they are all presently doing so. Ad finem venient, ad exitum venient (come to their departure/ exit/conclusion/end), exibunt (expire, pass on, go forth, go away, escape, pass away, perish), finem habebunt (have their end, come to an end), desinent (cease, come to a stop, end), interibunt (die, end, finish, perish, are lost, become extinct), finient (end, come to an end), exstinguentur (are extinguished, die, die out, are forgotten).

8. I remember losing this lovely scarf in London at a 'Spring Awakening' 2003, on the night of my twenty-third birthday (two years later), after a meal at **Les Portes des India**.

9. University of Reading, Berkshire, England: I am doing my final year, at **Wantage Hall** (Old Court).

Chapter 12 - Deserta Rajathania

1. **The Snake Mountain.**

2. **Rattan** (from the Malay rotan) is the name for climbing palms belonging to subfamily Calamoideae (from the Greek 'kálamos' = reed).Rattans are extensively used for making furniture and baskets. When cut into sections, rattan can be used as wood to make furniture. Rattan accepts paints and stains like many other kinds of wood, so it is available in many colours; and it can be worked into many styles. Moreover, the inner core can be separated and worked into wicker.

3. **Chāy masālā**, "tea spice". Tea vendors are known in India as "chai wallahs".

4. **Dromedary** (one-hump): Camelus dromedaries. Bactrian camel (two-humps, endangered): Camelus bactrianus. As tall desert-dwelling creatures, camels are iconic of deserts. Generally, the camel is a pleasant animal. If well

treated, the domestic camel is very docile and easy to manage. If ill-treated, they can become very stubborn. Camels can easily be identified by the unique one or two humps on their back and their long necks. When running, a camel can reach a speed up to 40 mph in short bursts, 25 mph for longer periods of time. Camels do not have hooves. The foot of a camel is made up of a large leathery pad, with two toes at the front, the bones of which are embedded in the foot. The padding makes the gait of a camel silent, and keeps it from sinking in the sand. The camel also has pads of thick leathery skin, on its leg joints, enabling it to kneel or lay in the hot sand. Similar to giraffes, camels move both legs together on each side of their body to walk. Camels are herbivores, they most commonly eat grasses and desert plants, although there are stories of camels consuming tents and just about anything else around. The inside of their mouth is lined with very thick skin that allows them to chew up thorny plants that other animals cannot consume. They can reach trees and limbs that are up to 11' high. The stiff hair on their noseallows them to forage in prickly or thorny plants. The diet of a camel requires salt, so the salty plants that grown in salt lakes and other areas are part of their normal diet. Camels are ruminant feeders and do not chew when they eat their food, but later regurgitate the cud and finish digesting it later. Camels travel in herds or caravans containing mostly females and calves with one dominant male. The other bulls (males) will travel in bachelor herds. The males (bulls) tend to become more aggressive during mating season. They will snap at each other and neck wrestle. When agitated, a camel will spit regurgitated food at the agitator. A camel's hump consists of fatty-tissue which minimizes heat-trapping insulation in the rest of their bodies, keeping them cooler. The fur or coat on a camel can reflect the sun and insulate the animal from the heat radiated from the desert environment Camels can withstand variations in temperature and water intake beyond what other animals can handle. Camels do not store water in their humps, the humps contain fat. The average life span of a camel is 40 to 50 years.

5. **The Aravali Range** (Hindi, lit. 'line of peaks') is a range of mountains in western India running approximately 692 km (430 mi) in a north-eastern direction across the Indian states of Gujarat, Rajasthan, and Haryana, ending in Delhi. It is one of the worlds' oldest mountain ranges. It dates back to a pre-Indian subcontinental collision with the mainland Eurasian Plate. The highest peak is Guru Shikhar in Mount Abu in Rajasthan. Rising to 5650 feet (1722 meters), it lies near the south-western extremity of the range, close to the border with Gujarat state.

6. **A Persian text** inscribed on Buland Darwaza, the imposing main gateway leading in to Fatehpur-Sikri, Isa [Jesus], son of Mary said: "The world is a bridge; pass over it, but build no house upon it. One should believe in the Day of Akherat [i.e., the Æon] and hope in eternity, for this world endures but an hour. So spend it in prayer and praise to God, in order to find serenity in the yet-unseen day." (trans. JDA) This text is close to Gospel of Thomas logion 42, "Become passers-by" or "wayfarers", in a spiritual Exodus to the Æon, not weighted down, "owned" by possessions (Mark 6:8-9), in the sense of παρεπίδημος; I Peter 1:1 suggests this was a term for Jesus followers, with its recurrence in 2:11 bearing the Thomas sense. Others read this logion as "Come into being as you pass away".

Chapter 13 - Jodphur

1. **Marwar** (Hindi) (also called Jodhpur region) is a region of southwestern Rajasthan state in North Western India. It lies partly in the Thar Desert. In Rajasthani dialect "wad" means a particular area. The word Marwar is derived from Sanskrit word 'Maruwat'. English translation of the word is 'the region of desert.' Dr D K Taknet: Marwari Samaj aur Brij Mohan Birla, Indian Institute of Marwari Entrepreneurship, Jaipur, 1993, p. 20

2. **Titans:** in mythology the sons and daughters of Uranus and Gaea, who were hurled from heaven by no less a one than Zeus himself. The Fort Mehrangarh Fort in Jodhpur is situated on a

steep hill and is described as the abode of Olympians in Jodhpur, 1925. 'An interesting and picturesque country', he wrote. In Huxley's day trains never averaged more than 14 miles an hour.

3. The warrior–ruling caste. This legendary dynasty was descended from the moon (Chandra), while the other principal houses, the Solar Dynasty (Suryavanshi) claims descentfrom the sun (surya). **Ilā** (Sanskrit) is an androgyne in Hindu mythology, known for their sex changes. As a man, he is known as Ila or Sudyumna and as a woman, is called Ilā. Ilā is considered the chief progenitor of the Lunar dynasty of Indian kings- also known as the Ailas ("descendants of Ilā").

4. In Hindu tradition, blue signifies the colour of the **Brahmin**.

Chapter 14 - Jaiselmer

1. **Jeysulmir** or Jaisalmer, a town in Rajputana about 140 miles W.N.W. of Jodhpur, situated in the middle of the Thar or Indian Desert. Kipling also refers to this town in chapter XVI, in "The Great Census" (collected in The Smith Administration), "Gemini", chapter IX of The Naulakha and in chapter X of Kim.

2. **The Ravanahatha** is an ancient musical instrument not unlike the violin. It's music is soulful and plangent; notes echo.

3. **Ker Sangri.** A combination of berries and dried beans cooked with yogurt and masalas. "Rajasthani cuisine is sensitive amongst Indian cuisines as people relish non-vegetarian dishes made from chicken, lamb and shikar which includes animal and birds like boars, venison, peacock, quail, duck, pheasant, rabbits and even camels etc. Vegetarian food comes in two varieties i.e. the food eaten by the common man that includes use of various spices and herbs and the food of the Marwari Jains that is prepared without using onions, garlic or for that matter any ingredient growing under the soil except for ginger and groundnuts. Rajasthan cooking in general has its own unique flavour where the simplest and the most basic of ingredients go into the preparation of delicious dishes. The harsh climate and the non-availability of ingredients in this region are a great influence.

Food that could last for several days and could be eaten without heating was preferred, more out of necessity than choice. The sparse rainfall is not conducive to growing fresh green vegetables. Due to this scarcity, whatever seasonal vegetables are grown, are sundried so that they can be used for the rest of the year." See his recipe portal www.sanjeevkapoor.com

4. **'Padharo Mhare Des'** means 'Welcome to my land'. Enthusiasm and courtesy are hallmarks of Rajesthani people. The word "Padharo", means 'welcome', as in, to a hospitable land. It is a land that held the guest supreme and even enemies were treated with grace on its soil. What better greeting could a prospective visitor hope to hear! Padharo also means come (in Hindi Aao but it's more like an invitation with pleasure). "Maare" means ours (in Hindi Hamare)."Des" means place/country/village/ town. Here it is used for Rajasthan. Phrase "Padharo Maare Des" is taken from Rajasthani song "Kesariya balam". It is one of the welcome phrase to invite people in Rajasthan and be a guest and enjoy their hospitality, know their culture and people. In simple it means "You are welcome to my country/village". Padharo Mhare Des is the name of a 2011 film documenting a 10-day, 2000 kilometre road trip from Udaipur to Jodhpur, Jaisalmer to Bikaner and Jaipur in India. Made by Gauri Warudi on digital format, using a 'Sony HD Handycam,' the film is narrated in English. The film is the outcome of a ten-day road trip through Rajasthan.

5. **Abhla bharat** or Shisheh, embroidery or mirror- work, is a type of embroidery which attaches small pieces of mirrors reflect metal to fabric. "Mirror embroidery is spread throughout Asia, and today can be found in the traditional embroidery of India. When merchant and traveller Marco Polo visited India in the 13th century, he commented that mirror work embroidery from India was more intricate and skilfully crafted than any other that he had seen. Mirror work, otherwise known as shisha, can be traced back to 13th century Persia. Tradesmen and travellers brought the handicraft to India in the same century, during the Mughal era, which consisted of Muslim rulers. Due to this, the

use of mirrors and the craft of mirror work stem from traditional Islamic beliefs: the mirrors help to trap or blind the evil eye, reflecting bad luck and evil spirits away from the wearer. This religious significance seeped into Hinduism and Jainism, where, historically, shisha torans were affixed to the front door in order to ward off evil spirits. A toran is a structural gateway often seen in Hindu and Buddhist architecture, and in mirror work, it is often made of cotton fabric embellished with mirrors, metals and embroidery." Unearth the Truth of Indian Mirror Work. https://strandofsilk.com/journey-map/rajasthan/mirrorwork/ history

6. **Krishna** was the eighth son of Devaki and Vasudeva. Based on scriptural details and astrological calculations, the date of Krishna's birth, known as Janmashtami, is 18 July 3228 BCE and he lived until 18 February 3102 BCE.

7. The first remake of Walt Disney's 1967 animation adaptation of the **Mowgli** stories from **The Jungle Book and The** Second Jungle Book by Rudyard Kipling was filmed here in 1994.

8. About the same time as my then parish church, **St.Mary's, High Offley, Staffordshire,** England, was built. I look around this 845-year-old fortification, and marvel at its contemporariness with the examples of Norman architecture I know, as a point of reference.

9. **The word haveli** is derived from Arabic haveli, meaning "partition" or "private space" popularised under Mughal Empire and was devoid of any architectural affiliations. Later, the word haveli came to be used as generic term for various styles of regional mansions, townhouse and temples found in India; when it was first applied in Rajputana by the Vaishnava sect to refer to their temples. Sarah, Tillotson (1998). Indian Mansions: A Social History of the Haveli. Orient longman. p. 72. In the northern part of India. Havelis for Lord Krishna are prevalent with huge mansion like constructions. The havelis are noted for their frescoes depicting images of gods, goddesses, animals, scenes from the British colonization, and the life stories of Lords Rama and Krishna. Bahl, Vani. "Haveli—A Symphony of Art and Ar-

chitecture". The New Indian Express. The havelis in and around Jaisalmer Fort (also known as the Golden Fort), situated in Jaisalmer, Rajasthan, of which the three most impressive are Patwon Ki Haveli, Salim Singh Ki Haveli, and Nathmal-Ki Haveli deserve special mention. These were the elaborate homes of Jaisalmer's rich merchants. The ostentatious carvings etched out in sandstone with infinite detail and then painstakingly pieced together in different patterns each more lavish than the next were commissioned to put on show the owner's status and wealth. Around Jaisalmer, they are typically carved from yellow sandstone. They are often characterized by wall paintings, frescoes, jharokhas (balconies) and archways. "Jaisalmer Havelis, Famous Haveli in Rajasthan India, Heritage Haveli Tours in Rajasthan India". Shubhyatra.com. "Patwon Ki Haveli - Patwonji Ki Haveli Jaisalmer - Patwon Ki Haveli In Jaisalmer Rajasthan". Jaisalmer.org.uk.

10. Located inside the mighty Jaisalmer fort, the **Laxminath temple** is dedicated to Goddess Laxmi (Goddess of Wealth) and her consort Lord Vishnu. One of the oldest temples in Jaisalmer, it was erected in the year 1494 during the rule of Rao Lunkaran. It is believed that the idols in the temple were installed by a learned Brahmin of the region, Sen Pal Shakdvipi. It is also said that the pillars of the temple were brought in here from Lodhruva village. The walls and ceiling of the Laxminath temple have beautiful paintings of other gods. Though the architecture of the temple is a simple one but the silver outline in the façade and the ornamentation add charm to the temple's beauty.

11. "Love within, our inherent nature. Man cannot create love. How to find out why it is not able to manifest itself. What is the hindrance? What is the difficulty? Where is the dam blocking it? If there are no barriers, love will show itself. It is not necessary to persuade it or to guide it. Every man would be filled with love if it weren't for the barriers of false culture and of degrading and harmful traditions. Nothing can stifle love. Love is inevitable. Love is our nature. The Ganges flows from the Himalayas. It is water; it simply flows – it does not ask a priest the way to the

ocean. Have you ever seen a river standing at a crossroads asking a policeman the whereabouts of the ocean? However far the ocean may be, however hidden it may be, the river will surely find the path. It is inevitable: she has the inner urge. She has no guidebook, but, infallibly, she will reach her destination. She will crack through mountains, cross the plains and traverse the country in her race to reach the ocean. An insatiable desire, a force, an energy exists within her heart of hearts. But suppose obstructions are thrown in her way by man? Suppose dams are constructed by man? A river can overcome and break through natural barriers – ultimately, they are not barriers to her at all – but if man-made barriers are created, if dams are engineered across her, it is possible she may not reach the ocean. Man, the supreme intelligence of creation, can stop a river from reaching the ocean if he decides to do so. In nature, there is a fundamental unity, a harmony. The natural obstructions, the apparent oppositions seen in nature, are challenges to arouse energy; they serve as clarion calls to arouse what is latent inside. There is no disharmony in nature. When we sow a seed, it may seem as if the layer of earth above the seed is pressing it down, is obstructing its growth. It may seem so, but in reality, that layer of earth is not an obstruction; without that layer the seed cannot germinate. The earth presses down on the seed so that it can mellow, disintegrate, and transform itself into a sapling. Outwardly it may seem as if the soil is stifling the seed, but the soil is only performing the duty of a friend. It is a clinical operation. If a seed does not grow into a plant, we reason that the soil may not have been proper, that the seed may not have had enough water or that it may not have received enough sunlight – we do not blame the seed. But if flowers do not bloom in a man's life we say the man himself is responsible for it. Nobody thinks of inferior manure, of a shortage of water or of a lack of sunshine and does something about it, the man himself is accused of being bad. And so the plant of man has remained undeveloped, has been suppressed by unfriendliness and has been unable to reach the flowering stage. Nature is rhythmic harmony.

But the artificiality that man has imposed on nature, the things he has engineered across it and the mechanical contrivances he has thrown into the current of life have created obstructions at many places, have stopped the flow. And the river is made the culprit. " Man is bad; the seed is poisonous," they say. I wish to draw your attention to the fact that the basic obstructions are man-made, are created by man himself – otherwise the river of love would flow freely and reach the ocean of God. Love is inherent in man. If the obstructions are removed with awareness, love can flow. Then, love can rise to touch God, to touch the Supreme. What are these man-made obstacles? The most obvious obstruction has been the opposition to sex and to passion. This barrier has destroyed the possibility of the birth of love in man. The simple truth is that sex is the starting point of love. Sex is the beginning of the journey to love. The origin, the Gangotri of the Ganges of Love, is sex, passion – and everybody behaves like its enemy. Every culture, every religion, every guru, every seer has attacked this Gangotri, this source, and the river has remained bottled up. The hue and cry has always been, "Sex is sin. Sex is irreligious. Sex is poison," but we never seem to realize that ultimately it is the sex energy itself that travels to and reaches the inner ocean of love. Love is the transformation of sex energy. The flowering of love is from the seed of sex." CHAPTER 1. SEX, THE GENESIS OF LOVE. From Sex to Superconsciousness by OSHO. Talks given from 01/8/68 to 30/10/68. Original in Hindi.

12. **Chapati** (alternatively spelled chapatti, chappati, chapathi, or chappathi, and also known as roti) is an unleavened flatbread from the Indian Subcontinent. The word chapat (Hindi: chapat) means "Flat", which describes the traditional method of forming rounds of thin dough by slapping the dough between the wetted palms of the hands.With each slap, the round of dough is rotated. Chapati is noted in the 16th-century document Ain-i-Akbari by Abu'l-Fazl ibn Mubarak, vizier of Mughal Emperor Akbar. Of Bread Ain-i- Akbari , by Abu'l-Fazl ibn Mubarak. English tr. by Heinrich Blochmann and Colonel Henry Sullivan

Jarrett, 1873–1907. The Asiatic Society of Bengal, Calcutta, Volume I, Chap. 26, page 61.

13. **Cyril John Radcliffe,** 1st Viscount Radcliffe GBE PC QC (30 March 1899 – 1 April 1977) was a British lawyer and Law Lord best known for his role in the partition of British India.

14. **Govinda** is a name of Lord Krishna. The sages call Krishna Govinda because He pervades all the worlds, giving them power. The Shanti Parva of the Mahabharata states that Shri Vishnu restored the earth that had sunk into the netherworld, or Patala, so all the devas praised Him as Govind (Protector of the Land). According to Bhagavad- Gita, Govinda means "master of the senses" or someone who satisfies the senses. In the Mahabharata, when Draupadi's saree was stripped by Dushasana in the court of Hastinapura, it is said that Draupadi prayed towards Lord Krishna, invoking him as "Govinda" at the instance of extreme distress where she could no longer hold her saree to her chest. For this reason, it is believed that "Govinda" is how the Lord is addressed by devotees when they have lost it all and have nothing more to lose. This may be the reason why in colloquial Tamil and Telugu the slang-term "Govinda" sometimes refers to the prospect of losing or failing in something important.

15. Sudden enlightenment. **Satori:** "The road that leads to satori." In the Zen Buddhist tradition, satori refers to the experience of kenshō, "seeing into one's true nature". Ken means "seeing," shō means "nature" or "essence." Satori and kenshō are commonly translated as enlightenment, a word that is also used to translate bodhi, prajna and Buddha- hood.

16. Also a medicinal plant, commonly called **Rohera** or Rehinee (Andersonia rohitaku). See: A dictionary in Hindee and English By John Thomas Thompson, MDCCCXLVI (1846). Printed by Baptist Mission Press, Calcutta

17. **Khaady bhandaar,** {khady bhaNDar} = LARDER(Noun). Usage : We faced an empty larder. Bhandaar: REPOSITORY (pr. {bhaNDar})(Noun). REPERTORY (pr. {bhaNDar})(Noun). Usage : the repertory of the supposed feats of mesmerism. In the

native slang, 'Bandar' means *Bhandaar* or store; *Bandar* also means port.

Chapter 15 - Rohet Gahr

1. Charles Bruce **Chatwin** (13 May 1940 – 18 January 1989) was an English travel writer, novelist, and journalist.
2. **Rohet Gahr** has been the ancestral home of the Singh family since 1622 AD. It was bestowed upon Thakur Dalpat Singh I for his exemplary courage and bravery in numerous military campaigns under the banner of the Rathores. Rohet became one of the most important Jagirs (fiefdoms) of the state of Marwar.
3. *The Songlines* is a 1987 book written by Bruce Chatwin, combining fiction and non-fiction. Chatwin describes a trip to Australia which he has taken for the express purpose of researching Aboriginal song and its connections to nomadic travel. (Bruce Chatwin, by Nicholas Shakespeare. Vintage; New Edition (6 April 2000))
4. **Siddharth Singh**, an eminent hotelier and polo player.
5. Rajasthan is famous for its exquisite artwork and vibrant culture. Embroidery is one of the main artwork and speciality of Rajasthani artists. **Embroidery** is the handicraft of making decorative designs on fabric or other materials with different and special types of threads and needles. Embroidery may include some other materials like beads, mirror, and metal pieces to incorporate better designs. Although, today machine embroidery has made embroider an easy task, but the machine embroidery is still not able to match the elegance and perfection of handmade embroidery by the expert artists of Rajasthan. The women of Rajasthan are experts in this field and make any article look totally different with their excellent embroidery work. Some of the women garments which have embroidery work on them are kaanchlis, ghaghras and odhnis. The masculine garments like angarakha, achkan and jama display very fine work of embroidery done with detailed hand work. While the do-

mestic embroidery is meant to be the field of women, the Rajasthani men are involved in other forms of embroidery like zardosi and danka. There are various forms of embroidery found in Rajasthani culture. In many parts of Rajasthan women live in very conservative communities, leading a restricted life, and are never allowed to learn to read and write. Due to this reason, embroidery becomes a medium of expression of their artistic temperament, allowing them to make living through their art. History The history of embroidery takes us back to 3000 B.C., where man started doing embroidery by the time he started wearing clothes. You can say that it is one of the first art forms known to the human civilization. The ancient paintings and artworks also depict some embroidery works which suggest that the art of embroidery is associated with the humans from the ancient ages. The paintings and record from medieval rulers of India prove that embroidery was an integral part of the royal life style. The painting of royal personalities depicts them in elegant dresses full of precious embroidery work. Mainly the Mughals and the Rajput rulers were very fond of embroidery. Their dresses were prepared by the finest embroidery artists of the state. There are many religious uses and beliefs related to the embroidery work. According to old Hindu beliefs, the shisha embroidery hanged at the doors of the houses and temples keeps the evil away. thread and needles, types of embroidery are Danke ka kaam, mukke ka kaam, zardosi, shisha embroidery, pakko Bharat, mocha surf Bharat, metal embroidery and many others. elements of Rajasthani embroidery is the creativity and imaginative skills of the embroidery artist. The artist first chooses the material on which embroidery is to be done. The next step is to draw a design on that fabric. Then according to the style of the embroidery selected, he picks the needles and the thread to be used for embroidery work. When the outlining of the design is done with thread, then the other elements are added to the designs using different materials like colourful beads, small pieces of mirrors, shiny metal parts. According to the design, the detailing of the embroidery is done by the use of thinner needles and threads. The metal embroidery is mainly done to make ornaments. In this type of embroidery, the metal pieces are attached to the clothe surface with the help of embroidery so extravagantly that it becomes impossible to differentiate the ground surface of the cloth. These ornaments are generally made for the royal personalities. The gold and silver threads are used in zardozi to prepare special handicrafts. The gold and silver pieces are passed through special dies in order to obtain fine threads for embroidery. The time taken to complete an embroidery work depends upon the design and the material of the work. It may take several days to accomplish a well detailed embroidery work. Jaisalmer is the centre for embroidery handicraft in Rajasthan. The handmade handicrafts by Rajasthani artists are recognised worldwide and are in great demand. Rajasthani artists portray the Indian tradition of art and culture perfectly in their artwork of embroidery. When you leave Rajasthan with one of the artistic embroidery work of the Rajasthani artists, you hold a proof of an artistic legacy and knowledge of Rajasthan which is passed from one generation to another from last several centuries.

6. **Jutti** or Joothis are traditional Rajasthani decorative Shoes, handmade, leather, usually colourful, embroidered in a range of styles and embellishments.

7. The Greek word for peacock was *taos* and was related to the Persian "tavus" (as in Takht-i-Tâvus for the famed Peacock Throne). The Hebrew word tuki (plural tukkiyim) has been said to have been derived from the Tamil tokei but sometimes traced to the Egyptian tekh. See: Burton, R F (1884). The book of the sword. Chatto and Windus, London. p. 155. ISBN 0-486-25434-8. The Indian peafowl or blue peafowl (Pavo cristatus), a large and brightly coloured bird, is a species of peafowl native to South Asia, but introduced in many other parts of the world. The Peacock Throne was a famous jeweled throne that was the seat of the Mughal emperors of India. It was commissioned in the early 17th century by emperor Shah Jahan and was located in the Diwan-i-Khas (Hall of Private Audiences) in the Red Fort of

Delhi. The original throne was subsequently captured and taken as a war trophy in 1739 by the Persian king Nadir Shah, and has been lost ever since. A replacement throne based on the original was commissioned afterwards and existed until the Indian Rebellion of 1857 (against the rule of the British East India Company). Muhammad Qudsi, the emperor's favourite poet, was chosen to compose twenty verses that were inscribed in emerald and green enamel on the throne. He praised the matchless skill of the artisans, the "heaven-depleting grandeur" of its gold and jewels, mentioning the date in the letters of the phrase "the throne of the just king". Poet Abu-Talib Kalim was given six pieces of gold for each verse in his poem of sixty-three couplets. The master goldsmith Said Gilani was summoned by the emperor and showered with honours, including his weight in gold coins, given the title "Peerless Master" (Bibadal Khan). Gilani produced a poem with 134 couplets, filled with chronograms. The first twelve reveal the date of the emperor's birth, the following thirty-two the date of his first coronation, then the ninety couplets giving the date of the throne's inauguration. Towards India he turned his reins quickly and went in all glory, Driving like the blowing wind, dapple-grey steed swift as lightning. With bounty and liberality, he returned to the capital; Round his stirrups were the heavens and angels round his reins. A thousand thanks! The beauty of the world has revived With the early glory of the throne of multi-coloured gems." Hasan, Mughal Poetry, pp. 56-61. Biography of Said Gilani Bibadal Khan in Nawaz Khan, Maathir, vol. 1, pp. 396-9

8. A Sankrit derivation of **mayura** is from the root mi for kill and said to mean "killer of snakes". Lal, Krishna (2007). Peacock in Indian art, thought and literature. Abhinav Publications. pp. 11, 26, 139.

9. **Kartikeya** (also known as Skanda or Murugan). A story in the Uttara Ramayana describes the head of the Devas, Indra, who unable to defeat Ravana, sheltered under the wing of peacock and later blessed it with a "thousand eyes" and fearlessness from serpents. Another story has Indra who after being cursed with

a thousand ulcers was transformed into a peacock with a thousand eyes. Anonymous (1891). Ramavijaya (The mythological history of Rama). Bombay: Dubhashi & Co. p. 14. In Buddhist philosophy, the peacock represents wisdom. Choskyi, Ven. Jampa (1988). "Symbolism of Animals in Buddhism". Buddhist Hiamalaya. 1 (1). Greek mythology the origin of the peacocks plumage is explained in the tale of Hera and Argus. The main figure of the Kurdish religion Yezidism, Melek Taus, is most commonly depicted as a peacock. Empson, RHW (1928). The cult of the peacock angel. HF & GWitherby, London. Springett, BH (1922). Secret sects of Syria and the Lebanon. George Allen & Unwin Ltd., London. Peacock motifs are widely used even today such as in the logos of the US NBC and the PTV television networks and the Sri Lankan Airlines.

10. **Tyrberg, T.**, (2002), "The archaeological record of do- mesticated and tamed birds in Sweden" (PDF). Acta zoologica cracoviensia. 45: 215–231. In Scandinavia the oldest record is of a male in the Royal ship-burial at Gokstad in Västfold, Norway (900-905 AD), proving that the Peacock was known to the Norse during the Viking Age. In Sweden however it is not definitely attested until the early sixteenth century when OLAUS MAGNUS (1555) states that they were bred in some numbers in Östergötland and Västergötland. The two Swedish subfossil records are both from Gothenburg and post-medieval (1600-1800 AD) and are possibly connected with the activities of the Swedish East India Company which imported large quantities of Far Eastern merchandise via Gothenburg 1732-1803.

11. **Gwyn, Peter** The King's Cardinal: The rise and Fall of Thomas Wolsey Pimlico 2000 p.113

12. **Partridge, E;** Beale, Paul (2002). A dictionary of slang and unconventional English. Routledge.

13. **Fitzpatrick, J.** (1923). "Folklore of birds and beasts of India". J. Bombay Nat. Hist. Soc. 28 (2): 562–565.

14. Bruce Chatwin's wife, **Elizabeth Chanler**. They married on 21 August 1965. Nicholas Shakespeare (1999). Bruce Chatwin. p. 181.

15. **Raga Bhairavi** for arthritis, Raga Hindol for backache, Raga Pooriya for hypertension, Raga Bhageswari for insomnia, and Raga Jaijaivanti for general pain.

16. "Tell him, Cebes, he replied, that I had no idea of rivalling him or his poems; which is the truth, for I knew that I could not do that. But I wanted to see whether I could purge away a scruple which I felt about certain dreams. In the course of my life I have often had intimations in dreams "that I should make music." The same dream came to me sometimes in one form, and sometimes in another, but always saying the same or nearly the same words: Make and cultivate music, said the dream. And hitherto I had imagined that this was only intended to exhort and encourage me in the study of philosophy, which has always been the pursuit of my life, and is the noblest and best of music." & "The dream was bidding me to do what I was already doing, in the same way that the competitor in a race is bidden by the spectators to run when he is already running. But I was not certain of this, as the dream might have meant music in the popular sense of the word, and being under sentence of death, and the festival giving me a respite, I thought that I should be safer if I satisfied the scruple, and, in obedience to the dream, composed a few verses before I departed. And first I made a hymn in honour of the god of the festival, and then considering that a poet, if he is really to be a poet or maker, should not only put words together but make stories, and as I have no invention, I took some fables of Aesop, which I had ready at hand and knew, and turned them into verse. Tell Evenus this, and bid him be of good cheer; that I would have him come after me if he be a wise man, and not tarry; and that to-day I am likely to be going, for the Athenians say that I must." (**Phaedo**, Sections 60d-61b, translated by Harold North Fowler, 1966, Plato in Twelve Volumes, Vol. 1; Introduction by W.R.M. Lamb. Cambridge, MA, Harvard University Press; London, William Heinemann Ltd. 1966. "**Music is concerned with harmony and rhythm**, so that you may speak of a melody or figure having good rhythm or good harmony-the term is correct enough; but to speak metaphorically of a melody

or figure having a "good colour," as the masters of choruses do, is not allowable, although you can speak of the melodies or figures of the brave and the coward, praising the one and censuring the other. And not to be tedious, let us say that the figures and melodies which are expressive of virtue of soul or body, or of images of virtue, are without exception good, and those which are expressive of vice are the reverse of good." (Sections 655a-b) Laws By Plato 360 B.C.E. Translated by Benjamin Jowett, The collected works of Plato (online at MIT and the Perseus Digital Library).

17. **Thakur SIDHARTH SINGH,** 14th and present Thakur Saheb of Rohet and Double Tazimi Sirayat of Jodhpur since 2nd February 2014. An accomplished polo player and successful hotelier, owner and operator of Mihir Garh, recent winner of the World Boutique Hotel Award (2013); married Thakurani Rashmi Singh, and has issue. Kunwar Avijit Singh & Baisa Jahnvi Singh. See: World of Royalty, 13 May 2016. http://members.iinet.net.au/~royalty/ips/r/rohet. html

18. **Thakur MANVENDRA SINGH,** 13th Thakur of Rohet , President, Jodhpur Cricket Association 1985/2014; Vice- President, Rajasthan Cricket Association; Member of the Board and Commitee of Mayo College, Ajmer; Member of the Board and Commitee of Chopasni Mayur School in Jodhpur; he served as the Up Zial Pramukh of Pali; married Thakurani Jayendra Kumari, and had issue, one son and two daughters. He died in a car accident on 2nd February 2014 near Pali. See: World of Royalty, 13 May 2016. http://members. iinet.net.au/~royalty/ips/r/rohet.html Thakur or Thakore (Sanskrit) is a feudal title and a surname used by various communities in India and Nepal The word Thakur means lord, god or master, The title was used by rulers of several princely states including Ambliara, Vala, Morbi and Varsoda. In the zamindari system, Brahmins & Rajput Thakurs were landlords who used to collect revenue in their jagir (feudatory estate). A Thakur's (e)state, called Thakorate, could occasionally reach salute state rank (mostly Maharajas or Nawabs -not all of those- or at last -few of the- Rajas) in the British Em-

pire of India. Page 915, Yule, Henry. Hobson-Jobson: A glossary of colloquial Anglo- Indian words and phrases... London: J. Murray, 1903. "Thakur Name Meaning". Ancestry.co.uk. Retrieved 2016-11-12. Powell, Baden Henry Baden (2015-09-27). "Full Text". The Land-Systems of British India, Vol. 1: Being a Manual of the Land-Tenures and of the Systems of Land- Revenue Administration Prevalent in the Several Provinces. Forgotten Books.

Chapter 16 - The Road to Benares

1. According to the *Vamana Purana*, the river **Varuna** was created by the gods alongside the Asi River. It is also mentioned in the *Mahabharata*. Varuna is a Vedic deity associated initially with the sky, later also with the seas as well as Ṛta (justice) and Satya (truth). He is found in the oldest layer of Vedic literature of Hinduism, such as hymn 7.86 of the Rigveda. He is also mentioned in the Tamil grammar work Tolkāppiyam, as Kadalon the god of sea and rain. He is said to be the son of Kashyapa (one of the seven ancient sages). In the Hindu Puranas, Varuna is the god of oceans, his vehicle is a Makara (crocodile) and his weapon is a Pasha (noose, rope loop). He is the guardian deity of the western direction. In some texts, he is the father of the Vedic sage Vasishtha. Makara appears as the *vahana* (vehicle) of the river goddess Ganga. In Hindu tradition, the theonym Váruṇa is described as a derivation from the verbal root *vṛ* ("to surround, to cover" or "to restrain, bind") by means of a suffixal -uṇa-, for an interpretation of the name as "he who covers or binds", in reference to the cosmological ocean or river encircling the world, but also in reference to the "binding" by universal law or Ṛta. Varuna is found in Japanese Buddhist mythology as Suiten. He is also found in Jainism.

2. The **Yamuna** (Hindustani: pronounced [jamuna]) is the second-largest tributary river of the Ganga and the longest tributary in India.

3. **Xuanzang** (602 – 664), born Chen Yi, was a Chinese Buddhist monk, scholar, traveler, and translator who traveled to India in the seventh century and described the interaction between Chinese Buddhism and Indian Buddhism during the reign of Harsha. He became famous for his seventeen-year overland journey to India (including Nalanda Monastery), which is recorded in detail in the classic Chinese text Dà Táng Xīyù Jì (Great Tang Records on the Western Regions), which in turn provided the inspiration for the novel Journey to the West written by Wu Cheng'en during the Ming dynasty, around nine centuries after Xuanzang's death.

4. **Advaita Acharya** (1434–1559), born Kamalaksha Bhattacharjee was a companion of the founder of the Gaudiya Vaishnava movement, Chaitanya Mahaprabhu, and guru of Haridasa Thakur (a prominentVaishnavasaint known for being instrumental in the initial propagation of theHare Krishnamovement).

5. **Dargah** is derived from a Persian word which literally means "portal" or "threshold." The Persian word is a composite of "dar" meaning "door, gate" and "gah" meaning "place". Many Muslims believe their wishes are fulfilled after they offer prayer or service at a dargah of the saint they follow. Devotees tie threads of mannat (Persian: "grace, favour, praise") at dargahs and contribute for langar and pray at dargahs. Dargahs dotted the landscape of Punjab. Dargahs in South Asia, have historically been a place for all faiths since the medieval times; for example, the Ajmer Sharif Dargah was meeting place for Hindus and Muslims to pay respect and even to the revered Saint Mu'in al-Din Chishti.

6. Mu'izz ad-Din Muhammad Ghori (Persian), born Shihab ad-Din (1149 – March 15, 1206), also known as **Muhammad of Ghor, was the Sultan of the Ghurid Empire** along with his brother Ghiyath ad-Din Muhammad from 1173 to 1202 and as the sole ruler from 1202 to 1206. He is credited with laying the foundation of Muslim rule in the Indian subcontinent, which lasted for several centuries. He reigned over a territory spanning over parts of modern-day Afghanistan, Bangladesh, Iran, Northern

India, Pakistan, Tajikistan and Turkmenistan. The Ghurids or Ghorids (Persian: self-designation:, Shansabānī) were a dynasty of Iranian origin from the Ghor region of present-day central Afghanistan, but the exact ethnic origin is uncertain. The dynasty converted to Sunni Islam from Buddhism, after the conquest of Ghor by the Ghaznavid sultan Mahmud of Ghazni in 1011. The dynasty overthrew the Ghaznavid Empire in 1186 when Sultan Mu'izz ad-Din Muhammad of Ghor conquered the last Ghaznavid capital of Lahore. At their zenith, the Ghurid empire encompassed Khorasan in the west and reached northern India as far as Bengal in the east.

7. **Wazir of Oudh. Asaf-ud-Daula** (b. 23 September 1748 – d. 21 September 1797) was the Nawab wazir of Oudh (a vassal of the British) ratified by Shah Alam II, from 26 January 1775 to 21 September 1797.

8. **Rafa'at wa Awal-i-Martabat Raja Sri Chait Singh Sahib Bahadur** (d. 29 March 1810) commonly known as Chait Singh was a ruler of Benares State in northern India. Chet Singh Ghat in Varanasi. Chait Singh was the eldest son of Raja Balwant Singh, and succeeded to the throne of Benares in 1770 after the death of his father. During the Eighteenth Century in northern India, the Mughal Empire was disintegrating, while the power of the East India Company was growing. Balwant Singh was a zamindar who took the title of raja, and rajas of Benares were still formally subject to the Nawab of Awadh (Oudh). The Nawab wished to hold total suzerainty over the zamindari. British authorities encouraged the Nawab to recognise Chait Singh as zamindar in 1773. In 1775 the Nawab, by now infuriated with the East India Company, transferred the domain to the Company under the direct control of the Governor-General of India, Warren Hastings. Under the new British terms, Chait Singh was empowered to contribute cavalry and maintenance grants for the Company's sepoy battalions. The Raja refused to do this and he began to secretly correspond with enemies of the Company in hopes of forcibly breaking the arrangement. The company discovered his plan, stripped him of his position and placed

him under house arrest in August 1781, pending an interview with Hastings. He escaped, killing his British guards and gathered his forces, appealing for assistance from nearby rulers, who did nothing. In severe battle with the Company's forces, Chait Singh's troops were defeated, the rebellion crushed, and the zamindari confiscated and given to his nephew Rafa'at wa Awal-i-Martabat Raja Sri Mahip Narayan Singh Sahib Bahadur on 14 September 1781. Chait Singh himself took shelter in Awadh, and then Gwalior, where he was granted a jagir for a while until it was later confiscated. He died in Gwalior on 29 March 1810 in obscurity, leaving three sons. The incident greatly tarnished Hastings' image and capability, leading to a failed attempt to impeach him by the British parliament.

9. **George Frederick Cherry** (1761–1799) was a British-born political officer of the East India Company, murdered in Benares by Wazir Ali Khan as part of a minor insurrection against the British. He was the British Resident at Lucknow until 1796, immediately prior to the period in which Wazir Ali Khan was removed as Nawab of Awadh by the British and replaced by Saadat Ali Khan II. The role of a resident extended to intelligence gathering, and at this, in the relative turbulence of late 18th century Awadh, Cherry excelled, running a network of spies and informers - such as Mirza Abu Taleb Khan, who wrote about some of his interactions with the East India Company. He had made sufficient enemies in Lucknow by 1796 that he was relocated to Benares, considered a less exposed town, to act as political-agent to the Governor General. In 1797 Wazir Ali Khan was deposed and required by the British to live in Benares with a pension. The young Ali - only 19 - was far from satisfied with his lot, and indications before 1799, and evidence of later enquiries suggests he was plotting against the British and with a view to regaining his lost position. By 1799, the British had come to the conclusion that Ali should be required to live in Calcutta - further from his power-base, and much more obviously under the eye of the British. It fell to Cherry to impart this news. Ali appears to have been informed of his fate in the early part of

January 1799, and his remonstrances fell on deaf ears. Appearing to acquiesce to the situation, he gave it out that he would relocate on the 15 or 16 January. On 13 January Cherry was informed that Ali would visit him the following morning, and on the 14th Ali appeared at breakfast time, leading a more-or-less normal 200-strong entourage. Cherry escorted Khan and four supporters into his house. Ali took the opportunity to complain loudly about his lot, to assert promises broken by the British, and to blame Cherry for failing to look after his interests. Then, in what looked like a choreographed movement, an associate, Waris Ali, restrained the sitting Cherry from behind his seat, Wazir Ali Khan struck Cherry with his sword, and Cherry was further struck by others of Ali's party. Cherry managed to struggle out of the house, but was quickly killed. Two of Cherry's colleagues were also killed: his secretary, Mr. Evans, was stabbed, escaped outside, and was shot whilst seeking to flee; and a Captain Conway, residing with Cherry, was also killed. Two other British residents of Benares were also killed, in what came to be known as the Massacre of Benares.-- Davis, Sir John Francis (1871). Vizier Ali Khan; or, The massacre of Benares: a chapter in British Indian history. London: Spottiswoode and Company. pp. 28–31, 40.

10. **Sigra or Si'ghra** is a downtown area in Varanasi district in the state of Uttar Pradesh.

11. **Sikraul** is a locality in Varanasi City in Uttar Pradesh State, India. It is belongs to Varanasi Division.

12. A **linga** or a lingam is a very complex symbol of Hinduism. It is associated with Shiva, supreme god in main gods of the Hindus. The Hindu scriptures say that a linga represents energy and strength. In almost all the temples of Shiva, Shiva is shown in the form of a linga.

13. **Sati** or suttee[note 1] was a historical Hindu practice, in which a widow sacrifices herself by sitting atop her deceased husband's funeral pyre. The extent to which sati was practised in history is not known with clarity. However, during the early modern Mughal period, it was notably associated with elite Hindu Ra-

jput clans in western India, marking one of the points of divergence between Hindu Rajputs and the Muslim Mughals. In the early 19th century, the East India Company, in the process of extending its rule to most of India, initially tolerated the practice; William Carey, a British Christian evangelist, noted 438 incidences within a 30-mile (48-km) radius of the capital Calcutta, in 1803, despite its ban within Calcutta. Between 1815 and 1818, the number of incidents of sati in Bengal doubled from 378 to 839. Opposition to the practice of sati by British Christian evangelists, such as William Carey, and Hindu reformers such as Ram Mohan Roy, ultimately led the British Governor-General of India Lord William Bentinck to enact the Bengal Sati Regulation, 1829, declaring the practice of burning or burying alive of Hindu widows to be punishable by the criminal courts. Isolated incidents of sati were recorded in India in the late 20th century, leading the Indian government to promulgate the Sati (Prevention) Act, 1987, criminalising the aiding or glorifying of sati.

14. **Bhairondth:** "The tliird deity visited was Bhairondth, the god of Benares, who keeps the city from evil spirits, and is armed with a danda or cudgel, which it is reported is freely used in the discharge of his duty. " Ah, this is a god to my liking surely," said Monohur. " His club ought to be a terror to the evil-minded." "And so it is," responded the Sunydst; "it effectually keeps the city clear of all knaves, mischief-makers, and evil-doers. But the god holds, nevertheless, a subordinate position, for he is only Mahddeva's chief officer of the peace." Speaking in this vein, they proceeded to the Manikarnika Ghat, which stands in the middle of the river-bank of Bendres, and is held sacred to Vishnu, though it derives its name from an earring of Mahadeva, or of his wife, having fallen into the sacred well."--*The Young Zemindár; His Erratic Wanderings and Eventful Return*; In Thtee Volumes. by Horatio Bickerstaffe Rowney, 1888. See also by same author: The *Wild Tribes Of India* (1882). "The reader will do well not to believe this story, but rather to conclude that much of the water when drunk is in a very unwholesome condi-

tion, and is the cause of disease. Probably the indications given of this temple may be sufficient to those with local knowledge to identify it. I can only suggest doubtfully that it is either the Bisheswar (or Golden temple of Siva), or the temple of Bhairondth. See: *The Sacred City of the Hindus: An Account of Benares in Ancient and Modern Times* by Rev, M. A. Sherring, 1868. ," p. 61.-- *Travels in India* by Jean-Baptiste Tavernier Baron of Aubonne: v. I: Translated from the Original French Edition of 1676 with a Biographical Sketch of the Author, Notes, Appendices, Etc.: v. I

15. Svarga (Sanskrit), also known as *Swarga* or Svarga Loka, is one of the seven higher lokas (esoteric plane) in Hindu cosmology. *Prithvi* or *Prithvi* Mata the Vast One" is the Sanskrit name for the earth as well as the name of a devi (goddess) in Hinduism and some branches of Buddhism.

16. In Indian religions, *Patala* (Sanskrit: *pātāla*, lit. 'that which is below the feet') or Pathalam, denotes the subterranean realms of the universe; the netherworld or hell.

17. Tripathagā f. "flowing through heaven, earth, and the lower regions", the Ganges etc.

18. Sādhanā (Sanskrit) is a generic term coming from the yogic tradition that refers to any spiritual exercise that is aimed at progressing the sādhaka towards the very ultimate expression of his or her life in this reality. It includes a variety of disciplines in Hindu, Buddhist, Jain and Sikh traditions that are followed in order to achieve various spiritual or ritual objectives. It is the long practice for attaining detachment from worldly things, which can be a goal of a Sadhu; done for attaining detachment from worldly things, which can be a goal of a Sadhu. It is the constant efforts to achieve maximum level of perfection in all streams in day-to-day life can be described. Everything can be sādhanā. The way you eat, the way you sit, the way you stand, the way you breathe, the way you conduct your body, mind and your energies and emotions – this is sādhanā. Sādhanā does not mean any specific kind of activity, sādhanā means you are using everything as a tool for your wellbeing. Sādhanā is a disci-

pline undertaken in the pursuit of a goal. Abhyāsa is repeated practice performed with observation and reflection. Kriyā, or action, also implies perfect execution with study and investigation. Therefore, sādhanā, abhyāsa, and kriyā all mean one and the same thing. A sādhaka, or practitioner, is one who skillfully applies...mind and intelligence in practice towards a spiritual goal.

19. Rishi Jahnu appears in the story of the Ganges and Bhagiratha. When the Ganges came to earth after being released from Lord Shiva's locks, her torrential waters wreaked havoc with Jahnu's fields and penance. Angered by this, the great sage drank up all of the Ganges' waters to punish her. Seeing this, the Gods prayed to the sage to release the Ganges, so that she could proceed on her mission to release the souls of the ancestors of Bhagiratha. Jahnu relented and he released the Ganges from his ear. For this, the Ganges river is also known as Jahnavi, meaning "daughter of Jahnu".

20. The Kali Yuga, in Hinduism, is the fourth and worst of the four yugas (world ages) in a Yuga Cycle, preceded by Dvapara Yuga and followed by the next cycle's Krita (Satya) Yuga. It is believed to be the present age, which is full of conflict and sin. "Kali" of Kali Yuga means "strife", "discord", "quarrel" or "contention" and Kali Yuga is associated with the demon Kali (not to be confused with the goddess Kālī).

21. The Sarasvati River (IAST: sárasvatī nadí) is a deified river mentioned in the Rig Veda[1] and later Vedic and post-Vedic texts. It played an important role in the Vedic religion, appearing in all but the fourth book of the Rigveda. s a physical river, in the oldest texts of the Rig Veda she is described as a "great and holy river in north-western India," but in the middle and late Rig Vedic books she is described as a small river ending in "a terminal lake (samudra)." As the goddess Sarasvati, the other referent for the term "Sarasvati" which developed into an independent identity in post-Vedic times,[4] she is also described as a powerful river and mighty flood. The Sarasvati is also considered by Hindus to exist in a metaphysical form, in which it

formed a confluence with the sacred rivers Ganges and Yamuna, at the Triveni Sangam. According to Michael Witzel, superimposed on the Vedic Sarasvati river is the heavenly river Milky Way, which is seen as "a road to immortality and heavenly afterlife."

22. The Satya Yuga (a.k.a. Krita Yuga), in Hinduism, is the first and best of the four yugas (world ages) in a Yuga Cycle, preceded by Kali Yuga of the previous cycle and followed by Treta Yuga. Satya Yuga is known as the age of truth, when humanity is governed by gods, and every manifestation or work is close to the purest ideal and humanity will allow intrinsic goodness to rule supreme. It is sometimes referred to as the "Golden Age".

23. Luc Paul Maurice Besson (French: born 18 March 1959) is a French film director, screenwriter, and producer. He directed or produced the films Subway (1985), The Big Blue (1988), and La Femme Nikita (1990). Besson is associated with the Cinéma du look film movement. He has been nominated for a César Award for Best Director and Best Picture for his films Léon: The Professional and The Messenger: The Story of Joan of Arc. He won Best Director and Best French Director for his sci-fi action film The Fifth Element (1997). He wrote and directed the 2014 sci-fi action film *Lucy* and the 2017 space opera film *Valerian and the City of a Thousand Planets. On India, Besson has said: "People don't go very fast here but they overtake recklessly. Now I understand why there are so many accidents in India,"; "People here look gentle but they drive crazy,"*

24. *Sannyasi, (Sanskrit: "abandoning" or "throwing down") also spelled sannyasin, in Hinduism, a religious ascetic who has renounced the world by performing his own funeral and abandoning all claims to social or family standing. On reflection he believe he is a Vedic Astrologer.* "You need to understand, India is not just about the Vedas or Vedic culture. Sage Vyasa, the person who compiled the four Vedas – his father was an Aryan and his mother was a Dravidian. In spite of that, in South India, they don't ascribe to the Vedas. Dravidian culture never went for astrology by looking at the stars, they made predictions by looking at people. Here,

we have what is called Nadi Joshyam. But the Aryan culture came with astrology. Astrology is an interpretation of astronomy. If you try to interpret something, invariably you miss a lot of points. So it is a mis-interpretation because you missed a lot of things. The reason why the Aryan culture looked at the stars so much is, they were nomadic. They were always travelling. Since there were no roads, they needed to figure out which is north, which is south, which is east, which is west. When the sun was up, they knew. Once the sun set, there was really nothing except fire and stars. So the Aryan culture revolved around fire and the stars. Even today, if people want to get married or do anything auspicious, they go around fire because nomadic cultures lived by fire and stars. Fire gave you light, heat, and protection from wild animals. The stars told you approximately which way to go. Slowly, observing the stars, they figured which way to travel. They kept looking up and their knowledge of the stars increased. Interpretations started, and they developed a certain mastery and knowledge about the stars. I only hope all predictions go wrong for you. Then it means your life is happening wonderfully. In India, for twenty-five rupees, or fifty cents, they will write your life. Let your life not be so bad. It does not matter what the hell happens, let something other than the prediction happen to you. Is that okay? May your predictions and dreams not come true. Because a prediction is just a compromised dream."

25. Sanskrit word prāṇa including breath or respiration; the breath of life, vital air, principle of life (usually plural in this sense, there being five such vital airs generally assumed, but three, six, seven, nine, and even ten are also spoken of); energy or vigour; the spirit or soul. Of these meanings, the concept of "vital air" is used by Bhattacharyya to describe the concept as used in Sanskrit texts dealing with pranayama, the manipulation of the breath. Thomas McEvilley translates prāṇa as "spirit-energy". The breath is understood to be its most subtle material form, but is also believed to be present in the blood, and most concentrated in men's semen and women's vaginal fluid.

26. Ashvamedha, (Sanskrit: "horse sacrifice") also spelled ash-wamedha, grandest of the Vedic religious rites of ancient India, performed by a king to celebrate his paramountcy. The ceremony is described in detail in various Vedic writings, particularly the Shatapatha Brahmana.

27. Manikarnika Ghat is one of the holiest[citation needed] cremation grounds among the sacred riverfronts (ghats), alongside the river Ganga, in the city of Varanasi in the Indian state of Uttar Pradesh. In Hinduism, death is considered as a gateway to another life marked by the results of one's karma. It is believed that a dead human's soul attains moksha, and hence breaks the cycle of rebirth when cremated here. Thus, scores of the elderly across the whole country seek to walk up to its edges, and spend their last days absorbing the charisma of the ghat making death painless and insignificant to be pondered upon. The ghat is named after Sati's earrings which fell here.

Chapter 17 - Fatephur Sikri

1. While Shari'ah refers to obeying the laid down religious laws, **Tariqah** refers to the spiritual way and the final stage of Haqiqah is recognising the inner truth. The Shahadah says— La ilaha illa 'Llah, Muhammadun rasulu Allah, meaning 'There is no god except God, Muhamad is the Messenger of Allah'.

2. **The Buland Darwaza** or Gate of Victory, one of the great masterpieces of Indian architecture and the most imposing monument in Fatephur Sikri. A towering archway topped with lines of minars and chattri cupolas. I have not seen anything like it in my life.

3. I am impressed by a Christian inscription. Emblazoned all around the arch is a panel of kufic script which reads: "Jesus, Son of Mary (on whom be peace) said: **The World is a Bridge, pass over it, but build no houses upon it.** He who hopes for a day, may hope for eternity; but the World endures but an hour. **Spend it in prayer, for the rest is unseen.**"

4. "**Akbar** took to wife the daughters of two great Rajput houses. He gave the chiefs or their brethren high rank in his armies, sent them with their contingents to command on distant frontiers, and succeeded in attaching the Rajputs generally. Under the early Mughal Emperors, the chiefs constantly entered the imperial service as governors or generals— there were at one time 47 Rajput contingents— and the headlong charges of their cavalry became famous in the wars of the empire. Jahangir and Shah Jahan were sons of Rajput mothers ; and Shah Jahan in exile was protected at Udaipur up to the time of his accession. Thus, whereas up to the time of Akbar, the Rajput clans had to a certain extent maintained their political isolation, though within limits that were always changing, from the end of the 16th century their chiefs became feudatories of the Empire—which is their natural and honourable relation to the paramount power in India. Count von Noer, whose interesting 'Life of Akbar' is published in translation by Mrs. Beveridge". [– Kaiser Akbar. Ein Versuch über die Geschichte Indiens im sechszehnten Jahrhundert. 1-2. 23+516, 12+600 p. Leiden 1881-85 (2. ed. by G. von Buchwald)], The Imperial Gazette, Vol. 11.

5. A **chhajja**is an overhanging eave or roof covering found in Indian architecture. Curved chhajja became popular in Mughal architecture particularly during and after the reign of Shah Jahan. By the time that buildings like the Jahangiri Mahal at Agra and the palace complex at Fathpur Sikri were built, it emerged as a popular and important architectural element of Mughal architecture. (Azam, N., 2003, "Development of Mosque Architecture Under Babur". Proceedings of the Indian History Congress. 64: 1406–1413).

6. **Diwan-i-Khas** or Hall of Private Audience, is a plain square building with four *chhatris* on the roof. However, it is famous for its central pillar, which has a square base and an octagonal shaft, both carved with bands of geometric and floral designs, further its thirty-six serpentine brackets support a circular platform for Akbar, which is connected to each corner of the building on the first floor, by four stone walkways. It is here that

Akbar had representatives of different religions discuss their faiths and gave private audience.

7. *The pursuit of reason ('aql) and rejection of traditionalism (taqlid) are so brilliantly patent as to be above the need of argument. If traditionalism was proper, the prophets would merely have followed their own elders (and not come with new messages)*-- **Akbar's sayings in A'in-i Akbari**, Naval Kishor, III, p. 179.

8. *The Diwan-i-Khas* is also known as The Jewel House.

9. *Jami Masjid* or the main congregational mosque of the town is the most important building here and houses two monumental gateways known as *Buland Darwaja* commemorating Akbar's victory over Deccan and Badshahi Darwaja, the reserved entrance for the emperor to the mosque. It also houses a big and beautiful courtyard with the splendid architectural masterpiece known as the Tomb of Salim Chishti, which is one of the most sought-after buildings in Fatehpur Sikri. The Jama Masjid is a 16th-century congregational mosque in the UNESCO World Heritage Site of Fatehpur Sikri in Uttar Pradesh, India. Constructed by Mughal Emperor Akbar, it is one of the largest mosques in India. It is a most sought-after pilgrimage site by the devotees. It is also one of the most visited tourist destinations in Agra district. Some of the designs of the mosque reflect beautiful Iranian architecture. Akbar commissioned the Jama Masjid as part of his new capital city of Fatehpur Sikri. The structure was one of the first sites constructed in the city, and was completed sometime between 1571 and 1574, according to its own inscriptions. The mosque was in honour of the Sufi Shaikh Salim Chishti, Akbar's spiritual advisor. It was also meant to serve as a khanqah (monastic school) for the Shaikh's descendants. In its time, it was extolled by various authors and travellers for its beauty and grandeur (Alfieri, Bianca Maria, 'Islamic Architecture of the Indian Subcontinent', 2000. The mosque played a part in Akbar's religious designs. In 1579, he delivered the khutbah (sermon) for a congregational prayer attended by the inhabitants of Fatehpur Sikri. The reading of the khutbah was typically reserved for an imam- hence was perceived as radi-

cal. Akbar also joined the people in their prayer, and was even seen sweeping the floors of the mosque. Akbar's was anything but your regular ruler! The Jama Masjid at Fatehpur Sikri remained a "symbol of Mughal heritage and pride" after Akbar's rule (Asher, C. B., 'Architecture of Mughal India', CUP, 1992, p. 202). The mosque was heavily admired by Akbar's son and successor Jahangir, who called it one of his father's greatest architectural achievements. Jahangir discussed the mosque complex at length with his son Khurram during a stay at Fatehpur Sikri in 1619. Khurram went on to become Mughal Emperor Shah Jahan, and cited this mosque as the model for his own Jama Masjid at Delhi. Buland Gate *Jama Masjid.* is surrounded by enclosure walls; just outside the southern wall is a large *baoli* (octagonal step-well). Similar to the rest of Fatehpur Sikri, the mosque is made of locally-quarried red sandstone. It also employs yellow sandstone, marble, and slate for decoration, and features Persian and Arabic calligraphy. At the time of its construction, the mosque was the largest in Mughal India. It represents a fusion of Islamic, Hindu, and Jain architecture, with a marked Gujarati influence. Asher asserts that the mosque draws elements from the Jama Masjid at Mandu, and the Jama Masjid at Chanderi, both pre-Mughal structures. Alfieri also sees an inspiration from pre-Mughal Jama Masjids, but instead cites those at Atala and Champaner. The mosque complex is entered via three gates. The eastern gate, known as the *Badshahi Darwaza* (Imperial Gate), was used by Akbar to access the mosque. It is decorated using cut mosaics. The northern and southern gates may have historically resembled each other - however, in 1573 the southern gate was rebuilt by Akbar as the Buland Darwaza (High Gate) to celebrate the success of his military campaign in Gujarat. It is the most prominent gate and a monument in itself, featuring hallways and rooms over its many floors. [Asher says that it is more likely the gate was built to emphasise Akbar's relationship with the Chishti Order. The sahn (courtyard) is of dimensions 165 m by 130 m. An ablution tank lies in its centre. The courtyard's northern, southern, and eastern sides are lined by *dalans* (arcades). These are shaded by a continuous, projecting *chhajja* (eave), which is supported by corbels. Chhatris top the parapets of these arcades. The inner bay of the arcades is divided into hujra (cells), probably used as sleeping quarters for devotees. Towards the northern side of the courtyard are the Tomb of Salim Chishti and the tomb of Islam Khan. The former is contrasted from the red sandstone of the Jama Masjid complex by its wholesale use of *makrana* marble. Underground water reservoirs lie beneath the courtyard. The rectangular prayer hall (dimensions 89 m by 20 m) lies on the western end of the courtyard, facing Mecca in keeping with Islamic tradition. Its facade is dominated by a grand *pishtaq*, which contains three arched entryways. Three domes rise from the roof, corresponding to the three bays into which the hall is divided. The central bay is square and richly decorated, featuring geometric marble inlays as well as polychrome floral paintings. Its western wall bears ornate mihrabs (prayer niches), bordered by mosaics and glazed tile. The two side bays are colonnaded halls, each containing a square chamber. These halls contain their own decorated mihrabs, and are supported by Hindu-style pillars. At the extremities of the prayer hall are zenanas (women's galleries).

10. *Diwan-I-Am* or Hall of Public Audience, situated near Agra Gate, was the place where Akbar heard petitions of the general public and did justice every morning. It is said that it was so built because of Akbar's belief in 'sun worship'. This chamber showcases a unique stone tiled roof and a exquisitely carved frieze. The chamber is broadly divided into three parts, with the space in front, the seat of the emperor in centre surrounded by the stone screens arranged in six-pointed star pattern and the portion masked by a beautiful screen meant for the royal ladies. A gracefully carved balustrade surrounded the chamber. The building is artistically prominent by skilful use of pillars, brackets, *chhajjas* and kiosks at regular intervals in a masterly composition. At the time of Akbar, both this complex and *Diwan-I-Khas* made ostentatious display of rich fabrics and other beautiful decorative items befitting the grandeur of the emperor.

11. **Ankh Michauli** (Blind Man's Buff Hose) was used by Akbar to play hide and seek with the women of his harem, Secret coffers and deep recesses in the walls of this building suggest that perhaps it was a treasury for valuable things such as gold and silver coins and secret documents. This building has three oblong halls of equal size with the central hall placed horizontally and two other halls placed at right angles on its either side. These halls have a central court and are interconnected by corridors with extremely wide openings. The walls are made up of rubble masonry and are very thick. *Ankh Michauli* has high ceilings. The bottom of the struts in the central hall supporting the beams of the ceiling have been beautifully moulded into the head of a truncated monster called 'Makar' in Hindu mythology, who is believed to be the guardian of treasures. The halls of this building also manifest simple mouldings and carved brackets lending them a grand look, while the wide *chhajja* around the central hall looks quite imposing. The two stairways to the east lead one to the roof.

12. **Pachisi** is a cross and circle board game that originated in Ancient India. It is described in the ancient text Mahabharata under the name of "Pasha". It is played on a board shaped like a symmetrical cross. A player's pieces move around the board based upon a throw of six or seven cowrie shells, with the number of shells resting with aperture upwards indicating the number of spaces to move. The name of the game is derived from the Hindi word paccīs, meaning "twenty-five", the largest score that can be thrown with the cowrie shells; thus this game is also known by the name Twenty-Five. Philologist Irving Finkel wrote: "The game of Pachisi was played by Akbar in a truly regal manner. The Court itself, divided into red and white squares, being the board, and an enormous stone raised on four feet, representing the central point. It was here that Akbar and his courtiers played this game; sixteen young slaves from the harem wearing the players' colours, represented the pieces, and moved to the squares according to the throw of the dice. It is said that the Emperor took such a fancy to playing the game on this

grand scale that he had a court for pachisi constructed in all his palaces, and traces of such are still visible at Agra and Allahabad."- Falkener 1892, pp. 257–58; quoting M.L. Rousselet: *India and its Native Princes*, 1876.

13. **The Deer Minaret** *Hiran Minar* was used by hunting parties from the ancient city of Fatehpur Sikri City of Victory Stone tusks protrude from the tower from which the royal party would shoot at animals Mughal Emperor Akbar built the city as his capital in 1569 but was later abandoned due to the acute lack of water Many of the red sandstone buildings still survive intact It is some 25 miles 40km from Agra and the Taj Mahal

14. **Tasawwuf.** is an Arabic term for the process of realizing ethical and spiritual ideals; meaning literally "becoming a Sufi," tasawwuf is generally translated as Sufism. The etymologies for the term Sufi are various. Sufism, or in Arabic, tasawwuf, is an umbrella term which refers to the inner mystical dimension of Islam. The same linguistic root also generates from the word for wool in Arabic; hence, a Sufi is one who wears a wool, or suf, garment. This refers to the practice of some ascetic mystics who would wear a simple wool garment. The word in Persian for those who wear wool is "Pashmina Push", a common reference in Sufi poetry. Sufism has a highly diverse set of traditions, with adherents from many different walks of life and with different levels of involvement.

15. **'To die before you die.'** The syncretic identity of the Sufis. The premise of *dying before you die* is to achieve self-liberation and become free from worldly concerns, while continuing to live in this physical life....When you die before you die, you release all of your attachment to your physical form, and the identity you have created for yourself in this life. *How can you live if you have not yet died?* To find joy within before one dies is key here. This reminds me of Jesus's saying: "Whosoever shall seek to save his life shall lose it; and whosoever shall lose his life shall preserve it." **Luke 17:33.**

16. **The Suffah** was not an enclosed space but was open on three sides and became a place which many of the poorer companions

would occupy. The great scholar of hadith, Hadhrat Ibn Hajr al-Asqalani (r.a), relates to us in his work Fath-ul-Bari that: 'As-Suffahh is the place in the back portion of the Prophet's Masjid. It had a covering and was prepared so that estranged people could stay there, people who had neither homes nor families'. (As-Sallaabee. The Noble Life of the Prophet. Vol.2. Pg.735.)

17. **The Ashab us-Suffah (Companions of the Bench),** In the early days of Islam the *Qiblah* (direction to face for prayer) was not the Baitul Haraam (Holy Ka'aba) but instead Muslims prayed towards Jerusalem (Bait-ul-Quds). The Holy Prophet (s.a.w) prayed towards Jerusalem out of obedience to the Will of *Allah* (s.w.t), however his heart was always inclined towards the *Ka'aba*. For this reason, when in Mecca, he would always position himself in the prayer so that he was facing both the Holy *Ka'aba* and Jerusalem. After the migration of the Muslims to *Medina* (hijra) the Holy Prophet (s.a.w) was not able to continue this practice (Jerusalem being north of Medina and Mecca being south of Medina) and the Holy Prophet (s.a.w), along with the companions, would pray only towards Jerusalem. The positioning of Jerusalem dictated that they would stand in the South-Western part of the Prophet's Mosque. This lasted until Allah (s.w.t) revealed the verse: "Verily, We see thee turning thy face often to heaven; surely, then, will we make thee turn to the *Qiblah* which thou likest. So turn thy face towards the Sacred Mosque; and wherever you may be, turn your faces towards it. And they to whom the Book has been given know that this is the truth from their Lord; and Allah is not unmindful of what they do." (The Holy Qur'an Chapter 2, verse 144) After this the Southern door of the Prophet's Mosque was closed and a new one opened in the Northern part of the Mosque facing the new *Qiblah* – Baitul Haraam (Holy Ka'aba). A shade was then erected, under the instructions of the Holy Prophet (s.a.w), which was fixed to the wall where the old *Qiblah* used to be (this was now the back wall of the Mosque). The type of shade, or raised bench, which was erected, is known in Arabic as a *Suffah* and therefore that quarter of the Mosque became known as *Al-Suffah*.

18. **Al-Fuqara.** Those who have more than half of their essentials in terms of money and assets are regarded as *al-Masakin*. Whereas, those who own less than half are from *al-Fuqara'*. *Al-Fuqara*: Those whose economic state is worse than the needy.

19. **Haji Syed Salman Chishty** is born on 9th March 1982 among the "Syed o Saddat" and "Chishty Sufi family of Ajmer Sharif" whose lineage goes back all the way to The Holy Prophet of Islam Hz.SYEDNA MOHAMMED through HIS blessed grandson Hz. SYEDNA IMAM HUSSAIN (A.S.) He being the 26th Generation Gaddi-Nashin (Hereditary Custodians/Key Holders) through His Chishty family which has been engaged in serving at the globally famed, acknowledged and renowned center of Peace and Unity for the whole of Humanity – THE BLESSED DARGAH AJMER SHARIF SUFI SHRINE of the 11th Century Sufi Grand Master Teacher Hz.KHAWAJA MOINUDEEN HASAN CHISHTY(R.A.) whose blessed Shrine's KEYS have been passed on to the present family of Gaddi-Nashins from generation to generation for the last 800 years. Since an early age he has been passionate about the World Sufi Spiritual Traditions with special focus on Chishty Sufi Order and after completing his basic education from Ajmer Sharif, got a Bachelors Degree in Economic and Commerce from Wilson College, University of Mumbai. During the following years he became completely dedicated towards his practical Sufi spiritual research studies on World Sufi Traditions and their impact on the different cultures and traditions of the world and vice versa.

20. **The Sufi saint Khwaja Moin-ud-din Chishti. (Chishtī Mu'īn al-Dīn Ḥasan Sijzī, 1143–1236),** He came to India from Persia in the year 1192 and continued to preach Islam until his death in 1236. He emphasized asceticism and taught a philosophy that included both love of God and love of humanity. biographical accounts of his life written after his death report that he received the gifts of many "spiritual marvels (karāmāt), such as miraculous travel, clairvoyance, and visions of angels" in these years of his life. Mu'īn al-Dīn seems to have been unanimously regarded as a great saint after his passing. As such, Mu'īn al-

Dīn Chishtī's legacy rests primarily on his having been "one of the most outstanding figures in the annals of Islamic mysticism." Additionally Muʿīn al-Dīn Chishtī is also notable, according to John Esposito, for having been one of the first major Islamic mystics to formally allow his followers to incorporate the "use of music" in their devotions, liturgies, and hymns to God, which he did in order to make the foreign Arab faith more relatable to the indigenous peoples who had recently entered the religion or whom he sought to convert.

21. The three levels of religious practice in Islam as expressed in the famous ḥadith of Gabriel: **1)** *Islām* (outward submission to the will of Allah), **2)** *Īmān* (faith), and **3)** *Iḥsān* (spiritual excellence). Texts from the *Qur'an*, *Sunnah*, and classical scholarly works are cited to distinguish these three levels of religion (dīn) from each other. The purpose of this knowledge is to lay out the big picture before the worshipper, the highest religious goals in Islam, what the author refers to as the "spiritual mountain." This includes a broad awareness of the Islamic disciplines: *Qur'an, Tafsīr, Tajwīd, Ḥadith, Sīrah, ʿAqīdah, Sharīʿah, Fiqh*, and purification of the soul or spirituality. The prophetic method of self-improvement and habit formation will lastly be presented as the primary means to achieve stronger faith and spiritual excellence. Having understood what Islam requires of us in matters of ritual worship, the next step is faith as revealed in the Qur'an and Sunnah and as it was understood by religious predecessors.

22. The last man (German: *Letzter Mensch*) is a term used by the philosopher Friedrich Nietzsche in *Thus Spoke Zarathustra* to describe the antithesis of his theorized superior being, the *Übermensch*, whose imminent appearance is heralded by Zarathustra. The last man is the archetypal passive nihilist. He is tired of life, takes no risks, and seeks only comfort and security. Therefore, The Last Man is unable to build and act upon a self-actualized ethos. "The opposite of the overman (*Übermenschen*) is the last man: I created him at the same time with that. Everything superhuman appears to man as illness and madness. You have to

be a sea to absorb a dirty stream without getting dirty." - Fragments November 1882 - February 1883).

Chapter 18 - Ashoka's Pillar

1. Representing the three figures of the Supreme.

PART IV: Dravidia

Chapter 19 - The Road to Madras

1. The **Theosophical Society**, founded in 1875, is a worldwide body whose aim is Universal Brotherhood based on the realization that life is indivisibly One. The Society imposes no belief on its members, who are united by a common search for Truth and desire to learn the meaning and purpose of existence through study, reflection, self-responsibility and loving service

2. H.P. Blavatsky began to outline a book which was advertised as 'The **Secret Doctrine,** a new version of Isis Unveiled', 1879: 'The Theosophical Society was 'to promote a feeling of Brotherhood among nations'. In 1882 the Founders of Theosophy undertook tours in India. Col. Olcott visited Ceylon and, in curing a paralytic person, discovered his remarkable healing powers. Madame Blavatsky went on a visit to Simla and from there journeyed into Sikkim to meet the two Masters who were the inner Founders of the Society. The Founders then left to establish themselves in a permanent International Headquarters, thus creating the first spiritual centre of the Society at Adyar, Madras, now Chennai. After reviewing The Secret Doctrine for W.T. Stead's Review of Reviews, Annie Besant, well known as a Social Reformer and Freethinker, sought out Madame Blavatsky and consequently joined the Society.

3. H.P. Blavatsky 'The Key to Theosophy and **The Voice of the Silence',** 1889.

1. **Chennai** is bounded by the open sea. Along the east, or rather running up to north-east, extends the continuous coast-line of the Bay of Bengal, stretching for nearly 1200 miles, from Kanyakamuri (Cape Comorin) to the Chilka Lake ; the western coast is formed by the shores of the Indian Ocean and the Arabian Sea, for about 540 miles. Off the south-east lies Sri Lanka (formerly the British Colony of Ceylon), separated by a shallow strait, across which runs the string of rocks and sandbanks known as ' Adam's Bridge.' The irregular northern boundary of Chennai (Madras) has been formed by acci- dents of history. On the extreme north-east is the Bengal Province of Orissa; next (proceeding westwards) come the wild highlands of the Central Provinces; then, for a long stretch, the Dominions of the Nizam of Haidarabad, separated by the Kistna river and its tributary the Tungabhadra ; lastly, on the north-west by west, the Districts of Dharwar and North Kanara in the Bombay Presidency. The State of Mysore occupies a large portion of the centre of the area.

2. **Mahabalipuram** is also known by other names such as Mamallapattana and Mamallapuram. The term 'Mahabalipuram' means city of 'great power'. Another name by which Mahabalipuram has been known to mariners, at least since Marco Polo's time is "Seven Pagodas" alluding to the Seven Pagodas of Mahabalipuram that stood on the shore, of which one, the Shore Temple, survives. The local traditions and the foreign accounts vividly refer to the submergence of six temples out of seven that existed here. Recent underwater archaeological explorations in the area have revealed many structural remains.

3. **The Shore Temple**, Rathas (Chariots) carved out of a single rock, Arjuna's Penance and several other cave temples are some of the famous wonders. Mahabalipuram was a place of pilgrimage even before the Pallava period and the Pallava king Narasimha Varman built these beautiful temples, including the

present Shore Temple, during the 8th century. Mahabalipuram was well known to earlier mariners as 'Seven Pagodas' since very early times ('pagodas' refer to the top-most part of a temple, i.e. kalash). It is generally believed that out of a total of seven temples originally constructed, all but one have submerged in the sea over a period of time and what is now known as 'Shore Temple' is remaining. European travellers in the 18th and 19th century have recorded this folk tradition. Mahabalipuram was also a famous centre of Pallava art and architecture and is said to have been a seaport right from the beginning of the Christian era. An 8th century Tamil text written by Tirumangai Al-war who described this place as Kadal Mallai, 'where the ships rode at anchor bent to the point of breaking laden as they were with wealth, big trunked elephants and gems of nine varieties in heaps'. The epigraphical sources also say that the Pallava kings had active overseas contacts with Ceylon (Sri Lanka), China and the Southeast Asian countries. A few Roman coins of Theodosius (4th century AD) were found , which suggest that Mahabalipuram had trade contact with the Roman world around the Christian era. Pallava king Sihmavarman led two expeditions by embarking two ships from Mamallapuram–Pallava embassy and Vajradanthi, the famous Buddhist monk (who introduced Mahayana Buddhism to Sri Lanka) sailed to China from Mamallapuram port. Archaeological excavations suggest this place could have served as an ancient port, such as long walls, steps leading to the raised platform, scattered rectangular dressed stone blocks and a broken stone statue which appeared to be a lion figure. Europeans referred to Mahabalipuram as Mavalipuram, Mavalivaram, Mavellipore, Mauvellipooram and Mahabalipur. It is also known by several other names such as Mamallapattana and Mamallapuram. Believed to be 'the city of great wrestler' (Mahabali). The Pallava kings ruled Mahabalipuram from Kanchipuram; the capital of the Pallava dynasty from the 3rd century to 9th century AD. Mahabalipuram literally means 'city of the Great Bali' in memory of tradition when Vamana (Vishnu's Dwarf Avatar) humbled the demon king Bali and caused his splendid beachfront palaces to collapse beneath the sea. Another name by which Mahabalipuram has been known to mariners, at least since Marco Polo's time is 'seven pagodas'. Carr refers to the account given by Chambers after his second visit to Mahabalipuram in 1776 that 'according to the natives of the place, the more aged people among them, remembered to have seen the tops of several pagodas far out in the sea, which being covered with copper, probably gilt, were particularly visible at sunrise as their shining surface used to reflect the sun's rays, but that now the effect was no longer produced, as the copper had since become incrusted with mould and Verde grease'. Similarly, there is another interesting narration referred by Ramaswami on Robert Sotheby's Curse of Kehama about the submerged remains of Mahabalipuram. The hinterland around Mahabalipuram is mostly covered by charnockite and migmatite group of rocks. Discrete bodies of granites are seen in some parts of the area, including the granatic promontories on the shore of Mahabalipuram. These outcrops may belong to the same age group of granatic activity that occurred in the central part of Tamil Nadu during the Protorozoic. The river Palar joins the sea on the southern side of Mahabalipuram near Sadras. The geomorphic feature like the Buckingham canal, is a backwater body located about 1.5 km west of Mahabalipuram, with outlets at Covelong on the north and Kalpakkam in the south. This area has contemplated stretches from Covelong on the north to Vayalur on the south with hinterland area of Vasavasamudram, a flourished port town during the early centuries of the Christian era. The coastline of Mahabalipuram region consists of long open beaches with casurina plantations. The shoreline is long and is oriented approximately N–S with a slight inclination to the coast. The beaches are appreciably straight, open and continuous. These exposed beaches have large subaerial and subaqueous sand storage. In the near shore zone off Mahabalipuram, the seabed is uneven with rocky outcrops of granitic boulders with occasional sand patches and it gradually slops down towards east.

There is a shoal called Tripalur reef, which is in the form of submerged rocks. A ridge is noticed to the southeastern side of the temple in about 8–10 m water depth that extends from South and narrows towards North and is more than 2 km in length and 0.5 km in width. Ancient Tamil literature does not directly mention Mahabalipuram, but a poem, *Perumpanarrupadai*. Underwater dressed stone blocks with huge marine growth at Mahabalipuram. Remains of underwater structures off Mahabalipuram. Steps leading to the platform found at Mahabalipuram. See: UNDERWATER CULTURAL HERITAGE 1236 CURRENT SCIENCE, VOL. 86, NO. 9, 10 MAY 2004. The local tradition does not mention how old the city is but associates it with the demon *Mahabali*, imparting the name, Mahabalipuram to this site. Since the early Tamil literature does not mention the name Mahabalipuram, it is reasonable to infer that the submergence of these structures is not earlier than 1000 years or so. If the Shore Temple (about 1200 years old) is the last surviving structure, then it is reasonable to believe that other submerged temples in the sea are also of the same age. The archaeology of Mahabalipuram commences from the early centuries of the Christian era, as a few Roman and Chinese coins were found. Two Pallava coins bearing legends read as Srihari and Srinidhi have been reported in and around Mahabalipuram. One of the inscriptions of **Narasimha I** mentions that he (Narasimha I) is the first person to introduce the construction of caves and temples in granite stones. The zenith of human habitation around Mahabalipuram was during the Pallava dynasty, therefore, and arguably, these temples may not be older than 1500 years. Megalithic burials, cairn circles, jars with burials were observed on the western side of Mahabalipuram. The site is about 1.5 km away as near Mallar region at Punjeri, located on the western bank of the inlet water, Bunkingham canal. The earliest date of Megalithic culture of southern India is not earlier than 1500 years BC and continued till early centuries of the Christian era. Mahabalipuram was a port before Pallavas. It became the principal port during Pallava rule and they had voy-

ages to Sri Lanka and Southeast Asian countries. The port continued to exist till the early British period, this idea is supported by the mention of a British ship that used to be anchored at Mahabalipuram. All these evidence's suggest that Mahabalipuram was an active port since the last 2000 years. It was during the Pallava regime that stone was extensively used for the construction of temples and bricks and wood for residential houses..
In Mahabalipuram, the stones are nicely dressed and chiselled properly. So far, the archaeology of Tamil Nadu does not refer to stone masonry older than the 4th–5th century AD. Therefore, the dates of submerged structures may be dated to later than early centuries of the Christian era. Krishnan and Mohapatra and Hariprasad point out that the major and important factor affecting Mahabalipuram coast is erosion. Severe erosion at Kalpakkam, south of Mahabalipuram owing to longshore sediment drift has also been reported. A recent study suggests the rate of coastal erosion in and around Mahabalipuram is 55 cm/yr. If the same rate prevailed since last 1500 years, then the shoreline at that time might have been around 800 m eastward and all the structures noticed underwater would have been on the land. As Pallavas encouraged the temple architecture at Mahabalipuram during 8th century AD, these structures may be assigned to be belonging to the same period. Mahabalipuram has served as a port during the Pallava period. Part of earlier Mahabalipuram town may have been submerged in the sea. The possible causes for submergence of these structures may be shoreline changes owing to erosion. Further, investigations are required to understand the nature of the submerged structures and their dates. Mahabalipuram was famous for its architecture in the past and will continue to be so as a centre for art and architecture, if it will survive nature's fury. See: Underwater investigations off Mahabalipuram, Tamil Nadu, IndiaSundaresh*, A. S. Gaur, Sila Tripati and K. H. Vora National Institute of Oceanography, Dona Paula, Goa 403 004, India.

1. The huge (41-metre-tall) statue of **Thiruvalluvar** situated near Swami Vivekananda Rock at Kanyakumari or Cape Comorin in Tamilnadu. Thiruvalluvar was a celebrated Tamil poet and the author of *Thirukkural*, a collection of couplets on ethics, political and economical matters, and love. The text is highly influential and legendary, widely cherished as the pre-eminent work of the Tamil literature.

2. The Bhagavathi Kumari Amman Temple is located in Kanyakumari in Tamil Nadu, at the southern tip of mainland India, thereby located on the confluence of the Bay of Bengal, the Arabian Sea, and the Indian Ocean. **Devi Kanya** is the manifestation of Parvatiin **the form of an adolescent girl child**. Devi is also known as *Shrī Bāla Bhadra* or *Shrī Bāla*. She is popularly known as *Shakti Devi*. She is also worshiped as an incarnation of the goddess Bhadrakali by her devotees. Sri Ramakrishna Paramahamsa is said to have performed the consecration of the temple. The goddess is believed to be the one who removes rigidity of the mind; devotees usually feel the tears in their eyes or even inside their mind when they pray to the goddess in devotion and contemplation. Kanyakumari Temple is one of the 51 Shakti Peethas (The Shakti Pitha are significant shrines and pilgrimage destinations in Shaktism, the goddess-focused Hindu tradition). It is believed that the right shoulder and (back) spine area of Sati's corpse fell here creating the presence of Kundalini Shakti in the region. As directed by his Guru Sri Ramakrishna Paramahamsa, Swami Vivekananda, came here to seek Devi's blessing in December 1892. It is in this location he decided to embark on the missionary work to a higher level of action rather than being passive like the usual Sanyasis. Swami Brahmananda (1863–1922) and Swami Nirmalananda (1863–1938), another two disciples of Sri Ramakrishna Parama Hamsa, also

worshiped Devi Kanyakumari. The worship of Devi Kanya Kumari here dates back to the Kumari Kandam (In Tamil mythology, Kumari Kandam is a mythical continent, believed to be lost with an ancient Tamil civilization, supposedly located south of present-day India in the Indian Ocean).

3. **The Periplus of the Erythraean Sea** (τῆς Ἐρυθρᾶς Θαλάσσης, Períplous tês Erythrâs Thalássēs), also known by its Latin name as the *Periplus Maris Erythraei*, is a Greco-Roman *periplus* (*Periplus* is the Latinization of the Greek word περίπλους (*periplous*, contracted from περίπλοος *periploos*), is "a sailing-around."). A *periplus* is a manuscript document that lists the ports and coastal landmarks, in order and with approximate intervening distances, that the captain of a vessel could expect to find along a shore. It is written in Koine Greek that describes navigation and trading opportunities from Roman Egyptian ports like Berenice Troglodytica along the coast of the Red Sea, and others along Horn of Africa, the Persian Gulf, Arabian Sea and the Indian Ocean, and southwestern regions of India. The text has been ascribed to different dates between the first and third centuries (AD 59–62).

4. **Our Lady of Ransom Church** is a centre of Indian Catholicism. The tomb stones unearthed at Kumari Muttom, near Kanniyakumari contain evidences to show that Catholics were living there for many centuries. The tomb stones dated 1496. In 1542 when St. Francis Xavier came to Cape Comerin (Kanniyakumari) he found 'Our Lady of Delights Grotto', at Kanniyakumari. Then it became a center for mission activities of the Jesuits. It is believed that Our Lady of Delights Grotto, in which St. Francis Xavier prayed, later became the church of Our Lady of Ransom. It is said that St. Thomas, one of the twelve disciples of Jesus Christ, visited Kanyakamuri. The tomb stones unearthed at Kumari Muttom, near Kanyakumari contains evidence to show that Catholics were living there for many centuries. In 1542 St. Francis Xavier came to Cape Comerin (Kanyakumari) he was delighted to find 'Our Lady of Delights Grotto', at Kanyakumari. Then it became a centre for mission

activities of the Jesuits. It is believed that Our Lady of Delights Grotto, in which St. Francis Xavier worshiped, later became the church of Our Lady of Ransom. Our Lady of Ransom is the Patron of the congregation in Spain which redeemed the Christians from the Muslim invasion in the year 1218. The people of Kanyakumari were delighted to combine the name Ransom with Delight and call their patron as *Alangara Upakara Matha*. The wooden alter elegantly depicts the artistic Roman Art. This church remains part and parcel of the new church. The foundation stone for the new church was laid on 31st May 1900 by Rev. Fr. John Consolvez. Mr. Pakiam Pillai of the Vadakkankulam was the architect of the new church. It is the model of ancient Gothic Art and culture. The length of the new Church is 153 feet, breath 53 feet and height is 153 feet. All these depict the breads of the Holy Rosary. In 1956 Rev. Fr. Josaphath Maria completed the front elevation and the pinnacles. In 2006 the parish celebrated the golden jubilee of the erection of the golden cross and 106th year of laying foundation of the church. There are about 12,839 in Kanyakamuri parish and two schools for children. I say a quiet prayer, desiring to grow in the love of Christ and praying for the blessings of our Lord Jesus Christ through the interceding of *Alangara Upakara Matha*.

5. In 1917 a foreign merchant ship got struck to the sand shore of Leepuram, Kanyakumari. The strenuous efforts of the crew and other experts to restore it did not help them. Hence they decided to abandon the ship and went in for an auction. **Flag-Mast-** Mr. Kayathan Villavarayan a merchant from Tuticorin paid the highest bid and assumed the ownership of the abandoned ship. He had donated the iron mast to Our Lady of Ransom Church, Kanyakumari. The catamarans of Kanyakumari were brought to Leepuram to take the mast to Kanyakumari. It is said that as soon as the mast was loaded on the kattumarams, the mast together with the catamarans sunk into the sea water. After a few minutes, the catamarans and the mast began to float.

6. Many people have been misled and deceived by false teachings, false doctrines, cultic rules, regulations, and beliefs. The New

Testament is clear that worship of false gods can open the door to spirits of idolatry **(I Corinthians 10:14-22)**. The Apostle Paul warned Timothy that in the last days, "some will abandon the faith and follow deceiving spirits and things taught by demons" **(I Timothy 4:1)**. Controlling cults or authoritarian religionists can cause soul ties to form which lead to demonic control. New Age spirituality is often tied to the occult. Involvement in other world religions can also open a person up to spirits of confusion, snake spirits, and other entities or dark spirits. A *boori atma* [evil spirit] could be to something one brings back from the Subcontinent. There are uncountable Hindu resources for an Indian who wishes to prevent or treat these kinds of conditions. However, though symptoms sometimes lessen after the application of pujas, mantras and reverse-cursing, only through Jesus Christ can the power of Satan be completely broken. *Prasad* includes food offered to idols, and eating it brings the special power and grace of the represented deity to anyone who eats it eating food offered to idols is one of only three prohibitions given to gentile converts in **Acts 15:29**. I have found freedom from demonic possession and harassment, only to suffer worse harassment after choosing to eat *prasad*. This reminds me of the story Jesus told of the demon who brought his friends to inhabit his old, empty home in **Matt 12:45**: "And the last state of that man was worse than the first." See: Anderson, Neil T., and Dave Park. 2001. 'The Bondage Breaker', Youth edition, Eugene, OR: Harvest House. Ferris, Winston, 'The Armor of God', Berrien Springs, MI: Word Alive Ministries, 1990. PUBLICATIONS BY DR. D. K. OLUKOYA: Dealing With Local Satanic Technology, Dealing With Witchcraft Barbers, Deliverance By Fire, Freedom From The Grip of Witchcraft, Prayer Warfare Against 70 Mad Spirits, Revoking Evil Decrees, The Serpentine Enemies, The Wealth Transfer Agenda, Victory Over Satanic Dreams, Violent Prayers Against Stubborn Situation,

7. **The Bhagavathi Kumari Amman** Temple is located in Kanyakumari in Tamil Nadu, at the southern tip of mainland India,

there by located on the confluence of the Bay of Bengal, the Arabian Sea, and the Indian Ocean.

8. *Theertha* literally refers to water. In Hindu sacred literature, it is referred to as the physical holy water body associated with a temple or deity. There exist privileged regions and places where energy in the form of terrestrial magnetism rises heavenward. As per Hindu spiritual literature, *apAna* (downward flowing energy) pulls life downwards, while *udAna* (levity) pulls life upwards. Such places are called *Tirtha* (ways), *Kshetra* (ways) or *pitha* (base). Sacred geography can identify sacred places and sometimes explain the importance of already known. The temple should be close to a water course or near a lake located to the east or north. Islands are also favourable places. For the building of a temple, it should have a lake on the left (north) or in front (east), and not otherwise. If the temple is built on an island, the presence of water all around is of good omen. Most of the Hindu temples are associated with a water body, typically a river or one or more Temple tanks.

9. **Vivekananda**, Swami Vivekananda; 12 January 1863 – 4 July 1902), born Narendranath Datta, was an Indian Hindu monk. He was a chief disciple of the 19th-century Indian mystic Ramakrishna. He was a key figure in the introduction of the Indian philosophies of Vedanta and Yoga to the Western world, and is credited with raising interfaith awareness, bringing Hinduism to the status of a major world religion during the late 19th century. He was a major force in the contemporary Hindu reform movements in India, and contributed to the concept of nationalism in colonial India.

10. In 1741, Maharaja Marthanda Varma defeated the Dutch East India Company at the famous Battle of Colachel (10 August 1741) between the Indian kingdom of Travancore and the Dutch East India Company. The Dutch never recovered from the defeat and no longer posed a large colonial threat to India. You see, it was the Dutch takeover of the black pepper trade that ultimately had serious repercussions on them and their trading in Kerala at large. In 1753, the Dutch signed the Treaty of Mave-

likkara, agreeing not to obstruct the Raja's expansion, and in turn, to sell to him arms and ammunition. This marked the beginning of the end of Dutch influence in India. VOC continued to sell Indonesian spices, sugar in Kerala until 1795, at which time the English conquest of the Kingdom of Kochi ended their rule in India.

Chapter 22 – Mudrai

1. The Epic and Early Puranic **period**, from c. 200 BCE to 500 CE, saw the classical "**Golden Age**" of **Hinduism**(c. 320-650 CE), which coincides with the Gupta Empire. In this **period**the six branches of **Hindu** philosophy evolved, namely Samkhya, Yoga, Nyaya, Vaisheshika, Mīmāṃsā, and Vedanta. South India in the 10th and 11th century CE under the imperial Cholas is considered as another Golden Age. The period saw extensive achievements in Dravidian architecture, Tamil literature, sculpture and bronze working, quasi-democratic reforms, maritime conquests and trade. The Cholas left a lasting legacy. Their patronage of Tamil literature and their zeal in building temples have resulted in some great works of Tamil literature and architecture. The Chola kings were avid builders and envisioned the temples in their kingdoms not only as places of worship but also as centres of economic activity. They pioneered a centralised form of government and established a disciplined bureaucracy. The Indian teachings differentiate the four world ages (yugas) not according to metals, but according to dharmic qualities (virtues), where the first age starts with the most and the last age ends with the least. The end is followed by a new cycle (Yuga Cycle) of the same four ages: Satya Yuga (golden age), Treta Yuga, Dvapara Yuga, and **Kali Yuga (dark age), of which we are currently in**. In Satya Yuga, knowledge, meditation, and communion with spirit hold special importance. Most people engage only in good, sublime deeds and mankind lives in harmony with the Earth. Ashrams become devoid of wickedness and deceit. Natyam. [the Arts, say for example dance, such as Bharatanatyam], according

to Natya Shastra, did not exist in the **Satya Yuga** "because it was the time when all people were happy". Satya Yuga (**Krita Yuga**) according to Mahabharata. Men neither bought nor sold; there were no poor and no rich; there was no need to labour, because all that men required was obtained by the power of will; the chief virtue was the abandonment of all worldly desires. The Krita Yuga was without disease; there was no lessening with the years; there was no hatred or vanity, or evil thought whatsoever; no sorrow, no fear. **All mankind could attain to supreme blessedness. Thomas Traherne,** the 17th century priest and poet from Hereford, often speaks of men being creatures of God, capable of celestial blessedness: "The end for which you were created, is that by prizing all that God hath done, you may enjoy yourself and Him in Blessedness. (Centuries, I. 12); "For in Him is the fulness of all Blessedness" (Centuries, I. 51), "Thy will, O Christ, and Thy Spirit in essence are one. As therefore Thy human will is conformable to Thy Divine; let my will be conformable to Thine. Thy divine Will is all wisdom, goodness, holiness, glory, and blessedness. It is all light and life and love. It extendeth to all things in heaven and earth. It illuminateth all eternity, it beautifies the omnipresence of God with glory without dimensions. It is infinite in greatness and magnifieth all that are united to it. Oh that my will being made great by Thine, might become divine, exalted, perfected! O Jesu, without Thee I can do nothing." (Centuries, I. 94). "...from the great blessedness and glory of the estate wherein we were placed, none of which can be seen, till Truth is seen, a great part of which is, that the World is ours. So that indeed the knowledge of this is the very real light, wherein all mysteries are evidenced to us." (Centuries II. 3); "...to have fallen from infinite glory and blessedness is infinite misery: but cannot be seen, till the glory of the estate from which we are fallen is discerned." (Centuries II. 4). "Ancient philosophers have thought God to be the Soul of the. World. Since therefore this visible World is the body of God, not His natural body, but which He hath assumed; let us see how glorious His wisdom is in manifesting Himself thereby. It hath not only represented His infinity and eternity which we thought impossible to, be represented by a body, but His beauty also, His wisdom, goodness, power, life and glory, His righteousness, love, and blessedness: all which as out of a plentiful treasury, may be taken and collected out of this world." (Centuries II. 21), "That you are a man should fill you with joys, and make you to overflow with praises. The privilege of your nature being infinitely infinite. And that the world serves you in this fathomless manner, exhibiting the Deity, and ministering to your blessedness, ought daily to transport you with a blessed vision, into ravishments and ecstasies...*By things that are seen the invisible things of God are manifested, even His power and Godhead,* because everything is a demonstration of His goodness and power; by its existence and the end to which it is guided." (Centuries, II. 24); "Contemplate therefore the works of God, for they serve you not only in manifesting Him, but in making you to know yourself and your blessedness." (Centuries II. 26). "He is infinitely more blessed than we even in our blessedness. We being so united to each other by living in each other that nothing can divide us for evermore." (Centuries II. 53). "And man, as he is a creature of God, capable of celestial blessedness..." (Centuries II. 43).

2. **Tat Tvam Asi,** a Sanskrit phrase, translated variously as "Thou art that," (*That thou art, That art thou, You are that,* or *That you are,* or *You're it*) is one of the Mahāvākyas (Grand Pronouncements) in Vedantic *Sanatana Dharma*. It originally occurs in the Chandogya Upanishad 6.8.7. See: Raphael, Edwin, "The pathway of non-duality, Advaitavada: an approach to some keypoints of Gaudapada's Asparśavāda and Śaṁkara's Advaita Vedanta by means of a series of questions answered by an Asparśin. Iia": Philosophy Series, 1992, Motilal Banarsidass.

3. A British cartographer, **Major James Rennell** prepared the earliest map that calls this area by the name Adam's bridge. In 1767 Lord Robert Clive, the then Governor of Bengal and Bihar, appointed him as surveyor-general of the East India Company's dominions in Bengal. James Rennell has been called the Father of Indian Geography, and for his pioneering work on oceanog-

raphy as the Father of Oceanography. Rennell was "of middle height, well proportioned, with a grave yet sweet expression of countenance. He was diffident and unassuming, but ever ready to impart information. His conversation was interesting, and he had a remarkable flow of spirits. In all his discussions he was candid and ingenuous." (Lee, Sidney, ed. (1896). "Rennell, James". Dictionary of National Biography. 48. London: Smith, Elder & Co.). After this Rennell was always accompanied by a company of Sepoys. In 1823, **Sir Arthur Cotton** (then an Ensign), was assigned to survey the Pamban channel, which separates the Indian mainland from the island of Rameswaram and forms the first link of **Adam's Bridge**. Geological evidence indicates that a land connection bridged this in the past, and some temple records suggest that violent storms broke the link in 1480. The western world first encountered it in Ibn Khordadbeh's Book of Roads and Kingdoms (c. 850), in which he refers to it as Set Bandhai or Bridge of the See: Suckling, Horatio John (1876). Ceylon: A General Description of the Island, Historical, Physical, Statistical. Containing the Most Recent Information. Chapman & Hall. pp. 58. The bridge starts as a chain of shoals from the Dhanushkodi tip of India's Pamban Island. It ends at Sri Lanka's Mannar Island. Pamban Island is accessed from the Indian mainland by the 2-km-long Pamban Bridge. Mannar Island is connected to mainland Sri Lanka by a causeway. Trade across the India–Sri Lanka divide has been active since at least the first millennium BC.

4. **Arulmigu Meenakshi Sundareshwarar Temple** is a historic Hindu temple located on the southern bank of the Vaigai River in the temple city of Madurai, Tamil Nadu, India. It is dedicated to *Thirukamakottam udaya aaludaiya nachiyar (Meenakshi)*, a form of Parvati, and her consort, Sundareshwar, a form of Shiva. The temple is at the centre of the ancient temple city of Madurai mentioned in the Tamil Sangam literature, with the goddess temple mentioned in 6th-century texts.

5. **The Dravidians** are indigenous to South India, preferring to speak Tamil over the Hindi of the Aryan and Moghul North. So it was that English was adopted as a trade-off between the two.

6. **Gopurams.** The Tamil derivation is from the two words: **kō** and **puram** meaning 'king' and 'exterior' respectively. It originates from the Sangam age when it was known as (ōnggu nilai vāyil) meaning 'imperishable gateway'. Siegfried Lienhard considers this Tamil derivation but offers a new derivation from the Sanskrit word, (*gopura*), is often translated as "town gate". Separately, it consists of two words go, with the possible meanings of "cow" or "sky", and *pura*, meaning city. See: S. Sundararajan, 'Ancient Tamil country: its social and economic structure', Navrang, 1991. The shrines of Meenakshi temple are embedded inside three walled enclosures and each of these have four gateways, the outer tower growing larger and reaching higher to the corresponding inner one. The temple has 14 *gopurams*, the tallest of which is southern tower, rises to over 52 m and was rebuilt in the late 16th century. The oldest *gopuram* is the eastern one built by Maravarman Sundara Pandyan during 1216-1238 A.D.. Each *gopuram* is a multi-storeyed structure, covered with sculpture painted in bright hues. The outer gopurams are high pyramidal tower serving as a landmark sign for arriving pilgrims, while the inner *gopuram* are smaller and serve as the entrance gateways to various shrines. The temple complex has 4 nine-storey *gopurams* (outer, raja), 1 seven-storey *gopuram* (Chittirai), 5 five-storey *gopurams*, 2 three-storey, and 2 one-storey gold-gilded sanctum towers. Of these five are gateways to the *Sundareshvara* shrine, three to the *Meenakshi* shrine. The towers are covered with stucco images, some of whom are deity figures and others are figures from Hindu mythology, saints or scholars. Each group or sets of panels in each storey present an episode from regional or pan-Hindu legend. The four tallest gopurams on the outer walls alone depict nearly 4,000 mythological stories.

1. **Babasaheb** (Devanagari: Bābāsāhēb) is an honorary title and given name. "Babasaheb" is a Marathi phrase which means "Respected Father" (Baba = father and Saheb = sir). Bibissaheb must be the female equivalent? A forthright matriarch? Bibi Saheb is the name of a female character in Shahnaz Zaidi's novel 'Baby's Breath' (2021): "Mariam hugged Bibi Saheb and looked at her, reassuring her she would look after Pari in London.

2. In October 1896 **Winston Churchill reached Bangalore**, then not a bustling megapolis but a small, sleepy, cantonment town. He liked the climate: 'the sun even at midday is temperate and the mornings and evenings are fresh and cool'. He liked the house alloted to him: 'a magnificent pink and white stucco palace in the middle of a large and beautiful garden'. And he was well served by his staff, who included a gardener, a water-carrier, a dhobi, and a watchman. Ramachandra Guha tells us in the Hindu that on December 21st, 2003: "Life in Bangalore was pleasant, but also very boring. A young army officer yearned for 'action'; but the only wars in India were then being fought at the other end of the subcontinent, on the Afghan border. So Churchill began a butterfly collection; this got to as many as sixty-five varieties, before it was attacked by rats. Simultaneously, he got down to the business of educating himself. Afer school he had been sent to the military academy in Sandhurst, and was consequently denied the benefit of an Oxbridge education. This left him with a serious chip on his shoulder, for whenever he met University men they would 'pose you entrapping questions or give baffling answers'. To get even, the young

Winston 'resolved to read history, philosophy, economics and things like that; and I wrote to my mother asking for such books as I had heard of on these topics'. The books arrived, and the autodidact got down to work. He read four or five hours each day: historians like Gibbon and Macaulay, philosophers like Plato and Socrates, economists like Malthus, biologists like Darwin. These varied readings led him to question the basis of his religion. No longer could he accept the Bible as an accurate rendition of history; but he was not prepared either to abandon his faith and declare himself an atheist. There was no real need, as he saw it, to attempt to reconcile the Bible with modern scientific and historical knowledge. As he put it, 'if you are the recipient of a message which cheers your heart and fortifies your soul, which promises you reunion with those you have loved in a world of larger opportunity and wider sympathies, why should you worry about the shape or colour of the travel-stained envelope; whether it is duly stamped, whether the date on the postmark is right or wrong?...What is important is the message and the benefits to you of receiving it'. This process of self-learning is described in his memoir My Early Life, in a chapter suitably entitled 'Education in Bangalore'. After eight months in Bangalore the young subaltern wrote to his mother summing up his life there. 'Poked away in a garrison town which resembles a 3rd rate watering place, out of season and without the sea, with lots of routine work and ... without society or good sport—half my friends on leave and the other half ill—my life here would be intolerable were it not for the consolations of literature....'. Apart from butterflies and books, there was also sport. In My Early Life there is a vivid description of a polo tournament in Hyderabad won by Churchill's regiment. Discreetly omitted from the memoir is what happened on that visit, outside the playing field. For it was in Hyderabad that Churchill fell in love for the first time. The lady's name was Pamela Plowden, and her father was a high official of the Indian Civil Service. She was, Winston wrote to his mother, 'the most beautiful girl I have ever seen—Bar none', and also 'very clever'. He hoped to take a tour of the city with her on elephant back, for 'you dare not walk or the natives spit at Europeans—which provokes retaliation leading to riots'. The ride was taken, but it got nowhere. For Pamela's father would not allow his daughter to enter into marriage with an impecunious army officer. So Churchill returned disconsolately to Bangalore. He now sought, as his biographer writes, 'an opportunity to expose himself to the fire of any enemy of England who happened to be available at the moment'. He wrote asking to join Kitchener's advancing army in Egypt, but they didn't want him there. Ultimately, after his mother had pulled a few strings in London, he was invited by General Sir Bindon Blood to join the Malakand Field Force, which was battling truculent tribes on the North-west Frontier. Churchill's son later wrote that his letters from Bangalore 'show that he thought he was in a prison'. So when the order for parole came he raced to redeem it. As he himself recalled, when Sir Bindon's telegram arrived 'I sped to the Bangalore railway station and bought a ticket for Nowshera. The Indian clerk, having collected from me a small sack of rupees, pushed an ordinary ticket through a pigeon-hole. I had the curiosity to ask how far it was. The polite Indian consulted a railway time table and impassively answered, 2, 028 miles. Quite a big place, India! This meant a five days' journey in the worst of heat. I was alone, but with plenty of books, the time passed not unpleasantly.... I spent five days in a dark padded moving cell, reading mostly by lamplight or by some jealously admitted ray of glare'. So the Indian countryside made as little impression on Churchill as had the sights in and around Bangalore. Books, English books, were preferable to either. 'Prison' or '3rd rate watering role'; that is how he seems to have regarded my home town. Bangalore left no traces on him; what traces did he leave on it? In Bangalore Churchill was bored, he was bookish, and he was butterfly-obsessed. And he was also (not that he reveals it in his memoirs) broke. Evidence of his financial penury is contained in the lounge of the Bangalore Club. There, under a display window, is a minute book open at a page where we can read, under the list of members who have outstanding dues, the name of 'Lieutenant W. S. Churchill'. The sum he owed (indeed still owes) the Bangalore Club was thirteen rupees. From his own testimony and that of his biographers, we know how Churchill lived in Bangalore. Many people in the city, most especially perhaps brokers in real estate, are keen to know where he lived. Not along ago a friend of mine moved to Bangalore. After a few months in rented premises he sought to buy a bungalow in Whitefield, since he had been informed that it had once been the home of Churchill. Luckily he consulted me before signing the papers. I told him that in fact every owner of an old bungalow in the city claimed that it was once Churchill's. I myself write this in a room the tiles of whose floor tell me that they were made in the year 1865 by the Standard Brick and Tiles Company, Yelahanka. The room forms part of a building which is no longer a 'magnificent pink and stucco palace'. And the once 'beautiful garden' was long ago colonized by concrete. Still, I have only to point the visitor in the direction of those faded but still lovely red tiles, and say: 'Lieuetenant Winston Spencer Churchill once lived here'. Education in Bangalore, My early life, Pamela Plowden, Churchill in India, Bangalore club."

3. The Greeks had visited Malappuram as evidenced by the coin symbols incorporated into the temple relief I saw earlier. In the heart of the Deccan Plateau there is one of the oldest land masses in the Indian Sub-Continent. **Megasthenes: Μεγασθένης**, 350 BC– 290 BC) was an ancient Greek historian, diplomat and Indian ethnographer and explorer in the Hellenistic period. He described India in his book *Indika*, which is now lost, but has been partially reconstructed from literary fragments found in later authors. Megasthenes was the first person to describe ancient India, and for that reason he has been called "the father of Indian history". Indika (Ἰνδικά; L. *Indica*) is an account of Mauryan India by the Greek writer Megasthenes. The original work is now lost, but its fragments have survived in later Greek and Latin works: *India is a quadrilateral-shaped country, bounded by the ocean on the southern and the eastern side. The Indus river forms the western and the north-western boundary*

of the country, as far as the ocean. India's northern border reaches the extremities of Tauros. From Ariana to the Eastern Sea, it is bound by mountains that are called Kaukasos by the Macedonians. The various native names for these mountains include Parapamisos, Hemodos and Himaos (the Himalayas). Beyond Hemodos, lies Scythia inhabited by the Scythians known as Sakai. Besides Scythia, the countries of Bactria and Ariana border India. At the extreme point of India, the gnomon of the sundial often casts no shadow, and the Ursa Major is invisible at night. In the remotest parts, the shadows fall southward, and even Arcturus is not visible... Megasthenes makes a division of the philosophers, saying that they are of two kinds - one of which he calls the Brachmanes (Brahmins), and the other the Sarmanes (śramaṇa- seeker, one who performs acts of austerity, ascetic; mendicant, is in verse 4.3.22 of the Brihadaranyaka Upanishad composed by about the 6th century 48 B.C. The concept of renunciation and monk-like lifestyle is found in Vedic literature, with terms such as yatis, rishis, and śramaṇas. The Vedic literature from pre-1000 B.C. era, mentions Muni (monks, mendicants, holy man); Rig Veda, for example, in Book 10 Chapter 136, mentions mendicants as those with kēśin, (long-haired) and mala clothes (dirty, soil-colored, yellow, orange, saffron) engaged in the affairs of mananat (mind, meditation). The word śramaṇa is derived from the verbal root śram, meaning "to exert effort, labor or to perform austerity". The history of wandering monks in ancient India is partly untraceable. The term 'parivrajaka' was perhaps applicable to all the peripatetic monks of India, such as those found in Buddhism, Jainism and Hinduism. The śramaṇa refers to a variety of renunciate ascetic traditions from the middle of the 1st millennium BC. The śramaṇas were individual, experiential and free-form traditions. The term "śramaṇas" is used sometimes to contrast them with "Brahmins" in terms of their religious models. Part of the śramaṇa tradition retained their distinct identity from Hinduism by rejecting the epistemic authority of the Vedas, while a part of the śramaṇa tradition became part of Hinduism as one stage in the Ashrama dharma, that is as renunciate sannyasins. Pali samaṇa has been suggested as the ultimate origin of the word Evenki самāн (samān) "shaman", possibly via Middle Chinese; however, the etymology of this word, is also found in other Tungusic languages...He with the long loose locks (of hair) supports Agni, and moisture, heaven, and earth; He is all sky to look upon: he with long hair is called this light. The Munis, girdled with the wind, wear garments of soil hue; They, following the wind's swift course, go where the Gods have gone before— Rig Veda, Hymn 10.136.1-2. Of the Sarmanes, Megasthenes tells us that those who are held in most honour are called the Hylobioi. Next in honour to the Hylobioi are the physicians, since they are engaged in the study of the nature of man. Besides these there are diviners and sorcerers. Women pursue philosophy with some of them. Megasthenes also comments on the presence of pre-Socratic views among the Brahmans in India. Megasthenes claims that before Alexander, no foreign power had invaded or conquered Indians, with the exception of the mythical heroes Hercules and Dionysus. However, it is known from earlier sources - such as the inscriptions of Darius the Great and Herodotus - that the Achaemenid Empire included parts of north-western part of India (present-day Pakistan). It is possible that the Achaemenid (Persian) control did not extend much beyond the Indus River, which Megasthenes considered to be the border of India. Another possibility is that Megasthenes intended to understate the power of the Achaemenid Empire, a rival of the Greeks. Megasthenes says that foreigners are treated well. Special officers are appointed to ensure that no foreigner is harmed, and judges hand out harsh punishment to those who take unfair advantage of the foreigners. Sick foreigners are attended by physicians and taken care of. I would contend that such hospitality exists to this day.

Chapter 24 - Ajanta Caves

1. Wherefore seeing we also are compassed about with so great a cloud of witnesses, let us lay aside every weight, and the sin which doth so easily beset us, and let us run with patience the race that is set before us. **Hebrews 12:1.** I have been crucified with Christ; and it is no longer I who live, but Christ lives in me; and the life which I now live in the flesh I live by faith in the Son of God, who loved me and gave Him-

self up for me. **Galatians 2:20I.** Then Jesus said to His disciples, *If anyone wishes to come after Me, he must deny himself, and take up his cross and follow Me. For whoever wishes to save his life will lose it; but whoever loses his life for My sake will find it.* **Matthew 16:24-25** Peter began to say to Him, "Behold, we have left everything and followed You. **Mark 10:28.**

2. *For it was I, the Lord your God, who rescued you from the land of Egypt. Open your mouth wide, and I will FILL IT with good things.* **Psalm 81:10.** *He FILLS my life with good things. My youth is renewed like the eagle's!* **Psalm 103:5.** At the sound of Mary's greeting, Elizabeth's child leaped within her, and Elizabeth was FILLED with the Holy Spirit. **Luke 1:41.** *Don't be drunk with wine, because that will ruin your life. Instead, be FILLED with the Holy Spirit.* **Ephesians 5:18.** *And this hope will not lead to disappointment. For we know how dearly God loves us because he has given us the Holy Spirit to FILL our hearts with his love.* **Romans 5:5.** I pray that God, the source of hope, will FILL you completely with joy and peace because you trust in him. Then you will overflow with confident hope through the power of the Holy Spirit. **Romans 15:13.**

3. **Nirvāṇa** (Sanskrit: literally, "blown out", as in an oil lamp) is a concept in Indian religions (Buddhism, Hinduism, Jainism, and Sikhism) that represents the ultimate state of soteriological release, the liberation from repeated rebirth in saṃsāra. In Indian religions, nirvana is synonymous with moksha and mukti. All Indian religions assert it to be a state of perfect quietude, freedom, highest happiness as well as the liberation from or ending of samsara, the repeating cycle of birth, life and death. "The ultimate goal is to stop this round of death and re birth, and to successfully and completely dissolve one's ego so that, upon death, you join the energy of the Universe, instead of being reborn. This is called Nirvana. Learned Lamas say that everyone, regardless of your spiritual training, has an opportunity after death to go into the light and enter Nirvana, dissolving one's ego. Most people, according to the Lamas, see the light and are faced with this decision after death but they experience only fear and doubt. This drives them to avoid the light and instead

head back to our "sphere" and be re-born again. Part of the spiritual training given to these monks is how to be peaceful and calm so that, upon death, they can dissolve into Nirvana." - 'Magic and Mystery in Tibet' by Alexandra David-Neel, 1929.

4. **OM SHANTI.** Oṃ śānti śānti śānti. Om (Oṃ). Like many mantras, this one begins with "Om". Om has no meaning, and its origins are lost in the mists of time. Om is considered to be the primeval sound, the sound of the universe, the sound from which all other sounds are formed. In the Brahminical tradition, from where Buddhism undoubtedly obtained mantra practice, Om is not just the universal sound, but the sound of the universe itself. For example in the (non-Buddhist) Mandukya Upanishad, it is said: Om! — This syllable is this whole world. Its further explanation is: —The past, the present, the future — everything is just the word Om. And whatever else that transcends threefold time — that, too, is just the word Om. Om is therefore a sound symbolizing reality. It represents everything in the universe, past, present, and future. It even represents everything that is outside of those three times. It therefore represents both the mundane world of time in which the mind normally functions, and the world as perceived by the mind that is awakened and that experiences the world timelessly. It represents both enlightenment and non-enlightenment. You could regard Om as being the equivalent of white light, in which all of the colors of the rainbow can be found. "A word of solemn affirmation and respectful assent , sometimes translated by 'yes, verily, so be it' (and in this sense compared with Amen); it is placed at the commencement of most Hindu works, and as a sacred exclamation may be uttered at the beginning and end of a reading of the Vedas or previously to any prayer; it is also regarded as a particle of auspicious salutation [Hail!]; Om appears first in the Upanishads as a mystic monosyllable, and is there set forth as the object of profound religious meditation, the highest spiritual efficacy being attributed not only to the whole word but also to the three sounds A, U, M, of which it consists." It's worth bearing in mind that Sanskrit was the language not only of later Buddhism, but

of the Hindu and pre-Hindu Vedic traditions as well. In Buddhist texts, as far as I'm aware, Oṃ is never seen as being comprised of A-U-M. Shanti (Pali: Santi) simply means "peace". It's a beautiful meaning and also a very beautiful sound. The shanti is repeated three times, as are many chants in Buddhism. In Buddhism as well as in Hinduism the threefold Shanti is generally interpreted as meaning the Threefold Peace in body, speech, and mind (i.e. peace in the entirety of one's being). Hindu teachings typically end with the words *Om shanti shanti shanti* as an invocation of peace, and the mantra is also used to conclude some Buddhist devotional ceremonies. [**Om Vajrapani Hum.** Vajrapani doesn't, to many newcomers to Buddhism, look very Buddhist at all. He is a Bodhisattva who represents the energy of the enlightened mind, and his mantra also symbolizes that quality. Vajrapani is pictured dancing wildly within a halo of flames, which represent transformation. He holds a vajra (thunderbolt) in his right hand, which emphasizes the power to cut through the darkness of delusion. Vajrapani looks wrathful, but as a representation of the enlightened mind, he's completely free from hatred].

5. **Bodhisattva** are enlightened beings who have put off entering paradise in order to help others attain enlightenment. The elaborate concept refers to a sentient being or sattva that develops bodhi or enlightenment — thus possessing the boddisattva's psyche; described as those who work to develop and exemplify the loving-kindness (metta), compassion (karuṇā), empathetic joy (mudita) and equanimity (upekkha). These four virtues are the four divine abodes, called Brahmavihara (illimitables).

6. **Maya**, (Sanskrit: "magic" or "illusion") a fundamental concept in Hindu philosophy, notably in the Advaita (Nondualist) school of Vedanta. Maya originally denoted the magic power with which a god can make human beings believe in what turns out to be an illusion.

7. *Beauty and truth are one, just as life is one.* "Ode on a Grecian Urn" is a poem written by the English Romantic poet John Keats in May 1819, first published anonymously in Annals of the Fine

Arts for 1819. "Ode on a Grecian Urn" was not well received by contemporary critics!!! It was only by the mid-19th century that it began to be praised, although it is now considered to be one of the greatest odes in the English language. A long debate over the poem's final statement divided 20th-century critics, but most agreed on the beauty of the work: "There are those who succeed too well, who swallow 'Beauty is truth, truth beauty ...,' as the quintessence of an aesthetic philosophy, not as the expression of a certain blend of feelings." I.A. Richards, *Practical Criticism*, 1929 pp. 186–187. Andrew Motion says that the poem "tells a story that cannot be developed. Celebrating the transcendent powers of art, it creates a sense of imminence, but also registers a feeling of frustration."- *Keats*, University of Chicago Press, 1999.

8. **Waghora River.** The caves, cut into the face of a mountain, form a horseshoe shape around the Wangorah River. Ajanta groups of caves is a World Heritage Site which overlooks a narrow sinuous gorge, through which flows the stream of Waghora. The river is descended from the head of the Cave 28 from a waterfall of seven leaps. *Waghore* means Tiger River in Marathi. They are an example of one of Indian's unique artistic traditions known as rock cut temples. Ajanta consists of thirty caves, each dedicated to the life of the Buddha.

9. **Cave 18, Ajanta.** Cave 18 is a small rectangular space (3.38 × 11.66 m) with two octagonal pillars and it joins into another cell. Its role is unclear.- "World Heritage Sites – About Ajanta Caves 01 to 29", Archaeological Survey of India, 2015.

10. **Cave 26,** has the impressive Mahaparinirvana of Buddha, or Dying Buddha. The sculptures in Cave 26 are elaborate and more intricate. It is among the last caves excavated, and an inscription suggests late 5th or early 6th century. Cave 26 is a worship hall (chaityagriha, 25.34 × 11.52 m) similar in plan to Cave 19. The major artworks include the Mahaparinirvana of Buddha (reclining Buddha) on the wall, followed by the legend called the "Temptations by Mara". The temptations include the seduction by Mara's daughters who are depicted below the meditat-

ing Buddha. They are shown scantly dressed and in seductive postures, while on both the left and right side of the Buddha are armies of Mara attempting to distract him with noise and threaten him with violence. In the top right corner is the image of a dejected Mara frustrated by his failure to disturb the resolve or focus of the ascetic Buddha.

11. **The Jataka tales** are a voluminous body of literature native to India concerning the previous births of Gautama Buddha in both human and animal form. The future Buddha may appear as a king, an outcast, a god, an elephant—but, in whatever form, he exhibits some virtue that the tale thereby inculcates. Often, Jātaka tales include an extensive cast of characters who interact and get into various kinds of trouble - whereupon the Buddha character intervenes to resolve all the problems and bring about a happy ending. The Jātaka-Mālā of Arya Śura in Sanskrit gives 34 Jātaka stories. At the Ajanta Caves, Jātaka scenes are inscribed with quotes from Arya Shura, with script datable to the sixth century.

12. **Chaitya,** chaitya hall, chaitya-griha, (Sanskrit: Caitya) refers to a shrine, sanctuary, temple or prayer hall in Indian religions. The term is most common in Buddhism, where it refers to a space with a stupa and a rounded apse at the end opposite the entrance, and a high roof with a rounded profile. Strictly speaking, the chaitya is the stupa itself, and the Indian buildings are chaitya halls, but this distinction is often not observed. Outside India, the term is used by Buddhists for local styles of small stupa-like monuments. Ajanta has rock-cut chaitya halls. Rock-cut chaityas, similar to free-standing ones, consisted of an inner circular chamber with pillars to create a circular path around the stupa and an outer rectangular hall for the congregation of the devotees. Over the course of time, the wall separating the stupa from the hall was removed to create an apsidal hall with a colonnade around the nave and the stupa. There is a chaitya arch around the window, of Cave 9, Ajanta. Cave 10 is a vast prayer hall or Chaitya, is dated to about the 1st century BC. Cave 10 features a Sanskrit inscription in Brahmi script that is

archaeologically important. The inscription is the oldest of the Ajanta site, the Brahmi letters being paleographically dated to circa the 2nd century BCE.[166] It reads: ????????? ???????? ????? ???? Vasithiputasa Kaṭahādino gharamukha dānaṁ "The gift of a cave-façade by Vasisthiputra" Katahadi.". Cave 19 drew upon on the plan and experimentation in Cave 9. Cave 19 is a worship hall (chaitya griha, 16.05 × 7.09 m) datable to the fifth century A.D. The hall shows painted Buddha, depicted in different postures. Cave 21, 22, 23 and 24 are all monasteries, representing the final phases of Ajanta's construction.

13. **Vajrapani Boddhisatva,**Vajrapāṇi (Sanskrit; Pali: Vajirapāṇi, meaning, "Vajra in [his] hand") is one of the earliest-appearing bodhisattvas in Mahayana Buddhism. He is the protector and guide of Gautama Buddha and rose to symbolize the Buddha's power. Scenes of Buddha using the vajra of Vajrapani as the "magic weapon" to perform miracles and propagate "superiority of his doctrine" are also common. Painting Vajrapani is beside the Buddha in Cave 1. In the western groups of caves, Vajrapani is depicted as a *bodisattva* with his *vajra* in a tableau, a votive panel of sculptural composition in which he in a standing posture (the only extant figure) over a lotus to the left of a Buddha in a *dhyanasana*. In this panel he is adorned with a tall crown, two necklaces, a snake armlet and holds the *vajra* in his left hand, and resting on a scarf tied across his hips. This close iconographic composition is at the entrance to the porch of cave 2 and in the incomplete porch of cave 1. Such votive carved panels with *Vajrapani* are also seen in the interior of *pradkssina* passage of cave 2 in which his presence is with other the ascetic *bodisattvas* like *Avalokiteśvara*; in this panel he has a crown in the form of a *stupa* with a scarf fastened over his left thigh. In the eastern group of caves at the entry to cave 6 in Aurangabad, *Vajrapani* is carved as a commanding persona in the form of a huge *dvarapala* along with *Avalokiteśvara*. Vajrapani image is flanked by a small attendant. He carries *Vajra*, his luminous weapon on the left hand, which rests on a scarf tied across his hip. His right arm is bent forward -perhaps he held a lotus like his *paredros Aval-*

okiteśvara. Both the bodhisattvas guarding the entrance to cave 6 are carved wearing princely headdresses (crowns).

14. **Vishwakarma,** or Vishvakarman (Sanskrit: Viśvakarmā, lit. 'all maker') is a craftsman deity and the divine architect of the gods.

15. **Bodhisattva Padmapani from cave 1** at Ajanta monastery in central India late 5th century, likely 477. This extraordinary mural painting survives from early medieval India, preserved in the interior of the rock-cut Buddhist monastery of Ajanta. It provides the earliest visual evidence of elaborate crowns being worn as signifiers of both princely and divine status. The crowns depicted are the antecedents of those used in Buddhist ritual today by the *Vajracharya* priests in Nepal.

16. **Sravasti Miracle.** "At Ajanta, rows of small Buddha images appear in the later caves, (Sravasti miracles, multiplication miracle, Ajanta cave 17, fifth century), usually in the rear shrine and its antechamber, and are specifically identified as the "1000 Buddhas" by inscription in cave 2. Walter Spink, 'Ajanta's Chronology: The Problem of Cave Eleven', *Ars Orientalis* 7 (1968): 164. The Sravasti miracles (that is, the multiplication miracle) are represented at Ajanta by the addition to the rows of Buddhas of two nagas upholding a lotus stem, and sometimes by the appearance of Purana Kasyapa. At the same time (in the fifth century A.D.) that the multiplication miracle was being depicted at Sarnath, it was also shown at Ajanta, where, however, Buddhas are arranged in rows and not in pairs as seen at Sarnath. It is apparent from the placement and form of the depictions at Ajanta that the multiplication has here become related to the Thousand-Buddha theme. What interests us most is a wall painting in cave 2, where a Buddha is shown performing the multiplication miracle while seated under a mango tree (Sravasti miracles, mango tree and multiplication miracles, Ajanta cave 2, fifth century.). The two major themes of the multiplication (See: Srvasti miracles (multiplication miracle), Sarnath, fifth century, sandstone. H. 94 cm. Indian Museum, Calcutta). Why the two themes coalesced, apparently for the first time at Ajanta, cannot be easily explained, although at

least two possibilities exist. One possibility is that the themes were first combined in texts that either have been lost or have not yet come to light. The second possibility is that the artists and monks of Ajanta were responsible for the new iconography, one that existed only in the visual tradition." Robert L. Brown, "The Śrāvastī Miracles in the Art of India and Dvāravatī", Archives of Asian Art , 'Duke University Press', 1984, Vol. 37, pp. 79-95.

PART V: West Bengal

Chapter 25 - Calcutta

1. **Albert and Victoria memorial.** The Victoria Memorial is a large marble building in Kolkata, which was built between 1906 and 1921. It is dedicated to the memory of Empress Victoria, and is now a museum under the auspices of the Ministry of Culture. The memorial lies on the Maidan and is one of the famous monuments of Kolkata. In January 1901, on the death of Empress Victoria,then Lord Curzon, suggested the creation of a fitting memorial. Lord Curzon proposed the construction of a grand building with a museum and gardens. Curzon said, "Let us, therefore, have a building, stately, spacious, monumental and grand, to which every newcomer in Kolkata will turn, to which all the resident population, European and Native, will flock, where all classes will learn the lessons of history, and see revived before their eyes the marvels of the past." The Prince of Wales, laid the foundation stone on 4 January 1906, and it was formally opened to the public in 1921. In 1912, before the construction of the Victoria Memorial was finished, Emperor George V announced the transfer of the capital of India from Kolkata to New Delhi. Thus, the Victoria Memorial was built in what would be a provincial city rather than a capital. The Victoria Memorial's architect was William Emerson (1843–1924). The design is in the Indo-Saracenic revivalist style (a revivalist architectural style mostly used by British architects in India in the

later 19th century, especially in public and government buildings in the British Raj, and the palaces of rulers of the princely states), which uses a mixture of British and Mughal elements with Venetian, Egyptian, Deccani architectural influences. The building is 103 by 69 m and rises to a height of 56 m. It is constructed of white Makrana marble.

2. **Kali Temple,** Dakshineswar is a locality in the north suburban region of Kolkata. This place is historically famous for the great temple of Goddess Kali, locally known as *Maa Bhabatarini Mandir.* It was built in 1855 by Rani Rashmoni. The temple is famous for its association with Shri Ramkrishna Paramhangsha Dev, a mystic of 19th Century Bengal. Large number of people gather at Dakshineswar throughout the year especially on the day of Shyama Puja, Shiva Chaturdashi, Bengali New Year's Day (naba barsha), Akshaya Tritiya and on 1 January every year on the occasion of Kalpataru Utsava (the day Shree Ramkrishna attained siddhi). As per the District Statistical Handbook, "Panchabati Ban is the place where Shri Ramakrishna Paramhansha Dev planted five (pancha) trees i.e. Asvattha, Bata, Bel, Asok and Amlaki, under which he used to meditate. The Panchamundi Asan is called so because there are five human skulls buried underneath and Shri Ramakrishna Paramhansha Dev used to sit and meditate on the asan (seat) and **attained siddhi (enlightenment/attainment with the Holy Spirit i.e. the God; in his case Goddess Kali)."** See: Enlightened by the Holy Spirit **(Acts 23:1-11): Matthew 10:17-20.** In my mind there is no doubt that Satan is a near equivalent to the goddess Kali. "The religion and philosophy of the Hebrews are those of a wilder and ruder tribe, wanting the civility and intellectual refinements and subtlety of Vedic culture." - *Henry David Thoreau* Goddess Kali, however, is not evil or against God, she serves God by keeping the souls in illusion who have turned away from God. Goddess Kali, the wife of Lord Shiva is the personification of material nature- God's external energy. A better equivalent of Satan would actually be the demon Kali, the personification of Kali-yuga. Maybe that's the Kali, meant. Anyhow, the idea that

God needs an evil opponent, in order to be good, is an igno-rant, primitive notion. Krishna says: Those miscreants who are grossly foolish, who are lowest among mankind, whose knowl-edge is stolen by illusion, and who partake of the atheistic na-ture of demons do not surrender unto Me. *(Bg 7.15)* "So far as I am able to judge, nothing has been left undone, either by man or nature, to make India the most extraordinary country that the sun visits on his rounds. Nothing seems to have been for-gotten, nothing overlooked. "Land of religions, cradle of human race, birthplace of human speech, grandmother of legend, great grandmother of tradition. The land that all men desire to see and having seen once even by a glimpse, would not give that glimpse for the shows of the rest of the globe combined." *--Mark Twain*

3. **The Hooghly River** (Hugli; Anglicized alternatively spelled Hoogli or Hugli) or the Bhāgirathi-Hooghly, originally and in local tongues the 'Ganga', and also called Kati-Ganga, is an approximately 260-kilometre-long (160 mi) distributary of the Ganges River in West Bengal, India.

4. **Howrah** is located on the western bank of the Hooghly River opposite its twin city of Kolkata. he name came from the word Haor—Bengali word for a fluvial swampy lake, which is sedi-mentologically a depression where water, mud and organic de-bris accumulate.The word itself was rather used in eastern part of Bengal (now Bangladesh), as compared to the western part (now West Bengal). On 11 October 1760, as a result of the Bat-tle of Plassey, the East India Company signed a treaty with Mir Qasim, the Nawab of Bengal, to take over the control of Howrah district. In 1787 the Hooghly district was formed and in 1819 the whole of the present-day Howrah district was added to it. The Howrah district was separated from the Hooghly district in 1843.

Chapter 26 – Shantiniketan

1. The name derives from the Bengali **'Shanti'** meaning peaceful, and 'niketan' meaning abode.
2. India folk **instrument.**
3. In **1901** by the Bengali poet, philosopher, educationalist and first Indian Nobel Laureate for literature (1913). In 1915 Tagore was knighted, but surrendered it in in protest against the Amritsar Masacre (1919).
4. "He that sinneth against me wrongeth his own soul. All they that hate me love death." **Prov., viii. 36.**
5. 'The Condition of Being a **Brahmin.**' Saṃyutta Nikāya 45. Connected Discourses on the Path 37. Brahminhood. At Savatthī. "Bhikkhus, I will teach you brahminhood and the fruits of brahminhood. Listen to that.... "And what, bhikkhus, is brahminhood? It is this Noble Eightfold Path; that is, right view ... right concentration. This is called brahminhood. "And what, bhikkhus, are the fruits of brahminhood? The fruit of stream-entry, the fruit of once-returning, the fruit of nonreturning, the fruit of arahantship. These are called the fruits of brahminhood."

Chapter 27 - Darjeeling

1. All substance that impacts with a diamond, is destroyed. So the *Dorje* symbolises that which is indestructible, enduring, powerful, invincible, and irresistible. Like a diamond, all inferior truth and beliefs will be shattered when confronted with the ultimate truth that we are the "observer," and that everything else is just illusion. Vajra is a Sanskrit equivalent of the Tibetan word *dorje* and it carries many meanings: Indra's thunderbolt, the lamas' sceptre, and diamond, but only in the sense mentioned above. It may also be used as a qualifying term for anything used in the tantric context. Thus the person who presides at tantric rituals is called the vajra master or *dorje lopon.*

2. The name of the **Cochil** or Chochile, resembles 'Coquille' resembles the French word for "shell". Perhaps the name comes from a mispronunciation of some native word, possibly for a river, or place? Some Indians say Cochile means: "where the land meets the sea and there you provide a living." That is, at least, among Lower Rogue River Athabascan tribes, in America, where it was another word for an estuary, where they did their fishing weirs and provided their living every year. Cochil was determined to come back to England with me. Sadly, I did not aid him in his forestated aim. I consider it unfortunate, both harsh and sad, that I went on without him.

3. Fashion is culturally vital and signifies the origins and gives a sense of belonging to the individuals of that group. There are wide cultural diversities in India but they all seem to take pride in wearing clothes from their culture roots. West Bengal is no different from every other Indian state, being a runaway version of itself- culturally rich, drenched in traditions and folklores. Bollywood is very important here. So too *Durga pujas*, *Rasgullas* or the term *Aami tumharo bhalo bhashi*. **Bengalis love the colour red.** Bengalis follow most of the Indian states: Men wear *dhotis*; women wear *sarees*. In the past, men from elite society used to wear *Uttorio*, a kind of scarf -- in addition to rest of their clothing; and women wore a veil called *Orna*. Bengali women prefer to wear *Banarasi sarees* in shades of red with a distinct border. The style of wrapping *sarees* is unique in this part of the country; it is wrapped in such a way that one end of *saree* is left over the shoulder, which is mostly used for tying keys or a tinkling ornament called *kinkini*.

PART VI: Old Delhi

Chapter 28 - Old Delhi

1. **Mewat** is a historical region of Haryana and Rajasthan states in northwestern India. Mewat region lies in between Delhi-Jaipur-

Agra. The region roughly corresponds to the ancient kingdom of Matsya, founded in the 5th century BCE. Mewati dialect, a slight variant of the Haryanvi and Rajasthani dialects of Hindi, is spoken in rural areas of the region. Mewati Gharana is a distinctive style of Indian classical music.

2. **The Aravalli Range** (also spelled Aravali) is a mountain range in Northwestern India, running approximately 670 km (430 mi) in a south-west direction, starting near Delhi, passing through southernHaryana and Rajasthan, and ending in Gujarat. The highest peak is Guru Shikharat 1,722 metres (5,650 ft).

3. **Gurugram,** formerly known as Gurgaon, is a city located in the northern Indian state of Haryana. It is situated near the Delhi-Haryana border, about 30 kilometres (19 mi) southwest of the national capital New Delhi

4. **The Yamuna** (Hindustani: pronounced [jamuna]) is the second-largest tributary river of the Ganga and the longest tributary in India. Originating from the Yamunotri Glacier (6,387 metres) on the southwestern slopes of Banderpooch peaks of the Lower Himalaya in Uttarakhand, it travels a total length of 855 mi. It merges with the Ganga at Triveni Sangam, Allahabad, which is a site of the Kumbh Mela, a Hindu festival held every 12 years. It crosses several states: Haryana and Uttar Pradesh, passing by Uttarakhand and later Delhi, and meeting its tributaries on the way. From Uttarakhand, the river flows into the state of Himachal Pradesh. After passing Paonta Sahib, Yamuna flows along the boundary of Haryana and Uttar Pradesh and after exiting Haryana it continues to flow till it merges with the river Ganga at Sangam or Prayag in Allahbad (Uttar Pradesh). It helps create the highly fertile alluvial Yamuna-Ganga Doab region between itself and the Ganga in the Indo-Gangetic plain. Nearly 57 million people depend on the Yamuna's waters, and the river accounts for more than 70 percent of Delhi's water supply. It has an annual flow of 97 billion cubic metres, and nearly 4 billion cubic meters are consumed every year (of which irrigation constitutes 96%). Like the Ganga, the Yamuna is highly venerated in Hinduism and worshipped as the goddess Yamuna.

In Hinduism she is the daughter of the Sun Deva, Surya, and the sister of Yama, the Deva of Death, hence also known as Yami. According to popular legends, bathing in its sacred waters frees one from the torments of death. The water of Yamuna is of "reasonably good quality" through its length from Yamunotri in the Himalayas to Wazirabad barrage in Delhi, about 233 mi; below this, the discharge of wastewater drains between Wazirabad barrage and Okhla barrage renders the river severely polluted. One official described the river as a "sewage drain". The main sources of pollution in the river: household and municipal disposal sites, soil erosion resulting from deforestation occurring to make way for agriculture, and resulting chemical wash-off from fertilizers, herbicides, and pesticides and run-off from commercial activity and industrial sites.

5. **Hastingpur,** is a city in the Meerut district in the Indian state of Uttar Pradesh. Hastinapur, described in Hindu texts such as the Mahabharata and the Puranas as the capital of the Kuru Kingdom, is also mentioned in ancient Jain texts. Hastinapur is located on the right bank of the Ganga River.

6. **The Naga Kingdom** [In the Mahabharata] is the territory of a hardy and warlike tribe called Nagas. They were also considered as one of the supernatural races like the Kinnaras. The word *Naga*in the Sanskrit language means *snake*or *serpent.* It seems likely that the Naga people were a serpent-worshipping group who were later described as *serpents* themselves in ancient Indian literature.

7. **Indraprastha** ("Plain of Indra" or "City of Indra") is mentioned in ancient Indian literature as a city of the Kuru Kingdom. It was the capital of the kingdom led by the Pandavas in the Mahabharata epic. Under the Pali form of its name, Indapatta, it is also mentioned in Buddhist texts as the capital of the Kuru mahajanapada. Modern historical research pin its location in the region of present-day New Delhi, particularly the Old Fort (Purana Qila). The city is sometimes also known as Khandavaprastha or Khandava Forest, the name of a forest region on the banks of Yamuna river which (according to the Ma-

habharata) had been cleared by Krishna and Arjun to build the city. It was one of the five places demanded for the sake of peace and to avert a disastrous war, Krishna proposed that if Hastinapur agreed to give the Pandavas only five villages, namely, Indraprastha (Delhi), Swarnprastha (Sonipat), Panprastha (Panipat), Vyaghrprastha (Baghpat) and Tilprastha (Tilpat) then they would be satisfied and would make no more demands. Duryodhana vehemently refused, commenting that he would not part with land even as much as the point of a needle. Thus, the stage was set for the great war for which the epic of Mahabharata is known most of all. The Mahabharata records Indraprastha as being home to the Pandavas, whose wars with the Kauravas it describes.

8. **Kaurava** is a Sanskrit term for the descendants of King Kuru (or simply Kurava in Tamil), a legendary king who is the ancestor of many of the characters of the Mahābhārata. **Kuru** is the name of the ancestor of the clan of the Kurus in the Mahabharata. He was the son of Samvarana and of Tapati, the daughter of the Sun. In the literature, Kuru is an ancestor of Pandu and his descendants, the Pandavas, and also of Dhritarashtra and his descendants, the Kauravas. This latter name derived as a patronym from "Kuru", is only used for the descendants of Dhritarashtra. King Kuru had two wives named Shubhangi and Vahini. He had a son named Viduratha with Shubhangi, and five sons with Vahini, named Ashvavat, Abhishyat, Citraratha, Muni, and Janamejaya.[44][45] Due to his merits and great ascetic practices the region "Kurujangal" was named after him. It has also been known as Kurukshetra since ancient Vedic times.

9. **Gerard Lake, 1st Viscount Lake** (27 July 1744 – 20 February 1808) was a British general. He commanded British forces during the Irish Rebellion of 1798 and later served as Commander-in-Chief of the military in British India. In spite of those victories, Viscount Lake was recorded as being an inveterate gambler who lost most of his family's fortune; a sad end for such a stalwart of Empire.

10. **The Gates of Delhi** were city gates in Delhi, India, built under dynastic rulers in the period that could be dated from the 8th century to the 20th century. They are the gates in the ancient city of Lal Kot or Qila Rai Pithora, also called the first city of Delhi (period 731-1311) in Mehrauli – Qutb Complex; the second city of Siri Fort (1304); the third city Tughlaqabad (1321–23); the fourth city of Jahanpanah's of (mid-14th century); the fifth city of Feruzabad (1354); the sixth city of Dilli Sher Shahi (Shergarh) (1534), near Purana Qila; the seventh city Shahjahanabad of (mid 17th century); and the eighth modern city New Delhi of British Raj (1931s) in Lutyens' Delhi of the British rule. In 1611, the European merchant William Finch[1] described Delhi as the city of seven castles (forts) and 52 gates. More gates were built after that period during the Mughal rule and during the British rule. Only 13 gates exist in good condition, while all others are in ruins or have been demolished. Like all gates denote, the direction of the destination station is the starting name of the gate

11. **Fergusson, J., History of Indian and Eastern Architecture, 1891,** Born in Scotland, James Fergusson (1808-86) spent ten years as an indigo planter in India before embarking upon a second career as an architectural historian. Although he had no formal training, he became one of the most respected researchers in the field and an expert on India's cave temples.

12. **The Red Fort** is a historic fort in the city of Delhi (in Old Delhi) in India that served as the main residence of the Mughal Emperors. Emperor Shah Jahan commissioned construction of the Red Fort on 12 May 1638, when he decided to shift his capital from Agra to Delhi. Originally red and white, its painting is credited to architect Ustad Ahmad Lahori, who also constructed the Taj Mahal.

13. **El Escurial.** Spanish for "among the rocks." It was meant as a dwelling for God on Earth, at a time when the Protestant Reformation was shaking the foundations of Catholic Europa. This unique building has come to symbolise the Counter-reformation. Architects of this were Juan Bautista de Toledo and his suc-

cessor Juan de Herrera. The construction works only lasted from 1563 to 1584.

14. **The *Naubat Khana*,** In the east wall of the court stands the now-isolated *Naubat Khana* (meaning "The Waiting Hall" in Persian, *Naubat*: and *Khana*: "House, Hall") also known as *Nakkar Khana*), the drum house. Music was played daily, at scheduled times and everyone, except royalty, were required to dismount. Later Mughal kings Jahandar Shah (1712–13) and Farrukhsiyar (1713–19) are said to have been murdered here.

15. **The *Diwan-i-Aam*,** The inner main court to which the Nakkar Khana led was 540 feet (160 m) wide and 420 feet (130 m) deep, surrounded by guarded galleries. On the far side is the Diwan-i-Aam, the Public Audience Hall. This was a place for the official affairs of commoners who sought after legal matters such as tax issues, hereditary complications, and *OuQhaf* (in Arabic) (in Islam, when a person leaves a piece of land for the charitable uses for the common good usage no one can ever buy or sell this building ever again. It remains to serve that purpose forever). The hall's columns and engrailed arches exhibit fine craftsmanship, and the hall was originally decorated with white *chunam* stucco ("A handbook for travellers in India, Burma, and Ceylon"). In the back in the raised recess the emperor gave his audience in the marble balcony (*jharokha*).

16. **The *Diwan-i-Khas*,** In Persian, Diwan:nmeans "The Official Hall", Khas: means "Special guests" and Aam: means "the common people". So this was a building for the official affairs and requests of the novelty and royal family. A gate on the north side of the Diwan-i-Aam leads to the innermost court of the palace (Jalau Khana) and the Diwan-i-Khas (Hall of Private Audience). It is constructed of white marble, inlaid with precious stones. The once-silver ceiling has been restored in wood. François Bernier described seeing the jewelled Peacock Throne here during the 17th century. At either end of the hall, over the two outer arches, is an inscription by Persian poet Amir Khusrow.

17. **The *Hira Mahal*,** ("Diamond Palace") is a pavilion on the southern edge of the fort, built under Bahadur Shah II and at the end

of the *Hayat Baksh* garden. The *Moti Mahal* on the northern edge, a twin building, was demolished during (or after) the 1857 rebellion. The *Shahi Burj* was the emperor's main study; its name means "Emperor's Tower", and it originally had a *chhatri* (an elevated, dome-shaped pavilion) on top. Heavily damaged, the tower is undergoing reconstruction. In front of it is a marble pavilion added by Emperor Aurangzeb.

18. **Connaught Place** (officially known as, Rajiv Chowk) is one of the main financial, commercial and business centres in New Delhi, India. Prior to the construction of Connaught Place, the area was a ridge, covered with kikar trees and populated with jackals and wild pigs. Residents of the Kashmere Gate, Civil Lines area visited during the weekends for partridge hunting. The Hanuman Temple attracted many visitors from the old walled city, who came only on Tuesdays and Saturdays and before sunset, as the return trip was considered dangerous. Residents of villages including Madhoganj, Jaisingh Pura and Raja ka Bazaar were evicted to clear the area for the construction of Connaught Place and the development of its nearby areas. The villages were once situated along the historic Qutab Road, the main road connecting Shahjahanabad, the walled city of Delhi (Old Delhi) to Qutab Minar in South Delhi city since the Mughal era. The displaced people were relocated in Karol Bagh to the west, a rocky area populated only by trees and wild bushes. However, three structures were spared demolition. These were Hanuman temple, a Jain temple in Jaisinghpura and the Jantar Mantar.

19. **Lakshmi,** is the goddess of wealth, fortune, power, luxury, beauty, fertility, and auspiciousness. She holds the promise of material fulfilment and contentment. She is described as restless, whimsical yet maternal, with her arms raised to bless and to grant. For centuries Hindus have invoked her thus:*Beautiful goddess seated on a chariot, / Delighted by songs on lustful elephants, / Bedecked with lotuses, pearls and gems,/ Lustrous as fire, radiant as gold, / Resplendent as the sun, calm as the moon, /Mistress of cows and*

horses —/ Take away poverty and misfortune / Bring joy, riches, harvest and children.

20. **Paharganj**(literally 'hilly neighbourhood') is a neighbourhood of Central Delhi, located just west of the New Delhi Railway Station. Known as *Shahganj*or King's ganj or market place during Mughal era.

21. **Cow veneration** in ancient India began during the Vedic era, and religious texts written during this period called for non-violence towards all bipeds and quadrupeds, and often equated killing of a cow with the killing of a human being specifically a Brahmin, (Krishna, Nanditha, 2014, *Sacred Animals of India*, Penguin Books Limited, pp. 80, 101–108): hymn 8.3.25 of the Hindu scripture Atharvaveda (1200–1500 BCE) condemns all killings of men, cattle, and horses, and prays to god Agni to punish those who kill. In Puranas, which are part of the Hindu sacred books, the earth-goddess Prithvi was in the form of a cow, successively milked for the benefit of humans. Prithu milked the cow to generate crops and end a famine. Kamadhenu, the miraculous "cow of plenty" and the "mother of cows" in certain versions of the Hindu mythology, is believed to represent the sacred cow, regarded as the source of all prosperity.

Chapter 29 - Jama Masjid

1. **Masjid-i Jehan-Numa** (lit.'World-reflecting Mosque'). The Jama Masjid was regarded as a symbolic node of Islamic power across India, well into the colonial era. It was also a site of political significance during several key periods of British rule. The Jama Masjid fell into British confiscation after The Indian Rebellion of 1857 (the major, but ultimately unsuccessful, uprising in India in 1857–58 against the rule of the British East India Company). At this time, it was barred from any religious use. The Masjid was eventually returned to the Muslim population in 1862. It was often a place of anti-colonial ferment. The function of the mosque as an autonomous political space has continued in the modern era. For example, in 2001 (in the aftermath of the 9/

11 attacks) the mosque was a site of protest against U.S bombings in Afghanistan. In 2019, massive protests occurred at the site due to the controversial Citizenship Amendment Act. There were explosions there in 2006 and a gun attack on tourists in 2010 (by the Indian Mujahideen ordered from Karachi, for the Iman allowing "semi-naked" foreigners inside it!).

2. At the time of its construction, it was the **largest mosque in the Indian subcontinent.** Shah Jahan claimed that the mosque was modelled after the Jama Masjid of Fatehpur Sikri, and this is reflected in the design of many exterior features, such as the facade and courtyard. The mosque predominantly uses red sandstone, and is set apart from its predecessors by a more extensive usage of white marble. Black marble also features as a decorative element. Arabic and Persian calligraphic pieces are found on various surfaces of the structure, whose content ranges from religious to panegyric. See: Asher, Catherine B. (1992). *The New Cambridge History of India: Architecture of Mughal India.* Cambridge University Press. p. 202. Having been built on a hill, the mosque is situated on a plinth elevated 10 metres above the surrounding city. The complex is oriented such that the back wall faces the west, towards Mecca.

3. **The muezzin** is the person who gives the call to prayer at a mosque. The muezzin plays an important role in ensuring an accurate prayer schedule for the Muslim community. The English word *muezzin* is derived from the Arabic: *mu'adh·dhin,* simplified *mu'azzin.* The word means "one by the ear", since the word stems from the word for "ear" in Arabic is *'udhun.* As the *mu'adh·dhin* will place both hands on his ears to recite the call to prayer. The call of the muezzin is considered an art form, reflected in the melodious chanting of the adhan. Historically, a muezzin would have recited the call to prayer atop the minarets in order to be heard by those around the mosque. Now, mosques often have loudspeakers mounted on the top of the minaret and the muezzin will use a microphone, or a recording is played, allowing the call to prayer to be heard at great distances without climbing the minaret. Today, with the pro-

duction of electronic devices, loudspeakers mounted on the top of the minaret, the muezzin will use a microphone and broadcast the call to prayer often without requiring the specialised skill of a muwaqqit (King, David A. (1996). "On the role of the muezzin and the *muwaqqit* in medieval Islamic society". In E. Jamil Ragep; Sally P. Ragep (eds.). *Tradition, Transmission, Transformation*. E.J. Brill. pp. 285–345.).

4. Another significant mosque is the Kali Masjid or '**black mosque**' so called from the dark colour given to it by time, and supposed to have been built by one of the early Afghan sovereigns; and the mosque of Roshan-ud-daula. The Kalan Masjid was built in 1387 by the son of Khan-i-Jahan Junan Shah, Prime Minster of Feroz Shah Tughlaq (r.1351-88). The mosque was built in Ferozabad, a section of Delhi, the city built by Feroz Shah Tughlaq but was later included in Shahjahan's new city Shahjahanabad. It is an imposing structure in a plain style, with the main upper storey approached via a flight of steps and crowned with a series of domes.

Chapter 30 - Chandni Chowk

1. Animals have been traditionally considered sacred in Hindu culture. So dressing up as one at a festival is a form of celebration and worship. The symbolic significance of animals in India are as vehicles of god or deities themselves. Not only animals are worship as sacred in India, Holy rivers, Sacred trees, land and birds are also worship in Indian culture. See: "Sacred Animals of India" by Dr. Nanditha Krishna and Maneka Gandhi, the animal rights activist. In Hinduism, **Jambavana**also known as **Jambavanta**is the **divine-king of bears**, created by the god Brahma to assist the avatar Rama in his struggle against the Lanka king Ravana (Patricia Turner, Charles Russell Coulter. *Dictionary of ancient deities*. 2001, page 248). Jambavanta is an Asian black bear or sloth bear in Indian epic tradition. In the Mahabharata, Jambavantha had killed a lion, who had acquired a gem called Syamantaka from Prasena after killing him. Krishna was suspected of killing Prasena for the jewel, so he

tracked Prasena's steps until he learned that he had been killed by a lion, who had been killed by a bear. Krishna tracked Jambavantha to his cave and a fight ensued. The combat between Krishna and Jambavan ensued for 28 days after which Jambavan began to grow tired. Then realizing who Krishna was, Jambavantha submitted. He gave Krishna the gem and also presented him his daughter Jambavati, who became one of Krishna's wives (Mani, Vettam, 'Puranic Encyclopedia: A Comprehensive Work with Special Reference to the Epic and Puranic Literature', Motilal Banarsidass, 2015).

2. **Church of St. James**, oldest church in Delhi. St. James Church also formerly known as 'Skinner's Church'. Colonel Skinner, an officer well-known in the history of the East India Company (See:(1851) 'Military Memoir of Lieut-Col. James Skinner', by James Baillie Fraser C. B., Volume 1 & 2). The church is situated at the junction of Lothian Road and Church Road in Delhi and is easily approachable by local transport and from Kashmiri Gate. built in 1836 by Colonel James Skinner. It was the church the Viceroy of India, attended until the Cathedral Church of the Redemption, near Gurudwara Rakab Ganj, was built in 1931. The only other church of that era, St. Stephen's Church, at Fatehpuri, Delhi was built in 1867. St. Stephen's is called the **Cathedral Church of the Redemption**, also the **Viceroy Church**, in New Delhi. It is located east of Parliament House and Rashtrapati Bhavan, formerly Viceroy House, which was used by then British Viceroy.

Chapter 31 - The End

1. The great Mughal to pen his account of India is **Abu'l Fazi.** "With Akbar there is a pre-modern vision of modernisation of India, a patriotism without revivalism. But what, in greater detail and depth, India meant to Akbar and his circle we have to go to his principal spokesman, Abu'l Fazl. There is no doubt that Abu'l Fazl was more conscious of the geography of India than any previous writer. In the north he considered the great mountain ranges to separate India from Turan (central Asia)

and Iran on one side and China ('Chin and machin') on the other. The following passage from his pen was long an aid to the arguments of those British strategists who would place the 'scientific frontier' of the Raj across the heart of Afghanistan: Intelligent men of the past have considered Kabul and Qandahar as the twin gates of Hindustan, one (Qandahar) for the passage to Iran, and the other for that to Turan. By guarding these two places, Hindustan obtains peace from the alien (raider) and global traffic by these two routes can prosper. It is significant that Abu'l Fazl considers India to be a peninsula." He says that the sea borders Hindustan 'on the east, west and south'. Akbar's sayings in A'in-i Akbari, Naval Kishore, III, p. 4, 179, 192. & V.A. Smith, Oxford History of India, p. 755 . M. Athar Ali, 'The Evolution of the Perception of India: Akbar and Abu'l Fazl', Social Scientist , Jan. - Mar., 1996, Vol. 24, No. 1/3 (Jan. - Mar., 1996), pp. 80-88.

2. **Cum grano salis,** L. With a grain of salt; with a bit of common sense and skepticism.

3. **Devas,** are benevolent supernatural beings in the Vedic era literature. Deva is a Sanskrit word that means "heavenly, divine, anything of excellence". They are rather like Angels, whereas Asuras are demons.

4. *Pars magna fui. L. A great part, i.e. Lux angelus quorum pars magna fui hoc volo.* I was a great part of the light of the angel whose only wish to be...I saw these terrible things, and took great part in them (... quaeque ipse miserrima vidi et quorum pars magna fui.) Virgil, *The Aeneid,* book 2, lines 5–6, p. 25. ("All of which misery I saw, and a great part of which I was." Aeneas was describing the sack of Troy).

Harry Matthews was born in the countryside near Stone, Staffordshire in 1980. He was educated in Shropshire and studied Philosophy at Reading University. It was while there he undertook during the summer holiday his journey to India. Since then he has written poetry collections and is engaged in doctoral research in English Literature.

Lightning Source UK Ltd.
Milton Keynes UK
UKHW051135070821
388395UK00006B/44